MODERN LEGAL STUDIES

RESHAPING PUBLIC POWER:
NORTHERN IRELAND AND THE
BRITISH CONSTITUTIONAL CRISIS

MODERN LEGAL STUDIES

RESHAPING PUBLIC POWER: NORTHERN IRELAND AND THE BRITISH CONSTITUTIONAL CRISIS

JOHN MORISON, LL.B., Ph.D.

AND

STEPHEN LIVINGSTONE, B.A., LL.M.

LONDON
SWEET & MAXWELL
1995

Published by
Sweet & Maxwell Limited of
South Quay Plaza,
183 Marsh Wall,
London E14 9FT

Computerset by York House Typographic Ltd, London
Printed in Great Britain by Butler & Tanner, Frome and London

A CIP catalogue record
for this book is available
from the British Library

ISBN 0 421 528907

04862478

Contents

Contents

Preface

This book calls for a re-conceptualisation of the way that we think about regulating public power in the United Kingdom. While the focus is directed towards mainstream British constitutional theory we draw upon the experience of Northern Ireland, a place where the failure of traditional British constitutionalism is most apparent, to uncover both new understandings about the way in which power is now exercised in the wider context of the United Kingdom and the genesis of a new way of controlling that exercise of power. The uncertain and contested British/Irish identity, of Northern Ireland and the experience of being constitutional lawyers from within a British tradition that does not seem to acknowledge the particular characteristics of this part of the United Kingdom, perhaps allows us to contemplate the British constitutional problem from the vantage point of a more advanced post-colonial perspective. Whatever the reason, we maintain that the experience from the edge of the Union is instructive more generally.

Indeed at a time when the national identity, as well as the basic constitutional arrangement of the polity, is under as much pressure as at any time since the acts of union, it is perhaps fitting that we should turn to an area where the strain on existing constitutional arrangements is greatest in order to try to see into the future. We do not say that the pace of change in Britain or the reasons for it are the same as in Northern Ireland but we do maintain that beyond the most obvious aspects of a constitutional crisis there is in Northern Ireland the beginnings of a new constitutionalism or at least a more developed response to the reshaping of public power that is occurring throughout the United Kingdom and beyond.

This book is essentially in two parts. In the first three chapters we look critically at orthodox constitutional thinking about both Great Britain and Northern Ireland. We see this as important because in a country without a written constitution a consensus of writing about the constitution can *become* the constitution. The traditional thinking must be challenged in order to clear a space for new approaches. We contend that both orthodox writing and the growing literature on reforming the constitution fail to capture the reality of a changing role for the state. New forms of international and supranational order as well as the realities of the exercise of political power in the last two decades in a changing polity are not reflected in a constitutionalism which, even in its reforming guise, concentrates almost exclusively on traditional parliamentary mechanisms and their capacity to curb excessive power exercised by a domestic executive. Public power is now qualitatively different from what is described by traditional scholarship. And it is still changing. Only a public law which starts from this understanding is likely to produce an adequate account of contemporary constitutional reality. Chapter one looks in some detail at the conflicts within existing ideas of constitutionalism. Some of the argument here is technical and, if there is such a person as the non-specialist reader, he or she may wish to pass over some of this and, indeed, some of the detailed discussion of proposals for reform that opens chapter two. It is in the second part of chapter two that we explain why that constitutionalism, even in its most ardently reforming guise, is not adequate to control the new forms of power as they exist in new sites. The changes in the nature of the state and in its exercise of power are discussed in some detail in the main part of chapter two. It is in chapter three that we turn to critically evaluating the Westminster approach as it has been applied to Northern Ireland. (An appendix containing a brief chronology of constitutional events is offered for those who do not have their own version of Irish history.) Here we argue how the experience of unsuccessfully attempting to modify orthodox British constitutionalism for Northern Ireland displays the endgame of the British approach more generally.

The second part of the book examines Northern Ireland as a case study of the developments sketched out in the first part. It is particularly apposite to look at Northern Ireland because two of the major trends we identify, the delegation of power to sub-units of government and increasing international influence, have been present for some longer time, even if for different reasons, than in the rest of the United Kingdom. Although our focus is on Northern Ireland this is not a book about the constitutional question of Northern Ireland and readers will not find an attempt to answer that question within these pages. Indeed in chapter three we observe that there is no shortage of "solutions" to the Northern Ireland question, the trouble is getting agreement on one of them. (We hope that talking about the macro-constitutional framework of Northern Ireland, rather than fighting about it, can continue as long as necessary—even if this a very long time indeed. We would not however, wish this to be a total distraction from the important job of democratising the exercise of power where it really is now in those sites above and below the level of the state as traditionally conceived. In Northern Ireland, as anywhere else, the genie can not be put back into the bottle: significant power is likely to remain outside the direct control of any institutional structure that may be produced by any future political deal.) Rather than offering solutions our concern is instead to examine certain changes in the way Northern Ireland has been governed and to consider what can be learned from these for constitutional lawyers further afield. In chapter four we look at the "real" constitution in Northern Ireland, those strategies of governance that can be seen in three over-lapping yet distinct phases. Chapter five provides a close analysis of the institutions and mechanisms that were developed within this real constitution to get the business of government done in the vacuum that was produced pending the long-awaited political stabilisation that would restore a political administration. It is here that the details of the incipient "new constitutionalism", based more on values than structures, are provided. That aspect of the new constitutionalism that relates particularly to the external dimension provided by international and transnational bodies and influences is discussed in chapter six.

In chapter seven we suggest that nascent in developments in Northern Ireland can be seen not only new levels of public power but also new ways of ensuring accountability and participation in the exercise of public power. This second element is important. Although we maintain that the claims of most constitutional reformers in the United Kingdom are ill suited to the changing circumstances this does not mean that we are simply apologists for the exercise of power, that we are content simply to point out that it has escaped to new levels where it will be even more difficult to contain. Rather our conclusion is that in order to revive democratic and constitutional values it may be necessary to undergo a more radical rethinking of premises than is presently being entertained in most areas of public law scholarship.

This book draws on literature from politics, public administration and economics as well as law. We make no apology for this as we feel it is high time that public lawyers made themselves aware of developments in other disciplines which affect the constitutional landscape they deal with. We do apologise to those working within such disciplines for our naivety and misunderstanding of such literature. At the very least correcting our errors may contribute to a much needed dialogue.

The authors have been in general agreement and it has perhaps helped that the Northern Ireland based author has been mainly concerned with the British viewpoint and the English based author with the Irish. We would like to thank Kevin Boyle and Stuart Weir of the Democratic Audit who encouraged us to consider these questions, though our inquiry may now have gone well beyond anything they would endorse. Piet Akkermans, Spyridon Flogaitis and other members of the European Group on Public Law, Bernadette Grant, Chris Moffatt and particularly Tom Hadden also helped in a variety of ways, most particularly by giving us opportunities to talk about these issues. We would also like to thank Karon Alexander and Louise Duggan for their valuable research assistance and the School of Law at Queen's University Belfast for funding their efforts.

Table of Cases

Table of Statutes

Chapter One

Constitutionalism Under Assault

Introduction

This chapter explores the increasing tensions within the British version of constitutionalism which render it in its traditional form increasingly unable to accommodate a range of developments in constitutional practice. Attention is given first to the traditional constitution as a series of comfortable ideas handed down from Blackstone to Bagehot and Dicey and now in the keeping of a host of modern textbook writers whose increased number provides a poor substitute for their lack of a response to recent innovations in the exercise of power. The reaction of this ancestral constitution to a number of changes in the actual exercise of power is critically examined. In particular, it is noted how developments arising from changes in the nature of the state's external relations, which increasingly place it within a web of international and supra national obligations, provide challenges which cannot be easily accommodated within the constitutional orthodoxy. Also, developments in domestic constitutional practice over a number of years, but particularly since 1979, are reviewed briefly for their impact on traditional ways of seeing the British constitution. The concern here is to see how orthodox constitutionalism fails to accommodate within even its own limited framework the most obvious developments which challenge it.

The traditional constitution

There is now perhaps the beginning of a trend towards bemoaning the complacency of the British constitutional tradition which is starting to replace the original complacent tradition.[1] Some of the more reflective accounts now begin by acknowledging dissatisfaction with the orthodox constitution before going on to provide the usual orthodox account of its operation.[2] The dominant paradigm, however, is still one where our constitution is seen as broadly satisfactory: it may be quirky but essentially it is capable of fulfilling its role. While there may be a growing lobby for reform, the modesty of the aims of almost of all there testifies to a general belief in the constitution's basic serviceability. This has remained remarkably consistent over a long period of great change. Advocates of the uniqueness and value of our ancestral constitution often distort the history of Parliament in Britain to bolster a claim that if Britain did not actually invent democracy then it certainly has the longest continuous history of parliamentary practice.[3] While the idea of describing as democratic the meetings in the period after the Norman conquest when the King summoned powerful subjects in order to take from them advice (and more importantly money) is maybe unlikely, the myth stresses an almost unbroken continuity. Some historians find in the parliaments of Edward I after 1272 some of the elements such as the fusing of principles of consent with those of representation and the embodiment of the sovereignty in the

---

[1] For example, in his "Review Article: The Constitution and its Discontents", *British Journal of Political Science* 21 (1991) Harden claims to detect "widespread dissatisfaction", and notices "numerous works written or edited by lawyers which have hammered home the case for constitutional reform" (p.489). He then goes on to discuss just five works, noting that the three that are anything more than simply mildly critical of some aspects of the Dicyean constitution find themselves "marginalised" (p.510). Then, in line with his own contribution (see, for example, *The Noble Lie: The British Constitution and the Rule of Law* (with N. Lewis) 1986) to what is in reality still a very small sub-genre within the scholarly literature, he concludes that "much of the case for reform should be understood as an argument for institutional change, based on *existing* constitutionality" (p.509 our emphasis). It seems that the radical nature of much of this trend disappears almost as completely as its claim to be widespread.

[2] See for example, Ganz, who in the preface to the second edition of *Understanding Public Law* (1994), simply notes the increased range of problems that have come to the fore in the seven years since the last edition, diagnoses the problem as resulting essentially from "a government exercising unrestrained power [who] can no longer be removed by constitutional means" (p. xvii) and recommends as a cure simply "restoring the checks and balances of the constitution" (p.137).

[3] See further J. Morison, "Annotated Bibliography of the UK Public Law: The Literature on Parliament" in *Revue Europeene De Droit Public / The European Review of Public Law / Eur. Zeitschrift Des Offent. Rechts / Revista Europea Di Dirritto Pubblico*, Vol. 6, No. 1 pp. 251–259.

crown-in-parliament that characterise later, more familiar forms of parliamentary government.[4] Such suggestions of continuity are taken up enthusiastically by constitutionalists who seem wilfully oblivious to the shuddering disjunctures provided by the Reformation or Cromwell's experiment in limited government. Sir David Lindsay Keir, surveying the constitutional history of Britain since 1485, is able to conclude

"continuity has been the dominant characteristic .... neither in its formal and legal, nor in its informal and practical aspect, has English government at any stage of its history violently and permanently repudiated its own tradition"[5]

Indeed, although the first modern European revolution was experienced in England in the 1640s, the resulting settlement of 1689 is minimised by seeing it as marking only the end of a more gradual movement involving the shift of power from the King to the King in Parliament. This suggests a more appropriately modern agent for exercising power in a constitution evolving slowly as society changes gradually and denies that this was the beginning of a radical shift that is still continuing, whereby absolutist power moved from the Monarch to Parliament to the House of Commons to the Cabinet to the Prime Minister and beyond. Seismic shifts to constitutional practice this century have been glossed over to contribute to the idea of a continuous, unwavering English tradition of excellence in constitutional arrangements. Fifty years ago Sir Maurice Amos was able to declare confidently that "the English Parliament is one of the capital facts not only of our national history, but of the history of civilisation".[6] The break-up of Empire and the trauma of disentangling from the colonial relationships with newly emerging nations throughout the world, did remarkably little to shake the faith of British constitutionalists in the British constitution. Indeed, Britain continued to think of itself as the "Mother of Parliaments" and sought to bequeath to its former colonies a "Westminster model" of government as the most stable and developed form of constitutionalism.

This unwillingness to acknowledge within constitutional theory changes that are undeniable in practice is captured well by Ferdinand

---

[4] See, for example, R.G. Davis and J.H. Denton, *The English Parliament in the Middle Ages* (1981) and R. Butt, *A History of Parliament: The Middle Ages* (1989).

[5] Sir David Lindsay Keir, *The Constitutional History of Modern Britain since 1485*, (1964) pp. 1–2.

[6] *The English Constitution*, (1930) p. 150.

Mount where he identifies the "continuity myth" in British constitutionalism.[7] The fiction of the constitution evolving only slowly and in a
gradual and organic way, is closely related to the fiction that Britain is in
some way unique or at least blessed with a history stressing an exceptional
degree of continuity and stability. This view has many adherents and
propagandists. Mount indicts a range of constitutional luminaries including Burke, Bagehot and Dicey, and quotes Jennings who recognised that
"political changes in the United Kingdom are marked by our use of
fictions. Institutions are rarely abolished; they continue in theory but
shorn of their essential functions. Names remain in constant use, but they
represent different things."[8] Mount offers a comic parade of distinguished
constitutionalists who have unwisely and inaccurately predicted that
certain constitutional events could never happen, such as the break-up of
empire, the abolition of the Northern Ireland Parliament and the appointment of another Prime Minster from the Lords. He then correctly
characterises and condemns "the glossing over of qualitative change, the
refusal to recognise the magnitude of the alteration in our arrangements
and attitudes over the centuries."[9]

Although the persistence of the belief that, as Dickens' Mr Podsnap
claimed, the English constitution is a matter for national pride and was
bestowed upon us by Providence,[10] is remarkable, it is now perhaps
untenable. Of course it is necessary to be very cautious in saying this. The
history of the various, admittedly limited, movements to reform the
constitution is littered with assertions that circumstances as diverse as the
decline of the monarchy, the extension of the franchise or the strengthening of the party system amount to a situation that was insupportable within
the present framework. (It perhaps says more about the vagueness of the
settlement rather than its much vaunted flexibility that all these features
have not only been incorporated but co-opted to become part of the very
tradition that they were once seen as assailing.) However, in the last 15 to
20 years a variety of issues have all variously contributed to a situation
where even within conventional constitutional thought it should be

[7] *The British Constitution Now* (1992) pp. 15–23.

[8] Jennings, *The Law and the Constitution* (3rd ed., 1943) quoted in Mount at p. 17.

[9] p. 19.

[10] "We Englishmen", Mr Podsnap told the foreign gentleman, "are very proud of our
constitution . . . it was Bestowed Upon Us by Providence". Charles Dickens, *Our Mutual
Friend* (1884–5).

evident that the framework of orthodox constitutionalism is under very serious stress. These range from the crisis in legitimacy of the 1970s and the experience of the Thatcher solution to that problem, to encompass also the simmering issue of devolution of parts of the polity and the problems of accommodating a European dimension.

The response to this from those just outside the circles of political power (those in power, or likely to attain power, have too much to lose) and the academic subset of auditors, chartists and commissioners of democracy has been to produce a series of proposals for constitutional reform. They recognise that in reality the United Kingdom is now the poor relation of many of its European neighbours in terms of its framework for controlling public power. As the century draws to a close it is becoming increasingly apparent that citizens in other countries do not, in fact, mind being blighted by the rigidity and legalism of their written constitutions and that they will continue steadfastly to refuse to clamour for all the advantages of an unwritten constitution as extolled by generations of British constitutionalists. However, as shall be seen in the next chapter, the range of these suggestions for reform remains very limited and many of the demands already come too late for a world where the exercise of power has moved on. What almost all of the reformers do not recognise is that the situation is worse than they thought. Not only have the developments of the last 20 years or so in Europe and in the domestic constitution produced fairly obvious tensions within the British tradition of constitutionalism but they have also produced huge changes in the locus of power which have been less well recognised than the symptoms they produce within constitutional theory. These are the source of the misfit between constitutional theory and the practice of government today and, while they are the subject of this whole account, they will be outlined in the next chapter.

While reformers think about ways of upgrading a seventeenth century constitution for their rather limited version of modernity what is the orthodoxy within constitutional theory doing? Regrettably most of it remains mired within the legacy of self-satisfaction which dominates much of the writing on the constitution. Traditionally this has referred to the particular historical circumstances of the United Kingdom to explain and then justify the claim that constitutionalism has reached its optimum expression within the well settled limits of the British textbook constitution of liberal-democratic descent. This idea has a long pedigree. As Poggi puts it, "the British polity stood in the imagination of eighteenth century European intellectuals as the embodiment not only of constitutional but also of representative government".[11] It required only the extension of the franchise to the new industrial middle classes in the early decades of the nineteenth century and the reforms of the middle part of the nineteenth century to usher in the classical liberal, representative state which remains, at least in the imagination of some more irredentist constitutional theorists, the acme of constitutional development. Even now the main textbook tradition[12] operates within the parameters set within a different age. A glance down the contents page of any of the main textbooks will reveal a world where the exercise of power is confined more or less neatly within the collection of institutions that the accidents of a long history have thrown up to take on those functions of the modern state that elsewhere are allocated to deliberately created (and controlled) bodies. In the United Kingdom Parliament still appears at the top the of this hierarchy of institutions, as if somehow it and the Crown operate a monopoly of public power. The privatisation of public power and the internationalisation of national authority that have radically altered the constitution in the last 20 or so years seem strangely absent in the mainstream of constitutional writing. Older textbooks have evolved into further editions without seeing the need to revise traditional categories and classifications. New works have adopted similar structures with apparently little realisation that the cosy world of Westminster where the destiny of the nation was hammered out on the floor of the House of Commons is now very far distant from the reality of public power at the end of the twentieth century. Notwithstanding the far-reaching changes in the distribution and exercise of power in the post modern world, the main substance of constitutionalism—at least as seen from the perspective of most constitutional law textbooks—remains almost exclusively the long established institutions and their formal behaviour. Thus, typically, the textbook view of the constitution emphasises the operation of Parliament along with a reactive examination of how changes in the wider world impact upon it. It offers detailed accounts of the Crown, the Lords and the other institutions that make up what one writer has dismissed as "the living dead of the constitution".[13] This traditional fayre is served up along with vignettes of

---

[11] G. Poggi, *The State: Its Nature, Development and Prospects*, (1990) at p. 56.

[12] See further the review of the textbook tradition provided by Morison and Doe in the annotated bibliography of United Kingdom public law in *Revue Europeene De Droit Public / European Review of Public Law /Eur. Zeitschrift Des Offent. Rechts / Revista Europea Di Diritto Pubblico*, Vol. 2, No.2. pp.495–502.

[13] Kingdom, *Government and Politics in Britain* (1991) at p. 253.

what might possibly occur within the bloodless and one-dimensional terms of its own study should the cut and thrust of politics produce a scenario where, improbably, it was left to the constitutional lawyer to resolve matters with his or her catalogue of laws, rules and conventions. This orientation is in contrast to the dominant paradigm in politic theory. There attention has moved away from the state and its institutions and towards political behaviour, parties, pressure groups and the deeper forces at work in the informal system which explain how things "really work".[14] Within legal writing the institutions have never lost their central importance. Perhaps the vocabulary of legal scholarship, with its emphasis on certainty, formality and rules, has not developed to express the uncertain, informal and "unruley" world of *realpolitik*.

Whatever the reason for this evolutionary direction, the theory of the constitution developed to underpin this set of understandings and practices has not needed to move much beyond the agenda set by those Victorian jurists, Bagehot and Dicey, whose deadhand on the throttle of constitutional doctrine has kept the engine of public law theory firmly steered in a direction away from developing a coherent, modern theory of the state and detailed limits on the control of public power. As Dearlove sees it,

"for most of this century the British constitution has been applauded as the best in the world in providing for a system of representative and responsible government and the liberal-democratic constitutional theory provided by Dicey has been seen as *the* theory to make sense of our system of rule".[15]

Even now the growing band of critics seldom think a prescription for a cure lies far beyond writing it all down somehow in an authoritative document and maybe adding a bill of rights and perhaps a measure of electoral reform.

This sanguine attitude towards constitutional arrangements could of course be contrasted with the reality of power, "the 'what actually happens constitution'" as JAG Griffiths terms it,[16] but this seldom surfaces in most constitutional writing. The prevailing way of regarding the constitution

---

[14] See further Dearlove, "Bringing the Constitution back in: Political Science and the State" (1989) 37 *Political Studies*, 521–539 for a critique of this development and an attempt to return the discipline to the issues which initially concerned it at the beginning of the century. See also Judge, *The Parliamentary State* (1993) as an example of the revisionist tendency which seeks to reinvigorate the study of the state and its structures.

[15] Dearlove, *op. cit.* at p. 535 (emphasis in original).

[16] JAG Griffiths, "Justice and Administrative Law Revisited" in *From Policy to Administration: Essays in Honour of William A Robson* (Griffith ed. 1976) at p. 205.

remains as an adaptable and flexible instrument for government that functions still with its historical anachronisms adding only charm to the pageant
of rule. The ad hoc-ery that generally is represented as a particular virtue of
the British way of ruling has its equivalence in a constitutionalism that
eschews the need for the abstract theorising that marks continental public
law or, indeed, even a developed idea of the state or a notion of public
power. Foreigners have states, the British have governments. With some
distinguished exceptions, constitutional scholarship remains atheoretical and
focused on institutions. The dominant tradition in Britain is, as Loughlin
puts it rather grandly in his detailed critique of contemporary thought in
public law, a "conservative variant of the normativist style" which "may be
found in formalism and the analytical method in public law and in the
belief that public law is concerned with the 'order of things' ".[17]

How exactly does this dominant tradition see the issues of public
power? What exactly is the detailed legacy from the orthodoxy that falls to
public lawyers today? There are a number of variations but essentially there
is always present the magpie's nest construction where what has lasted
from previous seasons is adapted and made to do in the belief that, as the
first Lord Falkland declared, if it is not necessary to change something then
it is necessary not to change it. The untidy construction that results is then
transformed by a series of short term, ad hoc solutions to deep-seated
problems with the result that while it may not be a success at least it can be
said to work. Over this untidy construction of mud and sticks the baubles
of monarchy and the glass beads of pageantry, history and "tradition"
preside and, with the mixture of nostalgia and conservatism which the
British establishment deploy so successfully, the whole inelegant nest
comes to be seen in the eyes of its builders as the perfect architectural
masterpiece.

There is thus, as Wolf-Phillips informs us, an "idealised view" of the
British system.[18] This remains as the legacy for public lawyers today.
Basically this sees government carried out in a liberal-democratic tradition
and in the public interest. The theoretical omnipotence of the sovereign
parliament is tempered by political and practical realities. The monarch,
widely admired and a focus for unity, is insulated from party politics. The

---

[17] Loughlin, *Public Law and Political Theory* (1992) at p. 139.
[18] Wolf-Phillips, "A long look at the British constitution" (1984) 37 *Parliamentary Affairs*
385.

government of the day is led by a Prime Minister who leads a parliamentary majority mandated by an electorate voting freely in open elections. Parliament both legislates in accord with the views of the electorate and scrutinises the work of government by controlling national expenditure and taxation and providing a public forum for redress of both collective and individual grievances. The convention of collective responsibility ensures that the government, composed of ministers of state (aided by a professional civil service), provides a focus for political accountability. The convention of individual responsibility means that each action within a given department's competence can be called to account within Parliament with the resignation of a particular minister or even the fall of a government a possible result of maladministration or incompetence. The House of Lords provides a forum beyond party politics where experience and maturity can be brought to bear to constrain popular government and provide a measure of continuity. The judiciary, meanwhile, provide a further check on power with the ordinary courts, guided by the principle of the Rule of Law, pronouncing on the legality of government action.

Within this idealised view the absence of a written constitution, or defined notions of the state and of public power, has been nothing of a disadvantage. On the contrary it has meant a measure of flexibility where conventions and understandings could grow up to cement the process of government in a pragmatic and realistic way. Although the basis of the constitution was established in a settlement dating back to the seventeenth century, the lack of a formal structure has meant that the institutions of government have been able to develop to meet modern requirements without the constraint of written rules or formal constitutional requirements.

All of this is supposed to work by a series of understandings, shared values and adherence to traditions of tolerance and freedom. While Parliament in strict theory may be able to legislate on what ever it wants, it is thought to be constrained in some way from doing so by some British sense of fair play or whatever. There is supposed to be a shared political culture which remains constant in government no matter who picks up the reins of power. The idea of a set of conventions, a code of political morality, is often held up to be the great glory of the British constitution and it is not uncommon for students commencing their studies through the orthodox texts to be surprised that conventions are not unique to the British system or to unwritten constitutions. Conventions were, of course, one of the twin pillars of Dicey's idea of the constitution—with the law of the constitution making up the other (and for him only legitimate one for study by lawyers).[19] Conventions are now, of course, legitimate subjects of study by even the most stuffy constitutionalists and these join a whole range of less specific customs, usages and "traditions" to provide the textbook explanation of why the whole unbounded structure holds together and why power does not escape the very loose limits of the British version of a constitution. This idea of a political morality astonishingly really still is central to the orthodox approach to the constitution. Even an authority such as Rodney Brazier, who appears in one guise as a thoughtful member of the reforming tendency,[20] almost seems to subscribe to this fiction of there being a self-limiting hold on power when he appears in the guise of a textbook writer. The phrases "serenity of historical continuity" (p. 9), "relatively high degree of homogeneity" and "widely diffused acceptance of traditional forms, gradualism and parliamentary methods" (p.10) all survive intact in the seventh edition of what is titled now *De Smith and Brazier: Constitutional and Administrative Law* (1994).

Could there be anything in these ideas of political morality even in an era when the Public Accounts Committee, commenting on a series of administrative and financial deficiencies within departments and other public bodies, concluded that "these failures represent a departure from the standards of public conduct which have mainly been established during the past 140 years"?[21] Even within the very heart of the orthodoxy it seems that there is in reality very scant regard for such ideas. Dicey, in arguing for a clause requiring a referendum to be attached to any Home Rule Bill, declared "This of course, it may be said, is unconstitutional. This word holds no terrors for me; it means no more than unusual."[22] Sir Ivor Jennings maintains that "to say that a new policy is 'unconstitutional' is merely to say that it is contrary to tradition".[23] More modern writers take an equally relaxed view. JAG Griffith declares "the constitution is no more

[19] See Dicey, *An Introduction to the Study of the Law of the Constitution* (8th ed.), pp. 27–31.
[20] See, for example, Brazier, *Constitutional Reform: Reshaping the British Political System* (1991); "Enacting a Constitution" (1992) 13 *Statue Law Review* 104.
[21] Committee of Public Accounts, *8th Report: The Proper Conduct of Public Business* (1994), paragraph 1. The *Economist* has felt able to go further, drawing upon the evidence of the Report to support of its suggestion that in the civil service integrity is slipping, impartiality is being undermined and parliamentary accountability is being eroded. (March 19, 1994, p. 35.)
[22] Dicey in *A Leap in the Dark*, quoted by Mount, *supra* p. 53.
[23] *The Law and the Constitution* (3rd ed. 1934) p. 59.

and no less than what happens".[24] Even Loughlin seems to come dangerously close to this when he asserts that "public law is simply a sophisticated form of political discourse".[25] Indeed, there is whole sub-genre within the textbook tradition which, in demonstrating its grasp of the gritty realities of power, appears almost to subscribe to the view that is occasionally heard from some politicians to the effect that the practice of government is really in itself the constitution. Thus it is that there is a range of cases and materials books which have expanded the usual ambit of such works from venerable statutes and hoary old cases to more unorthodox material. Turpin, Pollard and Hughes, and Allen, Thompson and Walsh all proudly include not only official reports from Parliament and its various committees but also administrative circulars, memoirs and political journalism.[26] Brazier goes even further. In his *Constitutional Texts: Materials on Government and the Constitution* (which insists on seeing government as extending really no further than parliament, the monarch and the judges) we are even offered a large selection of biographies, autobiographies, diaries and letters. While this may all be very practical and realistic it does seem to omit a surely essential factor of any constitution that it is trying to *control* how the powerful use power rather than simply celebrate it. The constitution should not be simply what *some* people say it is and, unless we are attempting the very interesting and ambitious task of providing a *sociology* of the exercise of constitutional power, it really ought not to be sought in the detritus of political life any more than in the contents of a Whitehall wastepaper bin or paper shredder. Indeed, we have more sympathy here with the reformer Anthony Barnett who tries to maintain a distinction between the power exercised within a constitution and the power of a constitution. In recognising that an unwritten constitution will generally benefit those political elites for whom it is unwritten, Barnett could be seen as pointing out the dangers in allowing the constitution as a set of rules

[24] Griffith, "The Political Constitution", (1979) 42 *Modern Law Review* at p. 19.
[25] Loughlin, *Public Law and Political Theory* (1992) at p. 4. To be fair Loughlin is concerned to root public law within its "social, political, economic, and historical context" and to embed his own inquiry with "the realities of the times" (p.4). Nevertheless, perhaps his wholly scholarly project, which reaches no practical conclusion much beyond exhorting us to consider more closely the work of Niklas Luhmann (pp. 250–264), would in fact be more realistic if it engaged more closely with public law's role in *controlling* power.
[26] Turpin, *British Government and the Constitution: Text, Cases and Materials* (2nd ed. 1990); Pollard and Hughes, *Constitutional and Administrative Law: Text and Materials* (1990) and Allen, Thompson and Walsh, *Cases and Materials on Constitutional and Administrative Law* (3rd ed. 1994.)

for power to become confused with the practice of those elites who "help to preserve the status quo by interpreting questions about the constitution as being about their decisions, not our freedoms."[27]

Tensions within the Orthodoxy

Of course the idealised view of the operation of public power, with or without its accompanying political morality, is not now accurate (if it ever was) and the constitutionalism which reflects it is not tenable. No longer can the orthodox constitutionalism of the textbooks offer much of a claim to make sense of how power is actually exercised in the United Kingdom. There have been massive structural changes in the nature of the state and in the actual practice of government which render a constitutionalism established in the seventeenth century, articulated in the Victorian age and preserved lifelessly in the twentieth century of little real value today. The changes have come from both external forces and from developments in the *realpolitik* of constitutional practice in the last century. They have produced massive fractures in the whole edifice of British constitutionalism.

The nature of the British state has altered fundamentally. The homogeneous nation state in which the idealised view of the British constitution is supposed to take its place no longer exists—if indeed it ever did. The forces of pluralism, nationalism and ethnicity that are transforming the rest of Europe and beyond have their impact in Britain too. There is far-reaching change occurring as a result of both internal and external forces. This is explored in more detail in the next chapter. Now, however, the impact of these changes on the orthodox constitutionalism can be briefly reviewed. It can be easily demonstrated how, while the actual practice of government has moved on (as indeed it must), the idea that there is any sort of constitutionalism at theoretical level that can explain and justify how public power is exercised is receding fast into a series of contradictions, inaccuracies and inconsistencies. The old principles and doctrines from the idealised constitution are wearing increasingly threadbare and the problems of stretching even the famously flexible British constitution to cover the bare patches where the practice has outrun the theory offers us

---

[27] Barnett, "Empire State" *New Statesman and Society*, July 29, 1992 at p. 20.

an indication of the extent to which there have been changes in the way power is distributed and exercised.

Except in the eyes of some of the more fiercely orthodox constitutional theorists, the practice within the domestic constitution has not stood still in the face of developments both within the state itself, and beyond it, which have challenged radically the form of the polity and the project of government. The exigencies of government have required that these realities be accommodated and while this has happened in practice the constitutionalism that for so long underwrote government in Britain has not of late proved to be as versatile and pragmatic as its adherents have claimed. There is now a gulf between practice and theory in the constitution. This operates with regard to *external* forces of change acting upon the constitution and *internal* factors necessitating a rethinking of the orthodoxies.

EXTERNAL TENSIONS

From the perspective of *external* change impacting on the constitution, the problems and inconsistencies that continuing developments in the later part of the twentieth century have brought to a constitutionalism rooted essentially in a seventeenth century settlement, are easily demonstrated. Reference need only be made to the increasing demands from Europe which provide a lens through which is refracted the incoherencies and inconsistencies of the orthodox constitutionalism in coming to terms with the reality of what it now means to be a single national entity in a political sea where the currents generated by economic, fiscal, trade and security imperatives do not respect the integrity of individual nations but instead flow over and around individual states controlling, directing, and occasionally overwhelming, their frail efforts to chart their own courses. The British constitutional tradition has experienced considerable difficulties in trying to accommodate the development of the international and supranational agencies that have grown up to deal with both the larger problems facing nations and the needs of individuals within those nations. This has ushered in not only a whole new set of institutions and structures but also a variety of principles and ideas such as subsidiarity, proportionality and guaranteed rights which are alien to the British common law tradition with its emphasis on parliamentary sovereignty. As Neal Acherson sees it, "Britain, like a spaceship nearing another planet, is now entering the gravitational field of very different constitutional ideas and very different ways of doing things".[28] The experience of attempting to reconcile parliamentary sovereignty with European integration and accepting the role of the European Court of Human Rights provide the most obvious examples of this problem.

In relation to the European Union it is necessary only to chart a few highlights in the process whereby the fundamental principle of parliamentary sovereignty, Dicey's "very keystone" of the constitution,[29] has been traduced (as the orthodox doctrine would have it) into some uncomfortable idea that, at best, parliament can utter some sort of clear imprecation—"an express positive statement"[30] of legislative virility forcing what might be a terminal crisis within the European Union—and only in this way legislate on whatever it wishes.[31] Early ideas of community law providing some sort of benign parallel legal system that would not overlap, or could perhaps be ignored, have disappeared from orthodox constitutionalism.[32] Now there is the clear judicial acknowledgement that the terms of the European Communities Act 1972 make it clear that it is "the duty of a United Kingdom court . . . . to override any rule of national law found to be in conflict with any directly enforceable rule of Community law".[33] Meanwhile community law mechanisms to ensure the primacy of

---

[28] Neal Ascherson, "Fuzzy Democracy", *New Statesman and Society*, March 11, 1994 at p. 24.

[29] *Introduction to the Study of the Law of the Constitution*, (10th ed., 1959) p. 70.

[30] *Per* Lord Denning M.R. in *Macarthys Ltd v. Smith* [1979] I.C.R. 785 at p. 789.

[31] See T.R.S. Allan, "Lord Denning's Dextrous Revolution" (1983) 13 *Oxford Journal of Legal Studies* p. 22–23 for discussion of a variety of arguments along the lines that parliament retains an ultimate overriding power to legislate so as to withdraw from the Community although it must accept a "manner and form" restriction in so far as an express positive statement is required and thus, at the very least, upset the traditional idea of implied repeal. See also Allan, *Law, Liberty and Justice: The Legal Foundations of British Constitutionalism* (1993) and Gravell's "Effective Protection of Community Law Rights: Temporary Disapplication of an Act of Parliament" [1991] P.L. 180.

[32] It is noteworthy perhaps that the present, edition of De Smith and Brazier *Constitutional and Administrative Law* (7th ed., 1994) is the first to drop De Smith's memorable description of the United Kingdom government wilfully indulging in "legislative schizophrenia" in the European Communities Act 1972 by seating Parliament on two horses, "one straining towards the preservation of parliamentary sovereignty, the other galloping in the general direction of Community law supremacy" (6th ed., 1989 at p. 82). The 2nd edition (1973) published in the year of the United Kingdom's accession to the European Community, flagged community law as "a constitutional innovation of the highest importance" (p.43) but offered only one-and-a-half pages of commentary and an appendix on the structure of the institutions.

[33] *Per* Lord Bridge in *R v. Secretary of State for Transport, ex p. Factortame Ltd* [1991] 1 A.C. 603 at p. 659.

European law have developed strongly and unequivocally.[34] One might think that surely this much less ambiguous acceptance of the primacy of community law in practice would force a more realistic approach no matter what the damage to the theory of the constitution. However, while the debate within political science may be over, with one commentator reporting that "talk of the destruction of parliamentary sovereignty in the 1990s has a quaint ring in the ears",[35] this issue still considerably exercises constitutional lawyers. Orthodox constitutionalism persists in constructing its whole intellectual edifice round Dicey's cornerstone. Even where some acknowledgement is made of the primacy of community norms it is grudging,[36] and the orientation of the whole agenda of the constitutionalism remains set by the domestic, traditional view.

The European Convention on Human Rights, and the requirements that it imposes on the law of the United Kingdom, is perhaps a less immediately pressing problem for government. However, there is still a parallel procrustean process whereby the traditional constitutionalism is tortured to fit the reality of international obligations. Here there is the

[34] See generally, Curtin, "The Decentralised Enforcement of Community Law Rights: Judicial Snakes and Ladders" in *Constitutional Adjudication in European Community and National Law* (Curtin and O'Keeffe ed. 1992), Steiner, "From Direct Effect to Francovich: Shifting means of enforcement of Community Law" (1993) 18 E.L.R. 3, Snyder, "The Effectiveness of European Community Law: Institutions, Processes, Tools and Techniques" (1993) 56 M.L.R. 19, Ross, "Beyond Franovich" (1993) 56 M.L.R. 55 and Martin, "Furthering the Effectiveness of EC Directives and the Judicial Protection of Individual Rights Thereunder" (1994) 43 I.C.L.Q. 26.

[35] Judge *The Parliamentary State* (1993), p. 209.

[36] For example, De Smith and Brazier conclude that although "the doctrine of parliamentary sovereignty has undoubtedly changed" this must be put into "the full Community political and legal context". Other countries have been equally reluctant and anyway "the expectation is that the national authorities will pass amending legislation" and so, presumably, salvage the forms of sovereignty at least. In any event, there is always the possibility of pulling the plug on community membership and then sovereignty "would fully revive in its traditional form if Parliament legislated to withdraw from the European Community". (*Constitutional and Administrative Law*, 7th ed., 1994, at pp.88–9). In *Wade and Bradley Constitutional and Administrative Law*, (11th ed., 1993) Bradley and Ewing consider the idea of a transfer of legislative power to the community and conclude "whether or not such an absolute limitation of the UK Parliament's legislative authority is theoretically possible, it is beyond doubt that this has not been achieved by the European Communities Act 1972, albeit that the devices called upon in that Act go a long way . . . to safeguard the primacy of community law as far as the UK courts are concerned." (pp.145–6). There then follows four pages of tight argument to establish that it is the British legislature, through s. 2(4) of the European Communities Act 1972, rather than European mechanisms that ensures conformity to E.C. law (pp. 146–9). Craig, offers a broadly similar defence of the orthodoxy from the assault of the *Factortame* decision in "Sovereignty of the United Kingdom Parliament after *Factortame*" (1991) 11 *YBEL* 221. The examples could be continued.

spectacle of the Judiciary having to accommodate an obligation taken on
by the Executive (through its Treaty making prerogative) which, within
the theory of the constitution, can really only be discharged by the
Legislature who must ensure that the standards set in the convention are
enshrined in the law. Thus there are a series of cases where individual
judges have attempted variously to: embrace the Convention as binding in
general and in preference to an act of parliament[37]; accept its validity in
assisting statutory interpretation[38]; deny its application to fill a gap in
common law[39]; employ it to clarify the common law[40]; assert that anyway
the standards of the convention are upheld in English law[41] and deny its
application altogether.[42] Meanwhile the European Court of Justice (and
perhaps the British legislature) maintain that it can be brought in via the
idea that fundamental rights of the Convention are the sort of common
legal tradition envisaged by article 164 of the Treaty of Rome which must
form part of the general principles of European Community law.[43]

All of this suggests a system not very happy with reconciling the realities
of increased and increasing international and supranational regulation
within a structure based on the supremacy of the domestic legislature. The
United Kingdom is not alone in having problems in grafting external
obligations on to its constitution. However, the fact remains that the

---

[37] As is well known, Lord Denning initially took a robust view where he stated in *Birdi v. Sec
State for Home Affairs* (unreported) that "if an Act of Parliament did not conform to the
ECHR, I might be inclined to hold it invalid". This view was soon retracted in *R v. Sec of
State for Home Affairs, ex p. Bhajan Singh* [1976] Q.B. 198 and in *R. v. Chief Immigration Officer,
ex p. Salamat Bibi* [1975] 3 All E.R. 846.
[38] *Waddington v. Miah* [1974] 1 W.L.R. 683.
[39] *Malone v. Metropolitan Police Commissioner* [1979] CH 344; *Gleaves v. Deakin* [1980] A.C.
477.
[40] Per Lord Fraser in *Attorney-General v. BBC* [1981] A.C. 303. Also *Derbyshire CC, ex p.
Times Supplements Ltd* [1992] 3 W.L.R. 28.
[41] Lord Donaldson in the Court of Appeal in *R. v. Secretary of State for the Home Department
ex p. Brind* [1991] 1 A.C. 696 maintained that "you have to look long and hard before you
can detect any difference between the English common law and the principles set out in the
Convention" (at p.717).
[42] *Brind v. Home Secretary* [1991] 1 A.C. 696.
[43] As long ago as *J. Nold KG v. Commission* (case 4/73 [1974] E.C.R. 491 the ECJ made it
clear that in protecting fundamental rights reference would be made not only to rights
contained in members' constitutions but also in international treaties which they had signed.
This was taken up in the United Kingdom context when Art. 7 of the ECHR (prohibiting
retroactivity in penal measures) was invoked to stop the prosecution of a Danish fisherman
operating in United Kingdom waters (*R v. Kirk* (case 63/83) [1984] E.C.R. 2689. See also
H.L. Deb. November 1992 col. 1087–1116 for discussion of this "back-door incorporation"
argument.

nature of political entities and individual affiliations have markedly altered without there being in the United Kingdom any corresponding qualitative change in the form of constitutionalism. Increasingly the nation state and the national constitution appear as too small for the big problems of life and too big for smaller problems. Thus issues such as economic viability, territorial integrity or environmental pollution are beyond the control of individual states and (in so far as they can be managed by public bodies at all) they are handled instead by the European Union, the United Nations or whatever. Meanwhile the state as a national political centre circumscribed by a domestic constitutional order, is simultaneously too large to be responsive to issues of local and ethnic diversity. Not only are affiliations and loyalties crossing national boundaries but the protection of individuals within existing states is being mediated increasingly by international and supranational bodies. For the domestic British constitution to accommodate these developments, and the alien institutions and mechanisms that they bring with them, demands more than ingenious tinkering with the existing constitution. It needs more than judicial ingenuity in interpreting conflicting requirements. It requires more than simply that a blind eye be turned to the fundamental contradictions in theory so that the practice can continue to work.

INTERNAL CHANGES IN THE PRACTICE OF GOVERNMENT

At the same time as constitutionalism in the Westminster sense has been assailed by fundamental changes operating externally there have been important *internal* changes also. The practice of government within the constitution has not stood still and this too has provided conflict between the orthodox theory of the constitution and its practice. The decade of change brought by the Thatcher administration in Britain introduced a radical, reforming government committed to a widespread re-constitution of the state and a reworking of the role of government. This, along with the external dimension alluded to above, has contributed to a major shift in the locus of power, the implications of which we believe have not even begun to be considered within orthodox constitutionalism. However, even within the limits of present constitutional thinking, with its idealised view of parliament sustaining and controlling government, the practice of government during the 1980s has demonstrated at last to most people many of the deep-seated problems in the British version of constitutionalism. The spectacle of watching a government, which never achieved more than 43 per cent of the popular vote, set about over-hauling the

welfare consensus of the past 50 years finally caused a number of constitutional commentators, particularly from the centre and left, to complain
that many of the apparently eternal veracities of the orthodox constitutionalism were not quite so enduring as they might have appeared. As Hirst
has remarked "In Mrs Thatcher Britain . . . found a politician to expose the
nakedness of constitutional checks and balances to public view".[44]

   In fact, Mrs Thatcher's reformist crusade was possible only because of a
coincidence of political will and circumstance, but it did show up in sharp
relief a variety of long-term trends in constitutional practice. The alternating two party system, and the link with democracy and choice that this
suggests, is an essential attribute of Westminsterism. It is one of the most
important unwritten aspects of the unwritten constitution. The split in the
Labour party towards a new centralist party weakened the Opposition and
denied to constitutional practice during the whole of the 1980s the
requirement of Westminster-style constitutional theory that there be a
strong second party to challenge government and offer an alternative to
(the small group of floating) voters who effectively control succession to
office when a government is threatened in Parliament. Without such a
challenge the British electoral system delivers to the winner of the most
seats in parliament almost total control over legislative and executive
power. It was this dominance that was handed to a conservative government committed to far reaching change.

   A very large academic industry has developed to analyse the impact of
the Thatcher government.[45] Certainly the fundamentals of the Thatcher
programme are well known. Essentially the radical Conservative government was able to follow a programme that has entailed a simultaneous
strengthening of central power with the dispersal of public power to the
free market economy. All alternative centres of power—nationalised
industry, trade unions, local authorities or whatever—were to be curtailed. At the same time the idea of big government taking on and
extending all the functions of the welfare state was unpalatable: it was
necessary to privatise government. The result is that the state while

---

[44] Hirst, *After Thatcher* (1989) at p.45.
[45] The offshoot of this that has considered constitutional, or even legal, theory specifically has
been perhaps surprisingly small. See further, for example, Graham and Prosser (eds.) *Waiving
the Rules: The Constitution Under Thatcherism*, (1988); Bogdanor, "The Constitution" in
Kavanagh and Seldon (eds.) *The Thatcher Effect: A Decade of Change*, (1989) pp.133–42; *Journal
of Law and Society—Special Issue Thatcher's Law* (Gamble and Wells eds 1989) and Morison
"How to Change Things with Rules" in Livingstone and Morison (eds) *Law, Society and
Change* (1990).

strengthened, is no longer the sole locus of power and its satellites exist beyond the remit of the constitution. In effect this means that there are an increased number of quangos and regulatory bodies performing an increased number of functions that once were the responsibility of the state. It also means that, perhaps stimulated by a drive for efficiency in government, executive agencies with doubtful degrees of accountability have been charged to assist the civil service. Beyond this even there is the imposition of market discipline on the delivery of services (such as education and health) by contracting out various aspects to the private sector. Monopolies and activities traditionally given shelter (and funding) by the state in a whole variety of area from the provision of telephone services and basic utilities to broadcasting, the universities and the arts were opened up to competition and the "discipline of the market". A central feature behind all aspects of this trend is, of course, the substitution of non-political for political methods of control. However, although the focus of government changed there has been no corresponding change in the focus of constitutional regulation. In general, and with only a very few limited exceptions,[46] the orthodoxy in constitutional theory has remained unmoved by the level and extent of a programme of change that has rendered much of it irrelevant.

For some the problem was not the constitution itself but the way that it was used. Thus, for Labour, who were denied power, attention remained fixed not on adjusting the framework of rule but on getting a chance to use it from the commanding heights of a House of Commons majority. Within the old, one nation Tory party bypassed by the radical government, it was held that essentially the game of government in this country is played by unwritten rules and gentlemen's agreements. For them the problem was simply that Mrs Thatcher was not a gentleman. However, the better view is that the governments of the 1980s were simply

---

[46] The citizen's charter, the Next Steps initiative and the on-going process of contracting out have elicited a limited number of accounts. See, for example, Harden, *The Contracting State* (1992); Barron and Scott, "The Citizen's Charter Programme" (1992) 55 *Modern Law Review* 526; Lewis, "The Citizen's Charter and Next Steps: A New Way of Governing", (1993) *Political Quarterly* 316; Freedland, "Government by Contract and Public Law", (1994) *Public Law* 86; Lewis, "Reviewing Change in Government: New Public Management and Next Steps", (1994) *Public Law* 105. Textbooks, however, remain largely unmoved by the changes profoundly effecting their remit. Only one or two textbooks (in administrative law) have taken serious notice of these developments. See, for example, Cane, *An Introduction to Administrative Law* (2nd ed., 1992) pp. 33–43 and Craig, *Administrative Law* (3rd ed., 1994) Chap. 3.

exploiting in the same way, but to a different degree dictated by their own particular doctrinaire political project, the conflicts and inconsistencies between theory and practice within the British constitution which successive governments had relied upon to progress their own, usually less dramatic political agendas.

This second view maintains that the British constitution has always displayed a disjuncture between the theory set out in its textbooks and the reality down in the dirt of political life and that governments have traditionally used the gap between theory and practice to cover the reality of exercising power in Britain. For example, the Labour government in the mid-1960s used retrospective legislation to overcome an inconvenient judicial decision about war-time damage to property and bullied local education authorities with a financially threatening administrative circular.[47] When orthodox commentators admire the flexibility within the British version of constitutionalism they normally do not notice that in part the true flexibility of the British constitution is that any structural constraints on power, such as might normally be associated with an idea of constitutionalism, are largely absent from the actual exercise of power.[48] In practice the majority party in Britain can govern as it wishes. Constitutionalists in the United Kingdom, with their belief in the pragmatic, empirical nature of the British constitution effectively disqualify themselves from complaining that this should be otherwise. Principles and values which elsewhere provide the aims to which constitutionalism is directed as an instrument, are largely absent. They are replaced instead by a constitutionalism which privileges institutions, fetishises political practice and emphasises structures above values, and customs and rituals above ideals and standards. From almost all ends of the political spectrum constitutionalism is fundamentally conservative. It stresses the way things are—and at best the difficulties of getting around this to change them—rather than the way they should be.

---

[47] See further examples in Oliver, "Law, Convention and the Abuse of Power", 60 *Political Quarterly* 1989 p. 38.

[48] In their investigation of the economic neutrality of the British constitution, measured in terms of "freedom to adjust the balance between private and public activity in the economy", Daintith and Sah conclude that there is a high degree of formal neutrality within present arrangements. (See "Privatisation and the Economic Neutrality of the Constitution" (1993) *Public Law* 465.) Presumably it was this that rendered it relatively straightforward to engineer the changes seen in the 1980s and 1990s. The question now remains as to whether it would be as easy to reverse such change and there is no doubt that the main, and indeed insurmountable, obstacles would not be constitutional ones.

It was against this background that the "Thatcher Revolution" took place *within* the constitution and the fact of it happening no less than some of the changes it wrought (which will be reviewed shortly) demonstrates the dissonance between the theory describing the idealised view and the practice of government within the real constitution. The experience of government during the 1980s has shown beyond doubt that in the United Kingdom the framework for rule is inadequate to control government within the limits normally associated with constitutionalism. Mention has already been made of many of the features of the orthodox constitutionalism which allowed this to happen so smoothly. These include variously the imagined historical continuity of institutions and doctrines; the unwritten, assumed nature of controls which elsewhere are given privileged status within a document establishing the very basis of the society; and the mystery of the traditional, tacit understandings that are supposed somehow to self-limit those in power. Beyond these, however, there are two elements which are perhaps worth highlighting again.

First, there is the pre-democratic inheritance which remains to underwrite much of the constitutional apparatus today. This is strongly linked to the continuity myth referred to above. Edmund Burke could refer to our "entailed inheritance" whereby "we have an inheritable crown; an inheritable peerage; and an house of commons and a people inheriting privileges, franchises, and liberties, from a long line of ancestors".[49] Although some have been able to dismiss this as Bentham did when he complained of "boasting and toasting" and questioned the "wisdom of barbarian ancestors" and the "virtue of barbarian ancestors",[50] it does remain actually part of the working constitution. Most obviously there is the prerogative power. While the history of the royal prerogative stresses the limitations and restrictions placed on it by the courts, the present day reality is that the prerogative has little to do in practice with the monarch. It provides government with a largely unchecked source of active power in key areas of treaty making, patronage and, indeed, warfare.

The pre-democratic character of the constitution can also be linked to an idea that Britain or the United Kingdom (the name is part of the problem) is a stateless society. In contrast to most of the rest of Europe, where states were deliberately created with limits ascribed to their separate parts in a written constitution, the United Kingdom does not have a

---

[49] Edmund Burke, *Reflections on the Revolution in France* (1790) (1969), at p. 119.
[50] Jeremy Bentham, *The Handbook of Political Fallacies*, 1824 (1962), pp. 155–6.

coherent idea of state as a political or legal actor. Instead the Crown stands in. Indeed, in Britain there is Her Majesty's government, Her Majesty's Loyal Opposition, and the idea of On Her Majesty's Service can encompass everything from the armed forces to the tax inspector or social security clerk. Loyalty is sworn by officials to the Crown rather than anything so prosaic as a constitutional document. The semiotics of the British passport are revealing here. Although the passport now bears the words "European Community", and it has changed from royal blue to a uniform maroon, it still carries the words in scrolly writing to the effect that "Her Britannic Majesty's Secretary of State Requests and requires in the Name of Her Majesty all those whom it may concern to allow the bearer to pass freely without let or hinderance, and to afford the bearer such assistance and protection as maybe necessary." This may conjure up an image of Phileas Fogg leaving Victorian London to travel around the world in 80 days with only the faithful Passepartout and a carpet bag containing twenty thousand pounds in Bank of England notes. However, it does recall accurately the ancient idea of a personal loyalty to the traditions personified by the monarch. Indeed, the political psychology of Ulster Loyalists demonstrates to the extreme how loyalty to any potentially perfidious political administration is contingent upon adherence to traditions that are represented by the Crown and the right to rebellion is retained for any breach of this Lockean social contract.[51]

The idea of the Crown standing in for a modern concept of state is, however, one that is serviceable enough for the modern age (notwithstanding the Ulster Loyalist) if one sees Crown government in terms of a constitutional system where Her Majesty's government, including the Cabinet and the Prime Minister with the civil service, acts as the *agent* of the Crown. As a former Head of the Home Civil Service writing on the duties of officials sees it, "for all practical purposes, the Crown ... is represented by the government of the day".[52] Within this understanding of constitutional principle, the government remains the chief mover within the system. Certainly the courts, in the trial of the civil servant Clive Ponting charged under the Official Secrets Act, had no doubt that the state

---

[51] In his *Two Treatises on Government* (1690) (1964), John Locke outlined his version of the social contract between rulers and ruled which entitles the people to remove the rulers if they either violate the rights of individual citizens or fail to provide the conditions under which the people may enjoy their rights.

[52] Sir Robert Armstrong quoted in Hennessy, *Whitehall* (1989), at p. 346.

and the Crown were synonymous with the government of the day.[53] Within this version of orthodox constitutionalism there are, of course, the checks and balances provided by parliament and the electorate, and it is these that are supposed to give legitimacy to the ancient system as it has evolved for modern times.

Of course the reality is quite different. The Crown is more than just an element of pageantry. It is not simply, in Bagehot's phrase, a "ceremonial" aspect to the constitution which runs alongside the "working" constitution.[54] Bagehot may well have been content with the belief that the monarchy was simply an example of Plato's "noble lie", a device for inducing into the masses a respect for their superiors and persuading them not to use their superior force of numbers to overthrow the social order. However, it is not true that, as he claimed, under the skirts of the monarch there arose a perfect republic. In fact government in the United Kingdom is not arranged much like government anywhere else, with a monarch simply adding glamour or consistency or whatever. The monarch is a remnant of another age and, although personally without significant power, the Crown has immense, pre-democratic powers from a former age. These pre-date the institutions of parliament and elections and modern democratic controls, and to a significant extent they evade the controls offered by these bodies. The Crown, as the government of the day, has inherited the sort of absolutist, divine right powers which Henry VIII took upon himself in his disavowal of the authority of the pope. As Tom Nairn argues,[55] in the context of Britain the Divine right thesis is essentially an early modern idea rather than a feudal one: without the authority of the Pope to buttress the regime at home, successive English Kings required alternative sources of legitimacy in asserting the degree of absolutist power of the monarch that came more easily in France. This was achieved most markedly by James I (James VI of Scotland) who acceded to the English throne and divine-right inspired, unqualified royal power in 1603. Of course the struggle to transfer power from the monarch to parliament was continuing,[56] but the point here is that the lines of this power were drawn by the monarchs and what was eventually wrested

---

[53] See *R v. Ponting* [1985] *Criminal Law Review* 318. See also Thomas, "The British Official Secrets Act 1911–1939 and the Ponting Case" [1986] *Criminal Law Review* 491.

[54] Bagehot, *The English Constitution* 1867 (1965).

[55] See further Nairn, *The Enchanted Glass: Britain and its Monarchy* (1988).

[56] L Wolf-Phillips provides a succinct account of this well-known historical struggle in "A Long Look at the British Constitution" (1984) 37 *Parliamentary Affairs* 385.

away from the monarchy was absolutist power. The old absolutism of the divine right kings has now been given to different personnel. The English parliament's victory in the Civil War was not a triumph for limited government: parliamentary absolutism was victorious. As Dicey put it, "the personal authority of the King has been turned into the sovereignty of the King in Parliament".[57] Dicey celebrated this as a successful transition from the pre-democratic, arbitrary power of the monarchy to a modern democratic arrangement which had the particular, additional advantage of retaining intact for the state the supreme central authority traditionally possessed by the Crown. However in reality of course there has not been a broadening of power but only a transfer. Parliament, or more accurately the Prime Minister and governing party of the day, is now in possession of a power whose ancient origin in the absolutism of the old monarchy makes it qualitatively different from that exercised within the limits of a written constitution in most comparable countries. One effect of this is that authority in the British state clearly flows downwards from the ruler rather than upwards from the people. This is related to the idea that people in the United Kingdom remain subjects rather than citizens: their rights and freedoms exist only in the interstices left by a sovereign parliament (controlled by an all powerful Prime Minister) which can largely do as it wishes without consultation, discussion, judicial scrutiny or constitutional check. Another effect is that the British system retains a higher degree of what Weber characterises as "traditional" and "charismatic" authority than other comparable states where "legal rational" authority tends to dominate. However perhaps the most important effect remains that the sovereignty of parliament, now harnessed by government, is directly linked to this venerable and pre-modern source. Although there are now the controls offered by parliament and the electorate, the powers and prerogatives from this reservoir of ancient, absolute power now lies largely at the disposal of the government of the day.

In Mrs Thatcher's time this power was deployed to its fullest extent. The constitution not only allowed it but facilitated it. During most of the period immediately prior to the 1980s the British constitution with its vague, ancestral basis might have been able to pass itself as quaint but adequate in comparison to those written constitutions that seriously profess to restrain government. Then each of the contestants for power in Britain was not far away from each other ideologically (as in the heyday of

---

[57] *Introduction to the Study of the Law of the Constitution* (10th ed., 1959) at p. 471.

Keynsian social democracy), and the traditional, inexplicit rules of what Marquand terms "club government"[58] meant that no-one would push the ambiguities and hazy compromises of the British constitution to their limit or use the huge battery of powers available to them to radically transform Britain. However, this was not the case in the 1980s. A government with a vision of deep-seated change was able to use the powers given to it in an ancient, largely pre-democratic constitution without much resistance from any paper barriers of a constitution. In the words of Charter 88,

> "the inbuilt powers of the 1688 settlement have enabled the government to discipline British society to its ends: to impose its values on the civil service; to menace the independence of broadcasting; to threaten academic freedom in the universities and schools; to tolerate abuses committed in the name of national security. The break with the past shows how vulnerable Britain has always been to elective dictatorship".[59]

The second of the elements to be highlighted relates to the focus on parliament which dominates orthodox constitutionalism. The main aspect of this is of course the fixation on parliamentary sovereignty. This is linked closely to the idea of parliament as the recipient of the pre-modern powers of the ancient constitution. Beyond this there is a more general view of all the institutions within the constitution being ordered with parliament at the apex. As we have said already, traditional constitutional theory generally still attempts to describe the whole system of government as if every exercise of executive power is traceable to a grant from parliament and ultimately accountable in parliament.

To some extent this academic conception of the importance of parliament accords with the reality of the struggle between political parties. What Bagehot noted as the "efficient secret of the English constitution" which was "the close union, the nearly complete fusion, of the executive and legislative powers",[60] has the effect of giving increased significance to parliament—at least as something that must be captured at election time in order to gain control of the whole apparatus of government. Bagehot wrote as a modern Victorian attempting to show that while the constitution was encrusted with venerable traditions it did function as a contemporary framework for government. Circumstances have, however,

---

[58] Marquand, *The Unprincipled Society: New Demands and Old Politics* (1988) Chap. 7.
[59] *Charter 88* (1988).
[60] *The English Constitution* (1867) (1963) p. 65.

moved on significantly. What was efficient for a more loosely articulated political system is now simply the key to largely unrestricted legislative and executive power. Bagehot's vision of the constitution did not foresee the rise of modern political parties and the massive powers of discipline and patronage available to the leader of the party in office to ensure almost complete domination of parliament in both its legislative role and where it seeks to scrutinise how that party exercises its executive role. No longer can parliament in any sense be seen to be the best expression of the will of the nation resulting from its direct connection with the people voting on any newly extended franchise for independent representatives—as perhaps could be argued from the perspective of newly minted Victorian Liberalism. The movement of power from the monarch to parliament may have reached a formal high point with the Bill of Rights in 1688, and then a political watershed with the various extensions to the franchise, but the process was not arrested there. As Mackintosh, most famously among a variety of commentators has pointed out,[61] from parliament effective executive power was transferred to a cabinet of ministers: cabinet government has, since the time of Churchill's wartime leadership, given way to Prime Ministerial government where now, the single office combines all the powers of the elected assembly.

Although the phrase "elective dictatorship",[62] was coined in the very different political climate of the 1970s, it did have a particular resonance during the period of Mrs Thatcher's premiership. Nevertheless, the "winner-takes-all" nature of government is something that suits both the major parties. While the 1980s were a lean time for Labour electorally, as a movement it has traditionally focused on the parliamentary road to socialism. Notwithstanding some recent flirtation with the idea of introducing proportional representation, the Labour Party knows well the benefits of capturing parliament. The idea of parliamentary sovereignty, the simple notion that, as Wade put it, "no act of the sovereign legislature (composed of the Queen, Lords and Commons) could be invalid in the eyes of the courts",[63] provides an irresistibly potent source of power to

---

[61] Mackintosh, *The British Cabinet* (2nd ed., 1968). Mount does point up something of a trend in constitutional thinking where he maintains that in recent decades the cabinet and prime minister have received too much attention from constitutionalists. He complains that indeed, "Sir Ivor Jennings and Professor John Mackintosh wrote as if nothing else really mattered". *Op. cit.* p. 113.

[62] Lord Hailsham, *Elective Dictatorship* (1976).

[63] H.W.R. Wade, "The Basis of Legal Sovereignty" (1955) *Cambridge Law Journal* 172 at p. 174.

politicians. Certainly parliamentary sovereignty can, as was seen in the 1980s, reward strong majority rule and take the emphasis away from dialogue and co-operation. Maybe it is even symptomatic of a style within British public life: democracy is a system of government at best rather than a style of life. For example in a financial context, the Treasury-City nexus is strong and although pension funds and insurance funds are the resources of the City there is little sign of any social priorities that these might suggest: there is no equivalent of German *lander* or Japanese MITI reflecting respectively a democratic and a bureaucratic qualification of the power of private capital. While we would not wish to push too far this idea of a national psychology underlying the exercise of power, it is undeniable that both the parliamentary system as it has evolved and the doctrine of parliamentary sovereignty have together allowed the distortion of constitutional practice away from the ideals of orthodox constitutional theory.

In saying this we are not claiming that parliament is in any way all-powerful, that it can meaningfully, as in Jennings famous example, legislate that smoking in the streets of Paris is an offence.[64] Indeed, part of the success of the Thatcher decade was to challenge this idea that the state could or should be expected to be omnipotent. Beyond this, indeed, we see the domestic parliament as having an increasingly restricted sphere of autonomy as the United Kingdom becomes increasingly enmeshed in interdependent supranational organisations and forces, and domestically power leaches out from government to other bodies and agencies. However, the emphasis on the power of parliament does have the important effect of establishing and legitimising the power of the *executive* to act as the state for all practical purposes independent of any meaningful controls by parliament. As Judge sees it in his review of the importance of parliament, there is a contradiction at the heart of the British constitution in that "the principle of parliamentary sovereignty [is] being used by executives to minimise their accountability".[65] In practical terms Ministers are now exercising the powers of parliament to legislate and controlling its powers to scrutinise. In this they are assisted by the civil service, those eunuchs guarding the political harem as Hailsham has styled them,[66] whose constitutional role is restricted to being simply instruments of government.

---

[64] Jennings, *The Law and the Constitution* (5th ed., 1959) at p. 170.
[65] Judge, *op. cit.* at p.210.
[66] Hailsham, "The Nation and the Constitution" in *The Crown and the Thistle: The Nature of Nationhood* (Maclean ed. 1979), at p.75.

The unnecessary levels of secrecy that persist in government help too. It is not too much of an exaggeration to say that the House of Commons is now less of a cockpit of politics or inquest of the nation than an elaborately managed press conference for the government (with perhaps a supporting role for the main opposition figures). The executive is largely immune to the controls of a parliament now dominated by party managers who seldom fail to organise effectively the members of their parliamentary party who make up the appropriate lobby fodder in the divisions.[67] In addition the government have the opportunity to manipulate the national economy in order to maximise the effective use of the prerogative to dissolve parliament. All this has the effect that the totality of the powers of the nation, although now reduced and circumscribed by international forces and agencies and dissipated throughout the polity, are at the disposal of the executive and can be used without any meaningful check by parliament.

The liberal theory of the constitution from the nineteenth century produced a model of democracy which saw parliament linking representation and accountability. The power of a sovereign parliament was directly linked to the electorate who were represented in the dominant House of Commons. Government was held to account in parliament through the doctrines of individual and collective responsibility and, in myriad informal and uncodified ways, the practice of the government was shaped and guided by parliament acting as the grand inquest of the nation. The link between government and the people was provided in parliament and, as Dicey saw it, "that which the majority of the House of Commons command, the majority of the English people usually desire".[68] The problem has come because this theory, with the central position that it gives to parliament, has been adhered to long after it could claim to have any connection with even Dicey's world where, for example, women not only did not, but according to him should not, have a right to vote. Now of course parliamentary sovereignty can no longer be seen sensibly by anyone as being underpinned by representative democracy. There is in no way any sort of continuous link between the governed and the governing:

---

[67] Griffiths and Ryle, *Parliament: Functions, Practice and Procedures* (1989), especially chaps. 8, 9, 10 and 11, provides an authoritative, detailed account of how government dominates parliament while from the perspective of modern political history Lenman's *The Eclipse of Parliament* (1992) demonstrates that this has been the case increasingly since the end of the 1914–18 war. See also Garrett, *Westminster: Does Parliament Work?* (1992).

[68] A.V. Dicey, *Introduction to the Study of the Law of the Constitution* (10th ed., 1959) at p.83.

election is separated from representation, and the right to select representatives is separated from the right to control them. The "single managed moment"[69] that occurs every four or five years when the party machine goes out to claim its "mandate" to do whatever it likes until the next time, has very little to with representing views at large or enabling the electorate to call government to account. However, the lip service that is still given to this idea within orthodox constitutionalism has the effect of giving government both the means and the legitimacy to do what it will with no check to its omnipotence. The incorporation of this model, with its focus on parliament, into British constitutionalism irrespective of fundamental changes in the way in which representative politics now operates in the United Kingdom, has resulted in the sort of largely unchecked elective dictatorship that was seen particularly in the 1980s. It has also, as J.D.B. Mitchell recognised in the 1960s, (1) stultified the emergence of a proper system of administrative law and (2) simultaneously led to too great a concentration on parliamentary controls.[70] This will repay closer examination.

(1) With regard to administrative law there has of course been a huge development since Dicey was able to claim proudly that there was no such thing as administrative law in England but only the rule of the ordinary law in the ordinary courts. Lord Diplock has referred to the establishment of a comprehensive system of administrative law as having been the greatest achievement of the English courts in his judicial lifetime, while Lord Woolf has described judicial review as the most vital and rapidly developing area of law ever. Although the doctrine might be well developed, and the academic specialism which this has spawned may be a particularly buoyant one, there must be some doubt as to the real, quantitative effect of the new body of judicial review doctrine on the actual exercise of public power. Access to the remedy, through the gateway of "sufficient interest", is narrow enough to suggest that it is intended for individual redress rather than more general scrutiny of the executive.[71] There has of course been a great increase in the use of judicial review: in 1994 there were nearly 3,000

---

[69] Tony Wright's phrase from *Citizens and Subjects: An Essay on British Politics* (1994) at p. 41.
[70] Mitchell quoted in Loughlin *op. cit.* at p. 193.
[71] See, for example, *R v. Secretary of State for the Environment, ex p. Rose Theatre Trust Company* [1990] 1 Q.B. 504 and *R v. Secretary of State for Foreign Affairs, ex p. World Development Movement Ltd* [1995] 1 All E.R. 611. See also Gordon, "Standing Room Only" (1995) 145 N.L.J. 116.

applications compared with 525 in 1980. However, an empirical examination of the trends and use of judicial review procedure in England and Wales for the Public Law Project, concludes that in practice its constitutional significance has been limited. Other than in the areas of housing and immigration (where particular factors apply and indeed have the effect of suggesting that figures indicate a low level of use) judicial review has not grown significantly in popularity as a remedy. Although judicial review is often depicted as a weapon in the hands of the citizen to be used against the over mighty powers of central government, the data suggests that this is not the case.[72]

There is also the view that while judicial review, and administrative law generally, may have expanded rapidly with the growth of government in the post-war period there are, as Freedland puts it, "some indications that our system of administrative law may have greater difficulties in coping with the rolling back of state activity [than] with the advance of that activity".[73] In particular, the re-structuring of public services involved in the agentisation of the Civil Service has exposed the inefficacy of administrative law controls. According to Freedland, contracting out should be regarded as an exercise of prerogative power and government certainly takes the view that the management of the civil service is a prerogative matter. The effect of this is that administrative law ideas, such as the principle against sub-delegation which might be thought to have application here, are effectively overwhelmed by the basic constitutional law principle that the exercise of prerogative powers is subject to only limited examination. Freedland argues moreover that the *GCHQ* case[74] (extending the courts' review jurisdiction into the prerogative power) is revealing because it illustrates not simply the administrative law daring of the House of Lords in reviewing the prerogative powers involved in the employment regime of a non-statutory agency of government but also, more significantly, their constitutional law caution in allowing the national security card to trump all others. There are likely to be further examples of the difficulties in using administrative law principles within a new framework

---

[72] See further Sunkin, Bridges and Meszaros, *Judicial Review in Perspective* (1993) especially pp. 100–101. See also Bradley, "Administrative Law: Is the System now in Place?" in *Constitutional Studies: Contemporary Issues and Controversies* (Blackburn ed., 1992), p.65 and the range of perspectives offered in *Administrative Law and Government Action* (Richardson and Genn ed. 1994).
[73] "Government by Contract and Public Law", (1994) *Public Law* 86 at p. 95.
[74] *Council of Civil Service Unions v. Minister for the Civil Service* [1985] A.C. 374.

of government that is achieved by a constitutional change putting agencies outside the administrative law remit and on to a contractual footing. In such a new situation traditional administrative law ideas based on controlling *decision-making* within government cannot easily come to grips with the more general task of overseeing government by contract.

There is of course always the Rule of Law which Dicey famously saw as a more than adequate substitute for a developed system of administrative law. Of course others have been less enthusiastic seeing the idea in practice as having a "Humpty Dumpty" quality whereby it is "a doctrine pregnant with ambiguity which means whatever its author would like".[75] We would tend towards this latter view, and indeed find of significance here a recent case which excited much attention. In *M v. Home Office*[76] the House of Lords confirmed that the courts do have the power to grant a mandatory interim injunction against an officer of the Crown. The details of English law do indeed make this a powerful and important judgement. However, is it not astonishing that constitutionalists should find it a breakthrough for the Rule of Law that the courts should be able to act against a Minster of the Crown who fails to comply with a mandatory judicial order? Secondly, it is perhaps even more disturbing that the Minister should have thought it safe to rely on legal advice, reproducing what was generally thought to be the settled position, and deliberately defy the court by returning an applicant for political asylum to Zaire despite his having made an apparently valid fresh application. Would not any central European county emerging into democracy or developing nation require this level of judicial control as a minimum?

(2) The other failing that Mitchell identified in the 1960s as coming about as a result of the emphasis on parliament is the concentration on parliamentary controls. Today this has led to both inadequate control and to misplaced control. Any control that is based in parliament is heir to the defect that parliament is ultimately in the control of the dominant political party. Parliamentary control is in reality reduced to a matter of internal party management. Although the forms and outward show of parliamentary control remain in place they are a fiction disguising only slightly the reality of stage managed party politics. Thus although standing committees may debate and set down amendments to legislation the only real hope for

---

[75] Ewing, "Trade Unions and the Constitution", *Waiving the Rules: The Constitution Under Thatcherism* (Graham and Prosser eds 1988) at p. 146.
[76] [1993] 3 All E.R. 537.

influence comes from the less vigorously whipped House of Lords or some passing political storm encouraging rebels to split the party. Other institutions similarly are in thrall to parliament and its embodiment of the political status quo. The Comptroller and Auditor General and the National Audit Office are inseparably linked to the Public Accounts Committee. The British version of Ombudsman is as a servant of parliament, a catalyst to parliamentary processes, and at best he or she appears as some sort of bolt-on foreign component sitting uncomfortably on the traditional coachwork of parliament. Despite occasional outbreaks of independence in the select committees they too inherit the party politics of parliament.[77] Underlying these devices, and their uneven effectiveness, there is the fundamental premise of ministerial responsibility. This has remained in place as the major mechanism long after it is meaningful to regard it as such and has distracted from the devising of alternatives. This is not the place to debate the extent of the demise of ministerial responsibility or the possibility of reviving it in any meaningful way. However, we must express some astonishment that within orthodox constitutionalism there are many who apparently believe that this doctrine, with its origins in the particular political practices of the early nineteenth century[78] provides the basis of a sufficient system of accountability today. For example, in a recent account Diana Woodhouse[79] seems to maintain that the very cornerstone of political accountability in the United Kingdom lies in the fact that government ministers are members of, and accountable to, parliament. She is apparently able to find in the mixture of political expediency, low ambition and just the occasional outbreak of honour that attend the case studies of resignation that she examines minutely, some sort of high constitutional principle that can act as an effective mechanism for controlling government. Other writers, with an interest less in grand constitutional principle than in the practical mechanics of power within the constitution, also (perhaps even more surprisingly) subscribe to this orthodoxy. Constitutional lawyers generally seem largely oblivious to the emptiness of the rituals within the old constitutional orthodoxies. Calls for

---

[77] Indeed, MP John Garrett takes the view that compared with the select committees of the last century their reports are "generally pallid, deferential and under-researched". *Westminster: Does Parliament Work?* (1992) at p.29.

[78] Birch sees the convention of collective responsibility as developing between 1780 and 1832 but dates the emergence of the concept of "responsible government" to 1829. See further *Representative and Responsible Government* (1962) Chaps 2, 3 & 10.

[79] D. Woodhouse, *Ministers and Parliament: Accountability in Theory and Practice* (1994).

resignations are usually not attended by expectations on either side that they will be heeded. The control exerted by party managers ensures that only political embarrassment (something very different from accountability) is fatal to a ministerial career. The emphasis on the disciplined organisation of the rival parties means that now the doctrine operates in reverse allowing ministerial irresponsibility by shielding inefficiency behind the machinery of the political party and the secrecy of government. Quite apart from questions as to whether ministerial responsibility is now a fiction (and indeed if we should even want ministers to resign if a Whitehall official makes a mistake) there is the issue of whether or not it even covers many of the agencies and individuals who now exercise executive functions. For example, Next Steps Executive Agencies have framework documents that define the responsibilities of, respectively, agency accounting officers or chief executives, departmental accounting officers and ministers. This division, and level of accountability for each, is premised on it being possible to distinguish between "policy" and "operational" issues: while ministers and departmental accounting officers are responsible for "policy" issues, the chief executives are accountable for "operations". However one looks at this there is a confusion or blurring of the traditional lines of responsibility. It may be that the doctrine of ministerial responsibility has still some limited jurisdiction[80] but this at best can mean only that the operation of these agencies is subject to a control that has been found inadequate in more conventional applications. Even if the concept remains broadly in place,[81] Parliament, through the individual member, can no longer turn to the minister responsible and ask him or her to account in the House. Now it is possible and indeed likely that instead the member of parliament's complaint on behalf of his or her constituent will be referred to the appropriate Chief Executive.[82] It may have been long a fiction that the minister actually knew anything about a particular constituent's problem but the orthodox theory at least established a line of accountability and a forum for realising it. There are of course other

---

[80] *The government reply to the Eight Report from the Treasury and Civil Service Committee (1988) Session 1987–88*, Civil Service Management Report: The Next Steps Cm. 524 contained the view that "the government does not envisage that setting up Executive Agencies within Departments will result in changes to the existing constitutional arrangements".
[81] The government reply to the Treasury and Civil Service Select Committee (*op. cit.*) admits that "establishing Executive Agencies within Departments will however involve some developments in the way in which external accountability is discharged".
[82] See Leopold, "Letters to and from 'Next Steps' Agency Chief Executives" (1994) *Public Law* 214 for an outline of some of the difficulties inherent in this.

methods of holding Next Steps Agencies accountable—including the right for a member to direct parliamentary questions at chief executives and for select committees to call them as witnesses in addition to a variety of financial accounting mechanisms. Whether or not these are adequate, and this is an issue we consider below,[83] there can be no doubt that they are separate from, and independent of, the traditional idea of ministerial responsibility and the exclusive focus on parliament that this entails. Meanwhile, the mechanisms based on the traditional parliamentary doctrines remain operating ineffectively except in so far as they keep the focus on parliament and block the development of effective alternatives.

Conclusion

In short it can be contended that the orthodox version of British constitutionalism is in serious trouble. It has failed to accommodate the new forms of international and supranational order that are of increasing importance. It has failed too to encompass the realities of political power historically and especially in the 1980s. Even within its own limited terms the orthodoxy is in trouble: fundamental ideas such as parliamentary sovereignty and the centrality of parliament as legislator and scrutiniser of the executive are being split apart by the formal practice of the very institutions they were supposed to control. Beyond this, as we have mentioned from time to time but will develop fully, the challenges to the idea of the nation state have simultaneously produced supra national agencies and mechanisms and dispersed public power away from formal, central institutions to a variety of bodies and forces, most notably the market. The regulation of authority from sources outside the traditional constitution is scarcely recognised as a problem let alone sorted out within the narrow view of traditional constitutionalism

We can not be content to simply allow government to happen and public power to continue to develop in a haphazard way fulfilling the criteria of those who use it rather than those on whose behalf it is supposed to be used. However, the question is, can the old apparatus of orthodox constitutionalism be given sufficient vitality for the role of re-shaping public power?

---

[83] See below at pp 67-83.

Chapter Two

Reviving Constitutionalism?—The Non Option of Reform

Introduction

At the end of the last chapter we asked the question whether orthodox constitutionalism could be re-vitalised to meet those challenges arising from both external relationships and changes in the practices of government which strain its conventional limits. The best hope of invigorating the orthodoxy comes from the burgeoning reforming tendency that is springing up at the intersection of constitutional scholarship and political debate. Despite the range of proposals proffered there it will not perhaps come as a surprise that we do not believe that reform can provide the answer to the problems of orthodox constitutionalism. It seems to us that the difficulties facing the traditional view of the British constitution are too far developed for even the most ambitious re-working of the existing constitutional structures to provide a complete or effective answer.

This does not mean of course that we are against reform of these structures. We are not attempting in some way to write off constitutionalism as false consciousness or some sort of strategy of legitimation by dead white males serving only to mask the undemocratic nature of capitalist relations. There can be no doubt that the basic institutions of the monarchy, parliament and government require revision to approximate to the standards achieved some time ago in comparable countries. There should be little objection to analysing and defining the responsibilities and duties of government, writing this down in a document and providing citizens with an instrument with which they can begin to assert rights. We should not deny the United Kingdom the sort of reforms that will update its seventeenth century constitution into the nineteenth century. However, plainly this is not enough. Reform of the traditional institutions and relationships will not authenticate the claim of orthodox constitutionalism adequately to describe or control the exercise of power either in those traditional institutions or in its new manifestations. Public power now operates at new levels and at new sites. Not only has the actual practice of government developed so that the ideals of representation and account-ability on which it is founded have little connection with its practical application, but there have been massive changes which have put much significant power out of the range of the institutions of central government and beyond the remit of even revitalised versions of the orthodox con-stitutionalism. There has been the rise of government activity in a welfare society which in turn is being superseded by the emergence of a post-industrial, post-welfare state where successive administrations have sought to change fundamentally the project of government. The locus of power has moved away into the market and to various satellite agencies which increasingly perform functions that were once felt to be the role of government. This process encompasses also changes in the nature of the society where power is exercised. There has been a development of diversity and of a politics of difference where a different, more vigorous civil society with a network of spontaneous and self-sustaining groups and networks interact with the state on a range of issues while never seeking to become or becoming directly part of government itself. Beyond this, power has become externalised and internationalised. New structures and mechanisms exist and, as we have already seen, these are seriously incom-patible with the fundamental ideas of parliament and sovereignty that make up orthodox constitutionalism.

All of this means that reforms to the traditional constitution of even the most ambitious design will fail to achieve the aim of controlling public power. This chapter surveys some of the approaches to constitutional reform at this formal level in order to point out the limitations of the whole reforming exercise. It then goes on to outline in more detail the ways in which the locus of power has shifted. Finally, the implications of this for our understanding of the nature of public power and legal regulation are examined.

Traditional Solutions to Traditional Problems

While the clamour for constitutional reform may well be growing it is yet far from deafening. However, as was sketched out in the last chapter, there are undeniable tensions within the orthodoxy even inside the limited terms it sets itself. There is an urgent need to reconcile the external dimensions of the constitution. The practice of government too has produced an obvious lack of fit between the orthodox doctrine and the reality of power. It is revealing that Craig, while acknowledging the extent to which society and government changed in the 1980s, actually finds it difficult to judge if this was carried out in an unconstitutional manner—given the flexible, unwritten nature of the very rules (that elsewhere would be shaping and controlling how government uses power).[1] Indeed, he concludes, whether the constitutional change was constitutionally improper depends solely upon a normative assessment of the changed position. While this may be true technically (and we shall return to Craig's normative assessments later) it is revealing that the constitution is so open textured that even a critic, attempting to be fair, must acknowledge that the fact of successfully achieving something has as much claim for legitimacy within our system as any idea of what *ought* to happen.[2]

Certainly governments generally have avoided undertaking much in the way of reform—even if they have been vociferous about the cause when in opposition. The alternating two party system of club government which delivers up to the party in power all the resources and powers available, has served government very well, certainly from 1945 to the 1980s—and there was always the expectation that the opposition would soon be given a turn. The lack of reform to the formal constitutional position has left government free to govern and, particularly in the case of the administrations since 1979, free to bring about huge changes in the actual practice of government that fundamentally re-constituted the state. High constitutional theory, meanwhile, remained largely untouched as the polity was re-ordered.

Any changes made at the formal level have been incremental only: another layer is added to the magpie's nest construction of the constitution. The focus on the old apparatus of parliamentary government, and in particular on the supposed scrutiny function of the House of Commons,

---

[1] Craig, *Public Law and Democracy in the United Kingdom and the United States of America* (1990), p. 210–211.

[2] Grant makes a similar point in his assessment of central and local government relations where he attempts to distinguish between changes that are simply "constitutional" in so far as they operate at the constitutional level and changes that may be "characterised in the normative sense 'constitutional' or, to make the point more clearly, as 'unconstitutional' ". "Central—Local Relations: the Balance of Power" in *The Changing Constitution* (Jowell and Oliver eds. 2nd ed., 1989) at p. 253.

has always been present. There has been a parliamentary ombudsman since 1967 and of course there is what many constitutional writers still persist in terming the "new" select committees introduced in 1979.[3] The ombudsman may well have facilitated the individual constituency work of the member of parliament, and the select committees may have invigorated the role of the backbencher and perhaps even supplied him or her with sufficient information to ask incisive questions. However, they have not seriously altered the basic balance of the formal constitution where the executive dominates parliament and ministerial responsibility sets the limits on inquiry as to how policy is made and carried out. Indeed, there has been a tendency for government in its reforming guise to limit and circumscribe the nature of any inquiry into reform. Commissions and inquiries, themselves often an alternative to action rather than a precursor, often have had strangely limited terms of reference. Most notably there has been the Royal Commission on the Constitution[4] which in fact was nothing of the sort but simply an inquiry into a particular devolution problem. Others, on the civil service, the honours system and tribunals of inquiry have been very much directed at specific issues rather than more general surveys of the whole constitutional edifice. Departmental committees of inquiry into constitutional matters have similarly been precluded from the big constitutional questions either by their narrow focus—as with, for example, the Franks Committee on section 2 of the Official Secrets Act[5] or the Radcliffe Committee on Ministerial Memoirs[6]—or by their terms of reference—as with the Fulton Committee on the Civil Service which was delimited from considering ministerial responsibility[7] or the Layfield Committee which looked at local government finance but not at its broader structure.[8] As Partington concluded, surveying the progress of the last 30 years in the mid 1980s, "these developments, though important, do not smack of grand strategy".[9]

---

[3] See, for example, *The New Select Committees: A Study of the 1979 Reforms* (G. Drewy ed., 2nd ed., 1989); Oliver, *Government in the United Kingdom: The Search for Accountability, Effectiveness and Citizenship* (1991) pp. 42–45; Thompson, *Textbook on Constitutional and Administrative Law* (1993) at p. 166; McEldowney, *Public Law* (1994) p. 45–6 & 318.

[4] Cmnd. 5460 (1973).

[5] Cmnd. 5104 (1972).

[6] Cmnd. 6368 (1976).

[7] Cmnd. 3638 (1968).

[8] Cmnd. 6453 (1976).

[9] "The Reform of public law in Britain: Theoretical Problems and Practical Considerations" in *Law, Legitimacy and the Constitution* (P. McAuslan and J. McEldowney eds., 1985) at p. 191.

The position has not improved in recent years even though pressure on the constitutional framework has been more intense. Government has directed most of its constitutional effort towards blocking the impetus from Europe and smothering devolutionary tendencies nearer home. Actual changes have been modest: for example, the introduction of a Data Protection Act 1984, an Official Secrets Act 1989 and a Security Services Act 1989 into the area of government secrecy, and the Police and Criminal Evidence Act 1984 reworking the relationship between suspects and the police. Indeed, even the idea of overhauling the constitution has not been given much encouragement by government. As Brazier notes, in the constitutional arena departmental committees of inquiry and Speaker's conferences, which require the initiative of the prime minister to set up, were rare during Mrs Thatcher's premiership and such constitutional inquiry as there was came from the House of Commons and House of Lords select committees which can be initiated more independently.[10] The Major government has tended to have inquiries thrust upon it, as with the Scott Inquiry on the arms to Iraq affair and the Nolan Inquiry into general standards of conduct of holders of public office. Other than this it has maintained a similar lack of interest in the big picture of constitutional reform[11] and any efforts here have been diverted into citizen's or consumer's charters and the rights to information required by these.

At the political level, in distinction to the governmental level, there has been considerably more activity. We do not intend to attempt a summary of all the suggestions.[12] Neither can we offer a detailed account of the related citizenship issue. This latter issue is a debate trapped in a language of pragmatism and political expediency that seems a long way from the

---

[10] *Constitutional reform: Re-shaping the British Political System* (1991) pp. 18–20.

[11] In a speech arguing against Labour's plans for a Scottish parliament, John Major expressed satisfaction with the existing constitution describing it as "an honoured, cherished, working, living, breathing balance of responsibilities". (*The Times* December 6, 1994).

[12] For an overview see, for example, Morison and Doe, "The Problem of Rights and the Literature of Constitutional Reform". *Revue Europeene De Droit Public / European Review of Public Law / Eur. Zeitschrift Des Offent. Rechts / Revista Europea Di Diritto Pubblico*, Vol. 3, No. 2. 1991. pp. 539–553 or Oliver "Written Constitutions: Principles and Problems" (1992) 45 *Parliamentary Affairs* 135. Smith, "Post-Modern Politics and the Case for Constitutional Renewal", (1994) 65 *Political Quarterly* 128 provides a similar account from a slightly different perspective. See also Loughlin's account of how generally the liberal normativist programme not only has an explicit political plan for constitutional reform but also has "an implicit form" through the work of public lawyers who have, he claims, "exploited the similarities in the normativist style in public law and constructed a radical reinterpretation of our tradition in a liberal rather than a conservative guise". *Public Law and Political Theory* (1992) p. 207 *et seq.*

optimism of T.H. Marshall's welfare state vision.[13] In place of it there is a squabble about which party thought of the idea first and whether citizenship is primarily a vehicle for social justice or a new basis for the provision of public services and reform in public administration. Are citizens to be the Left's "big idea" for the rest of the 1990s, part of a new European order or at least simultaneously a building block in, and an objective of, a new constitutional settlement?[14] Alternatively, are they to be active citizens watching their neighbourhoods and undertaking voluntary community work or simply consumers of new forms of public services with customer codes and the right of a rebate?[15] While such issues are important and the concept of "citizens" may eventually provide an organising principle for detailed reform as well as simply a rallying cry, this is not yet the case.

Turning to constitutional reform in the institutional sense naturally much of the interest and activity comes from the liberal centre and left of British politics. However, while the conservative party in power has shown itself reluctant to introduce reform, the broader Right has not always been, and indeed is not now, simply uninterested in changing the constitution. Lord Hailsham famously warned of the dangers of an "elective dictatorship" in the 1970s and urged the case for a written constitution and a bill of rights.[16] While Hailsham may have moderated his position slightly on the Conservatives' return to government,[17] there is an appreciation of (if not always an argument in favour of) reform within the conservative tradition.

At the active end of this spectrum there are proposals for change. F.A. Hayek, the inspiration for much of the Thatcherite right, has condemned the idea of unbridled parliamentary sovereignty and proposed a package of radical constitutional reforms to limit government.[18] Ferdinand Mount offers the suggestion of incorporating, and thus domesticating or "patriating", both European law and the European Convention on Human

---

[13] *Citizenship and Social Class* (1950); *Sociology at the Crossroads* (1963).
[14] See further, for example, Commission on Social Justice *Social Justice—Strategies for National Renewal* (1994); Meehan, *Citizenship and the EC* (1993); Speaker's Commission, *Encouraging Citizenship: Report of the Commission on Citizenship* (1990); Oliver, *Government in the United Kingdom: The Search for Accountability, Effectiveness and Citizenship* (1991) especially chap. 12.
[15] See further, for example, Lister, *The Exclusive Society* (1989); Barron and Scott, "The Citizen's Charter Programme" (1992) 55 MLR 526; Drewry, "Mr Major's Charter: Empowering the Customer" (1993) *Public Law* 248.
[16] See *The Dilemma of Democracy* (1978).
[17] See, for example, *On the Constitution* (1992).
[18] *The Political Order of a Free People* (1979).

Rights. For him this is not antithetical to conservative values: indeed, he remarks that "a really dedicated free-marketeer surely ought to welcome the installation of a supranational legal framework which would take the principles of free trade out of the reach of the political lobbyists".[19] Beyond this he sees certain developments, such as a Scottish assembly, as more or less inevitable in the medium term, and a supreme court protecting a variety of entrenched constitutional provisions as likely in the longer term. Frank Vibert from the Conservative Institute of Economic Affairs, also argues for the incorporation of the European Convention of Human Rights as well as the preparation of a constitutional document and, interestingly, an independent central bank.[20]

Generally however, notwithstanding the Hailsham position articulated in the 1970s when the prospect of Conservative government seemed distant, the much more typical conservative position is to counter attack in defence of the status quo. In doing so conservative constitutionalists frequently claim to be occupying the ground held by Burke and defending the virtues of a traditional constitution proved by history over any man-made construction. Thus since the war there have been a succession of conservative writers celebrating the British system of two party politics for producing an executive led parliament supporting a strong government within a political system where voter choice is restricted to giving either party a clear mandate every five or so years.[21] This is becoming more pronounced as the years in government pass by. The cynic might say that most conservative constitutionalists have learned the lesson that, as Kavanagh puts it, "the central issue in British politics has not been how to curb the elective dictatorship but how to capture it."[22] Thus there is the spectacle of John Patten joining the debate from the safety of cabinet office to opine that economic downturns generate discussions about the relationship between economic performance and structures of government. Long periods in office by an single administration, he believes, inevitably provoke calls by the opposition for changes in the existing arrangements in

---

[19] *The British Constitution Now* (1992) at p. 242. See also Vibert "A Free Market Approach to Constitutional Reform" in *Debating the Constitution* (Barnett, Ellis and Hirst eds., 1993) pp. 30–35.

[20] "Constitutional Reform in the United Kingdom—An Incremental Agenda" in *Britain's Constitutional Future* (Vibert ed., 1991) 15–36.

[21] See for example, *Some Proposals for Constitutional Reform: Being the recommendations of a Group of Conservatives* (1946) and, most famously, Leo Amery, *Thoughts on the Constitution* (1947).

[22] *Thatcherism and British Politics*, (1987) at p. 285.

the belief that "if you can't win, it is always best to try to change the rules"[23] Patten joins with those on the Right outside government who agree with his view that "penning a grand design for constitutional change is a simplistic exercise".[24] In particular there is Philip Norton who maintains that there is a negative case for retaining present arrangements— the case for change is not convincingly made—as well as a positive case.[25] This positive case seems to rest on no more that an endorsement of Westminsterism in its most traditional form.[26] As Norton quaintly puts it, such a model "combines Tory and Whig theory: the Tory emphasis on strong government and the Whig imperative of a strong Parliament, and of government operating within the limits set by Parliament".[27] He accepts that these conditions have never fitted exactly the Westminster model and that recently the balance inherent in the idea has been skewed towards the executive but perversely maintains that now it is shifting towards parliament.[28] He seems to find in the handling of poll tax and sunday trading issues in parliament, and in the demise of Mrs Thatcher, evidence of the potential of parliament to live up to the Westminster model—especially if it were strengthened in the usual ways.[29] From a more objective point of view, it is difficult to see how two local difficulties within the conservative party (both of which have since been patched over) and the political assassination of a leader by her own party can amount to evidence that parliament is in any sort of control or that the constitution is in balance. Indeed, as Mount says responding to the version of this argument outlined by John Patten, the sort of balance that the Westminster system had in mind was a much more sophisticated one between different parts of the polity—monarchy, church, barons and Commons, or government, parliament and judiciary—and not this idea whereby a regime either survives and governs as its wishes or gives way as prudent to popular indignation. In

---

[23] "Just Keep rolling along" *The Spectator* January 30, 1993, pp. 9–10.

[24] Patten, *Political Culture, Conservatism and Rolling Constitutional Change* (1991) at p. 22.

[25] Norton, "In defence of the Constitution: A Riposte to Radicals" in *New Directions in British Politics?* (Norton ed., 1991) and *The Constitution: The Conservative Way Forward* (1992).

[26] See further, for example, Norton, "The Norton View" in *The Politics of Parliamentary Reform* (Judge ed., 1983) 56–61.

[27] Norton, *The Constitution: The Conservative Way Forward* (1992) at p. 10.

[28] Norton, (ed.) *Parliament in the 1980s* (1985); *Parliament in Perspective* (1987).

[29] Norton, *The Constitution: The Conservative Way Forward* (1992) at p. 11.

contrast this view indicates a "coarse monolithic governmentalised conception of balance ... demonstat[ing] an alarming impoverishment of constitutional thought.[30] The political Left and Centre provide a greater range of reforming proposals. However, although there is a broad front, the variety of what is on offer is so limited as to suggest a similar "impoverishment of constitutional thought" here too. Despite the number of commissions, institutes and research centres there is a uniformity about the charters, draft bills of rights and written constitutions that they offer and the recipes for negotiating the obstacle of parliamentary sovereignty that they recommend. In part this coincidence of demands can be explained by the sheer scale of arguing for something approaching a modern constitutional settlement. It may also be a result of the uneasy relationship between constitutional pundits (whether inside a party think tank or swimming more freely) and the main political parties who must be persuaded to carry through any suggestion—at least as far as an election manifesto. In this atmosphere there is a perception that constitutional reform is unlikely to be a vote winner and this sentiment may be tempered with a temptation to use the status quo in the service of what might seem a greater political good.

Those contributing to the debate on constitutional reform offer only limited variations on the same essential themes. Presiding over most suggestions there is the idea that European Community law and the European Convention of Human Rights are in some way a good thing, at least in so far as they force the domestic administration to recognise a human rights dimension and the importance of social legislation. Lester[31] is representative of a view that sees Europe remedying the failure of the British parliament and ending the isolation of United Kingdom by bringing in the perceived advantages of civil law countries with their written constitutions, fundamental rights and developed systems of public law. The spectacle of the conservative government being taken to task by European structures in a way that it could not be by the domestic institutions of parliament and the courts may be satisfying. It is perhaps remarkable, however, that a supranational organisation, and one which stresses an idea of subsidiarity, should appear as answer to purely domestic problems. Indeed, further, as Blackburn remarks, "it might seem curious

---

[30] *The British Constitution Now* (1992) at p. 35.
[31] "The Constitution: Decline and Renewal" in *The Changing Constitution* (Jowell and Oliver eds., 2nd ed. 1985) pp. 345–369; "Fundamental Rights: The United Kingdom Isolated?" (1984) 46 *Public Law* 56.

to look to the European Union as a corrective to the oligarchic vices of British political structures, since the European Community itself labours under a 'democratic deficit'".[32]

Moving on to more specific proposals, there is the perennial issue of a bill of rights. This is a topic of enduring interest to academic writers who seem to debate almost ceaselessly the pros and cons of legalising political rights and politicising the judiciary as well as the difficulties of entrenching such an instrument. The content of such an document is debatable. Should it encompass social rights as well as political and civil rights? What is the role of the European Convention of Human Rights and can broad statements of value be accommodated within our judicial tradition? What are the virtues of the Labour party suggestion from the end of the 1980s of a Charter of Rights involving a range of specific acts of parliament? Can the judges be trusted? These issues make up much of the debate on this matter. It is perhaps a measure of the desperate nature of the reforming enterprise that the Institute for Public Policy Research has declared that "we need referees, *even bad referees*, to interpret and enforce the rules".[33] Meanwhile, however, as Ewing and Gearty conclude in their survey of civil liberties during the 1980s, many of the restrictions on political freedom have come not from legislation but judge-made initiatives authorising the extension of executive power. For them the "harsh reality is that we need to be protected by parliament from the courts".[34] The debate has not always remained an academic one however. There have been some half-dozen attempts in the last 20 years to introduce legislation in parliament to bring in a bill of rights.[35] Recently, however, the issue has increasingly been combined with more comprehensive packages of constitutional reform.

There is a burgeoning number of comprehensive reform packages, often with their own draft constitutions. They have all been given a considerable impetus from the list of aspirations provided by Charter 88. Generally they follow the format of desiderata set out there and cover, in

---

[32] "The Ruins of Westminster", (1991) *New Left Review* 5 at 23.
[33] Institute for Public Policy Research, *A Written Constitution for the United Kingdom* 1991, p. 9 (our emphasis).
[34] Ewing and Gearty, *Freedom Under Thatcher: Civil Liberties in Modern Britain* (1990) pp.270–1.
[35] See further Morison and Doe *op. cit.* p. 544. The most recent attempt, made by Lord Lester of Herne Hill in October 1994, took the form of a bill introduced to parliament allowing judges to interpret and apply the European Convention on Human rights in the way that they currently do with European Law.

addition to fundamental rights, the voting system, the role of the monarchy and the second legislative chamber, regional government and the modernisation of the House of Commons.

Thus, for example, there are calls for electoral reform, including proportional representation, from (especially) the Liberal Democrats but also parts of the Labour movement and a host of more independent commentators. The best arguments in favour of proportional representation arise from the basic unfairness of a system where, for example, in the last election the centre party received between one-fifth and one-quarter of the votes but less than 5 per cent of the seats in parliament and the link that the existing electoral system maintains with an unrelentingly adversarial style of politics.[36] All such calls are premised on the idea that it is possible and worthwhile to somehow shore up the *representative* parliamentary democracy that underpins and legitimates the orthodoxy of parliamentary sovereignty. This form of representation is, as we discussed in the last chapter, less a matter of a continuous process linking the governed with the governing, than allowing an electorate an intermittent opportunity to cast a single vote for one of the major political parties. The party that is successful will then seize upon this as a "mandate" justifying a process of government which makes few further connections to the electorate or the MPs in their representative roles. As Wright puts it,

"mandates are translated into governments without distraction, fragmentation or limitation . . . . citizens are reduced to voters, multiple arenas of citizenship narrowed to the periodic visit to the polling booth, professional party machines substituting for the authentic activity of democratic politics a politics of observation rather than of engagement".[37]

While anything that will reduce the starkness of the choice at election time is probably a good thing, it can not be said that any system of proportional representation will really connect the electorate to what is being done in their name.[38] Indeed, if the only result of introducing proportional representation were to give a degree of credibility to the traditional idea

---

[36] See further, for example, Holme, "Parties, Parliament and PR" in 1688–1988: Time for a New Constitution (Home and Elliot eds., 1988) p. 129.
[37] *Citizens and Subjects: An Essay on British Politics* (1994) at pp. 62 and 75.
[38] There are of course extra dangers with proportional representation. For example, there is the threat that such a system may indeed usher in an element of power broking by minorities that would further distance people's preferences from policies as is so apparent in Israel where fundamentalist politicians frequently hold the balance of power and use it to considerable effect.

that the demands of democracy are satisfied by a professionally managed election every five years, giving some kind of democratic blessing to a government prepared to use the crude and anti-democratic instrument of parliamentary sovereignty and all the pre-democratic inheritances of prerogative powers, then it should be resisted.

Similarly the various calls for parliament to be reformed and modernised are worthwhile in themselves, and in so far as they go, but only if they do not underwrite a claim that we will then have *responsible* government. Ideas, ranging from Labour and the Liberal-Democrats' ambitious schemes to decentralise government to their more modest plans to introduce a reformed upper house and further regularise working hours and enhance clerical support in the Commons, are to be valued.[39] However, they do not amount to a *sufficient* remedy to secure responsible government. The traditional mechanisms and doctrines, even in combination with revitalised select committees, and indeed Public Accounts Committees, working in a new streamlined and more modern looking parliamentary environment cannot by themselves ensure the responsibility of the state to its representatives or the people. Even increased local government will not provide a democratic antidote to central power if it simply mirrors the party politics of Westminster and avoids introducing constitutional mechanisms to fracture and restrain power.

One of the reforms, simultaneously the most radical and the most traditional on offer, illustrates well the drawbacks of the whole reforming enterprise. Tony Benn's Commonwealth of Britain Bill[40] basically seeks to create a democratic, federal and secular Commonwealth of England, Scotland and Wales by its 54 clauses and four schedules. It is a worthy enterprise and one that is carried out in a manner that would be worthy of any nineteenth century architect of a bourgeois revolution. According to the proposal, the monarchy is to lose its constitutional status and its residual prerogative powers are to pass to a President, elected for a fixed term, who exercises these powers strictly on the advice of the Prime Minister and the new Commonwealth Parliament. This is to be a bicameral body with a

---

[39] See the Labour Party's *Meet the Challenge Make the Change—A Modern Democracy: Report of the Policy Review Group on Democracy for the Individual and the Community* (1989). Also, Brazier, "Labour's Plans for the Constitution", (1990) 41 NILQ and Loveland, "Labour and the Constitution: The 'Right' Approach to Reform?" (1992) 45 *Parliamentary Affairs* 173. For the Liberal Democrat position see *We the People . . .* (Liberal Democrat Federal Green Paper No. 13 1990) and *Here We Stand* (Liberal Democrat Federal White Paper No. 6 1993).
[40] Bill 161 (1990–91) given its first reading on May 20, 1991.

new House of the People replacing the House of Lords and exercising a review function. It will sit for a fixed period. Legislation passed by this body is to prevail over European Community law. New regional parliaments will be elected for England, Scotland and Wales. (Jurisdiction in Northern Ireland is to be abandoned). The Church of England is to be disestablished and religious freedom and equality declared. A Charter of Rights, detailing certain social entitlements as well as basic freedoms, is to be introduced and entrenched and a new court will police this.

This proposal gets about as close as the Westminster system can to a modern arrangement such as might have been appropriate in the nineteenth century. There is much that would be gained in the unlikely event that this proposal were to be realised. However, it would not by itself secure a meaningfully representative and responsible system of parliamentary government, let alone deal with the new forms of public power. The Commonwealth of Britain is to be just that: it is not a republic and, although parliament is to be slightly impeded by the Charter of Rights, it is supreme. The basic feature of the British system, whereby power operates from the top down, is retained intact. Despite some radical sounding tones, this constitution does not empower and authorise government on behalf of the people: it rather hopes that democracy will grow up in the space allowed by government. In contrast to the continental idea of popular sovereignty residing with the people and a written constitution authorising the parliament, here it is parliament which remains supreme. It can only be a hope that it operates in a democratic, accountable way for it is not compelled to do so.

All of the discussion on constitutional reform and bills of rights is subject to a secondary debate which often seems to threaten to overwhelm the main issues. This too is indicative of the impoverished nature of the basic constitutional settlement that the reformers are anxiously attempting to update. The *means* of reform are the subject of much doubt and debate. There is the issue of how the legislation required for reform could be politically engineered within parliament.[41] There is also the related and more dominant issue of how such legislation could be made to stick. This comes about as a result of the basic tenet of classic constitutionalism that, as Anson puts it, "Parliament . . . is omnipotent to change, but cannot bind

---

[41] See further, for example, Lester, "An Agenda for Real Reform" *Political Quarterly* (forthcoming 1995)

itself not to change, the constitution of which it forms a part."[42] Parliamentary sovereignty, and all the celebrated flexibility that this is supposed to bring to the constitution, is a significant problem for the reformer. The obsession with sovereignty that, as we noted earlier is so prevalent within the textbook project, is present also at this more daring end of constitutional scholarship. The whole issue of reform, expressed within terms of a written constitution, a bill of rights, a new second chamber or whatever, is almost invariably, as Craig puts it, "premised on the idea that a way round the 'traditional' view of sovereignty must be found".[43] The slavish adherence to the doctrine that is demanded by traditional Westminsterism diverts much of the energy of constitutional scholars who seem to feel the need to come up with ever more sophisticated variations and revisions to the traditional doctrine as well as practical mechanisms for entrenchment provisions or Constitutional Commissions to ensure that their reforms last beyond the next government. This stumbling block of sovereignty should really alert the reformers to what is a basic problem within the constitution rather than just a historical curio to be circumvented. While power can be limited, shared and supervised by other bodies; sovereignty cannot. Any system which blocks off meaningful control in such a way rightly raises suspicion. As Wright sees it

> "parliamentary sovereignty provides a cloak of legitimacy for executive and party dominance. It permits British government, with only a minority of electoral support, to claim a bogus majoritarianism. It produces a system which is allegedly strong, but which is notoriously weak in terms of such democratic criteria as representation, accountability, participation and openness".[44]

---

[42] *Law and Custom of the Constitution* (5th ed., 1922) at p. 8.
[43] Craig, "Public Law, Sovereignty and Citizenship" in *Rights of Citizenship* (R. Blackburn ed. (1993) at p. 324. Craig's own attempt, in his analysis of the possibilities of citizenship within a sovereignty based system, is one of the very rare efforts to actually explore rather than simply evade the theoretical issues. While he does not deny the need for reformers to come up with ingenious ways of circumventing the doctrine (p.324) there is an effort made to explicate what exactly it is that lies behind the very different ideas of Dicey, Wade and Blackstone which make up the "traditional" view that is usually set up in opposition to the "new view" (sic) of Jennings, Heuston and Marshall. On finding the historical, political and legal assumptions and justifications which informed the traditional view unsuitable for today, Craig seems to recommend simply that we ignore the usual meaning of the doctrine by referring to Dworkin's idea of the integrity of law as involving ideas of "fit" and "justification". We can then apparently say that it would be a good idea if sovereignty was not what everybody thought it to be and, once we face the idea even the traditional doctrines involved normative choices, we are then free to make other choices.
[44] *Op. cit.* p. 6.

The reformers' first target should be the very idea of sovereignty which presently bestrides our constitutional history as its beginning and its end. It is this which ushers in a formalism which cuts off completely debate long before we come near anything radical such as federalism or regional government within a United States of Europe. The almost universal acceptance of this formalism and the resulting timidity of the reformers' agenda should be instructive.

All this is beginning to force us towards the conclusion that, as M.P. John Garrett observes, "if we were starting from scratch" it is doubtful "if the Westminster model would get a look in".[45] Certainly all efforts to reform traditional Westminsterism are heir to a number of basic difficulties relating to the fundamentally undemocratic nature of the ancestral constitution. Developments such as an extended franchise and elective politics may have been superimposed on the existing constitution but essentially, as we discussed in chapter one, the pre-democratic constitution remains in place. It has been adapted and patched up only a very little even when very obvious changes in political practices—such as the development of the party system—have destroyed any claim that it might be able to advance that it delivers representative or responsible government. It is not clear to us that further tinkerings with the old contraption will yield a worthwhile return: it is likely the old mechanisms were worn away beyond repair about the same time as the institutions of the state outgrew their original bounds and any capacity that the traditional parliamentary machinery might have had to control them. Any attempts to shore up the high constitution of parliament and central government are more likely to end up providing a spurious justification to executive abuses of power within parliament while at the same time missing out altogether on that whole range of power that exists outside Westminster .

However, we would not like to leave the impression that we are actively against constitutional reform. Anything that at least fractures power at any level is worthwhile and we endorse many of the proposals while recognising that they are refracted through the prism of a version of liberalism where rights are generally narrowly drawn and power is falsely seen as the almost exclusive preserve of central government and exercised through parliament. Most of these reforms are at least aimed at creating a democratic, pluralistic political system which can yield an effective and accountable government. We want this too. Everyone should wish to see

---

[45] *Westminster: Does Parliament Work* (1992) at p. 25.

the concept of the British subject replaced by a modern idea of the citizen as more than a customer. Basic human rights guaranteed in a written constitution or a least via a constitutional change which will give the ECHR a privileged place, are an important first step in providing an instrument to develop human rights practice. Sources of unaccountable prerogative powers, both inside and outside parliament, should be subject to controls. Competence should be given to regional assemblies if desired and Westminster simultaneously reinvigorated perhaps with a new upper chamber and arguably a voting system that reflects better the wishes of the range of voters. All this and more is overdue.

This faint praise is not intended to dam out of hand any attempts to modernise the British constitution to a level attained, at least formally, elsewhere in Europe some years ago. However much more than this is required. The idea of a written constitution that seems so daring in the eyes of British constitutionalists is hardly likely by itself to cure all the ills of government. We do not see reform as in any way sufficient to remedy most of the problems within orthodox Westminsterism. Even updated to the limited degree envisaged by most of the schemes, such a reform misses out on the fact that it is not just the institutions that need to be upgraded but the whole system which requires democratisation. There are indeed normative choices to be made as Craig repeatedly reminds us. A constitution is more than just the nuts and bolts of the procedures and mechanisms that appear in the cold print of the textbook: there are values and attitudes inherent there.[46] The values and attitudes of the United Kingdom constitution are rooted in its pre-democratic past and orientated almost exclusively around parliament and the formal institutions of high constitutionalism. A democratic culture should mean more than simply periodically giving the people the chance "to kick the rascals out"—however efficiently this is engineered. The wider issues need to addressed urgently.

In addition to this argument, that it is the system that requires democratic reform and not just the institutions, there is the related point that constitutional reform along the lines considered is now largely obsolete because time and the nature of public power have moved on. Power has leached out from the domestic institutions of parliament, the cabinet and the civil service upwards to supra national bodies. It has simultaneously leaked away downwards into new levels and structures in a newly

---

[46] See further, for example, M. Foley, *The Silence of Constitutions* (1989).

constituted and still rapidly changing civil society. The problems of controlling the real public power as it exists at these new levels, and in new sites, are well beyond the reforming strategy reviewed here. It is to these new sites that we now turn.

The Moving Locus of Power

Orthodox constitutionalism has concerned itself almost exclusively with the institutions of big government. It should not really be surprising therefore that the reforming tendency that now is increasingly augmenting the orthodoxy is oriented towards trying to repair the institutions of the state, and in particular, reinvesting parliamentary controls with a virility that perhaps they never really had, even when dealing with the very different circumstances for which they were designed.

However, it seems to us that the focus of attention now, and increasingly, lies above and below the level of the individual nation state and its particular institutions. Power has leached upwards towards international and transnational bodies and groupings and, simultaneously, it has percolated downwards and outwards to a greater range of quasi state bodies and agencies and into a more diverse and vital civil society. The capacity of the state, and of its individual organs of government, to actually do very much in isolation is limited. Modern post-industrial states are held within a web of international relations and obligations which informally and formally restrain their ability to act alone and for themselves. At the same time, the whole project of government is changing at the internal, national level. It is now almost politically unthinkable to raise taxation and so the horizons of what government can hope to achieve are reduced. There has been the obvious withdrawal by the state from some of its welfare state responsibilities and the less obvious but more significant re-ordering of how remaining responsibilities are discharged at arm's length from government through quangos, agencies and contract. Meanwhile, civil society, Edmund Burke's "little platoons", has regrouped into intermediate associations, social networks and charitable and commercial groupings. In a sense they compete with the state not only as providers but also in offering a rival focus to traditional politics and its institutions.

Even the most sophisticated elements within the reforming wing of orthodox constitutionalism have not begun to recognise the reality of the change that has already occurred, or the possibility of it accelerating to maroon completely a version of constitutionalism that already looks fairly isolated in the modern world. Constitutionalism in the British sense seems still to be predicated on some nineteenth century idea of the state as an all-powerful actor possessing public authority and the right to make laws, enjoying a monopoly of legitimate force within a defined territory and interacting equally, at least formally, with other sovereign states in a world context. It does not see the modern state as caught in a network of supranational obligations and relationships and simultaneously under-mined in its national project by a fracturing civil society and a multiplicity of points of focus that are alternative and additional to the state. Identities have spilled out of the containers provided by national boundaries as roles and loyalties are divided along political, racial, ethnic, sexual and religious lines of fracture. The state is now a broker of myriad interests and a facilitator for pressure groups as much as a direct provider for their diverse needs. The state itself and its institutions are no longer so much a prize to be won by competing factions as an arena in which to pursue a variety of smaller conflicts without incurring the responsibilities which government entails. This is a long-term, global trend. However, in part too it is a result of Thatcherism: the conflicts between public and private, state and market, and society and the individual all moved in favour of the latter at the expense of the former during this period. Of course this trend is not complete. We do not live in a world where there are only individuals as Mrs Thatcher famously claimed. While there may be fewer people involved in the traditional groupings of political parties and trade unions, there are a host of intermediate groups and social networks often based around a single issue—such as environmentalism—or a particular stigmat-ised identity—such as feminism. The examples given are not wholly representative as they suggest movements but often these groupings are as likely to be locally based as they are to be globally orientated. There may well be the beginnings of an international civil society with groups like Greenpeace and Amnesty International operating not to take command of the state but to save the whale or insist upon humane treatment of political prisoners, but there are also groupings around highly personal yet political issues such as sexual and reproductive identities and controls.

At the same time as orthodox constitutionalism in its reforming guise maintains a distorted and inadequate view of the state, it operates within a limited and impoverished conception of power and law. There is an international and transnational dimension as well as implications from the fragmenting nature of civil society to this too, which orthodox constitu-tionalism with its focus on national institutions and hierarchical law can not accommodate. Public power does not now mean just government power. Neither does it mean only power that was once wielded by government and has now been privatised, contracted out or simply abandoned to a variety of private companies, agencies or charities— although this is certainly involved. Power now both spills over and penetrates national boundaries. It does not restrict itself to what traditionally was seen as public space but instead increasingly penetrates all areas of private intercourse regulating, shaping and facilitating as much as, and indeed more than, controlling, sanctioning and straightforwardly ordering. Power should not be conceived of as narrow and repressive and coming only from the state. Civil society contains a multiplicity of micro worlds and micro power relations where the points of power and conflict are multiplied through exploitation, oppression, victimisation and marginalisation. Such power relations exist in all the categories of family, culture and consumption as well as in more traditional areas of government, policing and work. They come to the surface in issues previously thought to be apolitical like reproductive politics, sexuality and the family. These produce new points of conflict and create new resistances in networks which, although more complex and indeterminate than the simple top down of constitutionalism, are more authentic and should equally be the subject of constitutional control. Such a complex and multi-layered conception of power does not see parliament or indeed any aspect of the traditional constitution having a monopoly or even a particularly significant share of power. It certainly does not encourage us to try to shore up a constitutionalism which not only purports that government has a legitimate monopoly of power but also pretends that it operates to ensure that power is exercised by the people through its moribund institutions.

Similarly, the idea of law that is contained within orthodox constitutionalism is equally one-dimensional and inadequate. The hierarchical, direct nature of law that is presupposed in orthodox constitutionalism seems to match the narrow focus of power that the orthodoxy also suggests. The notion of sovereignty requires that state law is privileged above all else: indeed, the very idea of law often seems to be modelled on the nation state legislating freely and directly. There is little understanding of how law operates to implement, facilitate, restructure as well as indirectly and at an ideological level. The supposedly supreme character of domestic law predominates: sovereignty is either to be retained or given away, lost or won. The legal order is, within this view, a hierarchy of subordinate and supreme authorities. There can be no admitting an overlapping of jurisdictions or a sharing of competence as the new European order would seem increasingly to require. Similarly there is a limited understanding of the role of law in steering institutions and practices in line with values or processes as opposed to simply constituting and policing institutions and structures.

Of course the change in the nature of state, public power and law is partial and incomplete: it contains contradictory elements and divergent trends. Ties of religion, culture and ethnicity redefine communities in ways that run counter to both the concept of a national state and the supranational trends which overlie this. Diversity sits alongside transnational order. At the same time as we see metablocs in trade, security and other globally conceived issues, there is a resurgence of nationalism and emphasis on an idea of community. Regionalism exists contemporaneously with internationalism. National law and an idea of subsidiarity operate alongside supranational systems that seem poised to set us free of all lesser jurisdictions. We must be careful: Dyson, whose analysis of the state is influential here, warns of "crack-pot ideas" and "the tyranny of the fashionable".[47] There is certainly much hyperbole and fanciful speculation about the end of the state and much nonsense about what will replace it. However, there is much of value and certain important trends can be discerned. In what remains of this chapter we will sketch out some of the globalising pressures on the idea of state and some of the influences from a changing and fragmenting civil society which undermine the traditional state as predicated by even the most ardently reforming version of orthodox constitutionalism. (This complements the analysis in the previous chapter of how certain of the legal ramifications that have already been produced from Europe, and certain of the changes in the practice of government, are causing problems within the orthodox constitutionalism.) Closely related to this changing and fragmenting nature of civil society there is the increasing tendency for government to operate at a distance. We survey briefly the regulatory state, quangos and the next steps initiatives. We then conclude the chapter by making some general observations about how these changes impact upon our understanding of public power and the nature of law.

I. The Globalising State

The idea that modern, developed states are now held increasingly within webs of international obligation and dependency which operate to

---

[47] Dyson, *The State Tradition in Western Europe* (1980) at p. 287.

reduce their autonomy and independence is certainly not a new one. The work of Laski, Dyson, Poggi, Offe and others[48] have persuaded many that the sort of state as imagined in classic nineteenth constitutional theory no longer exists.

Indeed, there is now a trend towards taking this insight a good deal further than is justified and concluding that there is now a new world order beyond the struggle of the old ideologies of left and right where liberal democracy, free trade and international law prevail.[49] Whatever exaggerated claims have arisen there can be no doubt that the idea of state as predicated within traditional constitutionalism no longer exists. No longer do we live within a clear configuration where a set of institutions exist within a defined territorial area and perform the function of providing a framework of rule with an effective and exclusive competence to control national affairs, make law, deal with disputes and enforce decisions. As Dyson puts it, "a combination of international, economic and technological developments cast doubt on the viability of the state itself as the fundamental unit of politics".[50]

Within the paradigm of British parliamentary constitutionalism, and constitutional law in particular, there is, as we noted in the last chapter, a reluctance to theorise about the state and a preference to talk about the Crown or the government in its place. There is however (at the very least) an implicit assumption which sees a territorially defined association embracing all the people within that territory and having a common government which possesses the monopoly of violence giving it the capacity to guarantee the finality of decision in political disputes.[51] It is a somewhat monolithic vision of the state where there is a centralised authority based in, and justified by, parliament. Power is exercised by a variety of institutions which all derive their authority in a hierarchy from

---

[48] Laski, *Studies in Law and Politics* (1932); Dyson, *op. cit.*; Poggi, *The Development of the Modern State* (1978); *The State: Its Nature, Development and Prospects*, (1990); Offe, *Contradictions of the Welfare State* (1984). See also, Middlemas, *Politics in Industrial Society* (1979); Wolfe, *The Limits of Legitimacy* (1977); Dunleavy and O'Leary, *Theories of the State* (1987); Chomsky, *World Orders, Old and New*, (1994); Held, (ed.) *Prospects for Democracy* (1993) and Archibugi and Held (eds.) *Cosmopolitan Democracies The Agenda for a New World Order* (1995).

[49] Much of this trend can be traced to the publication of Fukuyama's *The End of History and the Last Man* (1992).

[50] *Op. cit.* at p. 282.

[51] This description is based on the definition offered by Finer, *Comparative Government* (1970) at p. 24. It is one that is quoted by Allen, Thompson and Walsh, *Cases and Materials on Constitutional and Administrative Law* (3rd ed., 1994) at p. 39 in one of the very few examples of a textbook even approaching this issue.

parliament who maintains an unrivalled and complete competence within the national territory. The narrowness of this viewpoint is disappointing. In many ways constitutional lawyers are at the forefront of globalising developments through international law, agreements such as those emerging from the Conference on Security and Co-operation in Europe (CSCE—now the Organisation for Security and Co-operation in Europe, OSCE) and the General Agreement on Tariffs and Trade (GATT), and of course European Community law and the jurisprudence from the European Court of Human Rights. There ought to be a better appreciation in legal circles of the network of international obligations within which a developed state operates. Nevertheless, there remains a stubborn adherence to the idea of viewing the United Kingdom as an isolated sovereign state. Of course when we recall the ingenuity which constitutional lawyers bring to the task of denying and mitigating the impact of E.C. law, then this commitment to the nation state becomes more explicable as it becomes joined with the notion of legal sovereignty—that incunabula of traditional legal theory.

Of course legal sovereignty is different from economic and political sovereignty and from the ideas of autonomy and independence which they suggest. However, orthodox constitutionalism is closely linked to, and very much depends upon, the idea of the state as an actor possessing a monopoly of power within its own territory and able to negotiate with other similar monopolies. Of course this idea of economic and political sovereignty is now no longer any more tenable than is the associated idea of legal sovereignty. There is a world economy with an infrastructure quite detached from nations. Global capital is stronger than the governments of mere nations and there has grown up a variety of institutions including the International Monetary Fund, World Bank, G7 and GATT, designed to service the needs of multinational and transnational corporations, banks and investment houses. Similarly global production and trade throws up corporations and interest groupings that are stronger than the state which is often reduced to facilitating and assisting transnational corporations as they seek to shift production to low wage countries and aim their marketing at privileged sectors within national economies. This has produced international economic interdependence which has essentially overwhelmed the whole Kenysian project of the 1940s aimed at giving economic control back to the nation state. It is not yet true that we can no longer speak of a national economy at all. However, control of exchange rates, employment rates, inflation and growth is now increasingly moving beyond the remit of national governments.

All this has been assisted by technological developments. The revolution in the handling of information and in communications has the effect that developed economies now rely increasingly on complex electronic infrastructures. Developing countries still have an emphasis on agrarian production where their farm produce and natural resources are their saleable assets. Second level economies are still based on industrial production and are dependent on cheap manual labour, raw material and energy, and on export markets. They are more likely to retain an integrated national economy and rely on the state infrastructure. However, the most advanced economies, or, more precisely, the most developed sectors of advanced economies, do not rely on raw materials, energy or the capacity of the nation state to organise these. They are based on knowledge and technology. They sell expertise such as financial services and banking, management consultancy, television, computer software, etc. Powerful transnational businesses are creating information networks and highways that by pass the nation state framework. Even in stable, advanced countries such as the United States, Japan, Germany and the United Kingdom the state is increasingly no longer the most relevant socio-economic entity or the significant political configuration. Regions, such as Orange County, California, Ruhrgebiete in Germany or Osaka in Japan are emerging as areas with pre-eminent economic status within a national territory. The growth of the City of London as a major financial centre in the 1980s can be seen in this light. It was a commercial revolution made possible by a technological revolution producing an area of economic activity with a rate of development and a field of operation separate from the wider unit in which the accidents of geography, time zones and entrepreneurial flair placed it. It is not perhaps too fanciful to imagine that the real decision-making powers of the future will be transnational business groups in conjunction with city-regional governments.[52] Such economies, based on information, communications and technology transcend the nation state and reveal its increasing incapacity to act independently.

On the political side there is a developing global interconnectedness which has the effect that many of the traditional areas of state activity and responsibility, including defence, the administrative and legal system as

---

[52] The idea of a Europe of the Regions by-passing national governments for European Union purposes, and the establishment of the Council of the Regions, keeps open up the possibility that the European Union may one day find it more practical to recognise this trend and reverse its present structures which reserve the decisive role for national governments.

well as economic management cannot now be achieved without international collaboration. A glance down the table of contents of the European Union Treaty 1992 (the Maastricht Treaty) provides simultaneously a list of the basic functions of government within the classic formulation of the nation state, and an indication of how they are no longer the sole preserve of national government. There are provisions relating to: citizenship, a single economy with a European System of Central Banks and a single currency, education, culture and public health, foreign and security policy and justice and Home affairs. (And of course all these are augmented by the social chapter on employment and working conditions from which the United Kingdom presently has opted out.) These operate in addition to the law making powers of the Union and the jurisdiction of the European Court of Justice. It is remarkable that these items correspond almost exactly with the list of characteristics of the nineteenth century constitutional state as Poggi, for example, provides.[53]

Commentators, such as Mulgan who claim to see "the embryo of a single global community conscious of a common interest and common values",[54] are overstating the position. There is much uncertainty about the role and influence of many of the expensive, overlapping bodies. However, there are a range of European and world-wide transnational bodies which reflect the division of the world into blocs based on trading, defence as well as economic interests. Clearly these operated to reduce the sovereignty of individual nations in so far as their independence and autonomy is restricted. Only old-fashioned dictators in the developing world or local warlords in Bosnia can claim sovereignty in the sense that they are free to act independently—at least until the United Nations or the United States of America chooses to intervene. The sphere of autonomy of governments in developed countries, including the United Kingdom, is diminishing. The North Atlantic Treaty Organisation (NATO) and its extensions the North Atlantic Co-operation Council (NACC) and the Partnership for Peace (PFP), the Western European Union (WEU), the United Nations, and a variety of informal alliances and understandings restrict even the basic freedom of the state to wage war. (There is even an embyronic European army with Eurocorps, established under the WEU.)

---

[53] See, Poggi *The Development of the Modern State* (1978) at p. 93. See also Hall and Ikenberry, *The State* (1989) Chap. 1.
[54] Mulgan, *Politics in an Antipolitical Age* (1994) at p. 201.

At the same time, the power to make law, another fundamental aspect in the traditional idea of state, is circumscribed by conventions and treaties and subject to higher authorities and over-arching jurisdictions. Transnational bodies can operate to limit autonomy by setting aspirations, as with the United Nations Universal Declaration of Human Rights and the subsequent UN charters of rights, as well as the Paris and Helsinki accords from the CSCE. They can establish standards and provide a mechanism for adjudicating on those standards (while leaving enforcement of the standards to the individual nation) as with the European Convention on the Protection of Human Rights in the British context.[55] Alternatively, and most dramatically, treaties can grant jurisdiction to transnational bodies as with the European Union. Jacques Delors' famous statement about the "displacement of the centre of decision making" and his prediction that within a few years 80 per cent of economic legislation, and possibly fiscal and social law as well, would originate from Brussels,[56] indicates the most spectacular reduction of the nation state's command of the legislative function. Several thousand pieces of legislation are passed each year by the European Union: there were more than 15,500 regulations between 1990 and the end of 1993.[57] Other documents, including Commission communications to the Council, budgetary items and proposals for legislation, also flood out of Brussels. The inability of the United Kingdom parliament to cope with such a deluge of material, as well as its relative feebleness in executing the scrutiny role that it does undertake,[58] suggests that the United Kingdom parliament has in practice ceded its control over the

---

[55] With over 5000 complaints reaching the Commission annually (908 from the United Kingdom in 1992 and 648 in 1993), and some 2000 applications being registered annually (187 of these from the United Kingdom in 1993) as well as more than 30 cases from the United Kingdom reaching the Court and requiring the national law to be changed on some half-dozen or more occasions, the effect of this treaty is practical as well as directory. (See Council of Europe, *Survey of Activities and Statistics* (1993)).

[56] Speech to the European parliament reported in *The Times* July 7, 1988.

[57] Recently the volume of proposals from the European Commission has actually declined. (There were 200 proposals for legislation in 1990 and less than 50 in 1994). However, as we noted earlier in Chap. 1, other, less direct means of imposing a European order now increasingly characterise the operation of the European Union and the relative decline in formal legislative proposals does not disturb an overall trend towards increased law making in institutions beyond those of the national state.

[58] Garrett, *op. cit.* pp. 218–224 provides a scathing critique of the reality of parliament's role in shadowing and scrutinising the European Union institutions and of the government's efforts to keep such a role beyond the attentions of the House of Commons. Griffith and Ryle, *Parliament: Functions, Practice and Procedures* (1989) pp. 407–8; 436–9 and 490–492 provide a more standard outline of what should be happening.

process of European government just as thoroughly as it has in theory yielded its sovereign monopoly to legislate. Qualitatively of course the legislation is rather mixed with up to about two-thirds of that coming from the Commission relating to agriculture. However, there are sufficient matters of importance to lead even a conservative constitutionalist such as Mount to declare that "the European Community has, in effect, endowed us with a written constitution and a Bill of Human Rights".[59] Powers of taxation, another fundamental aspect of nationhood and a defining feature of government, are now also yielded to the European Union.[60]

It is obvious that the political sovereignty of the nation state has been breached and that the transnational institutions that have grown up to express relationships within wider interest blocs now exist side by side with more orthodox national and local institutions. As Hirst observes, there is now a "changed conjecture", whereby politics is centred "less and less on a single structure of authority; supra-national, national, regional and non-state forms of governance are all possible contenders to influence policy".[61] It is also true, however, that as well as there being a number of different levels at which power and politics takes place, there are a range of structures and mechanisms at each level.

As well as the direct impact from the main institutions of the European Union and the European Convention on Human Rights there are various infrastructural changes that encourage a more European-wide viewpoint. Despite the cagey approach of the British government to the European game, the institutional reality from Brussels is encouraging the other players to play under its rules. For example, the British political parties are linked into transnational groupings in Europe.[62] It is increasingly common

---

[59] *The British Constitution Now* (1992) at p. 223. Presumably Mount has in mind the ECJ's duty by article 164 to ensure the observance of general principles of law in the interpretation and application of the Treaty and the body of case law that has built up in the last twenty years drawing upon the European Convention of Human Rights as just such a general and common standard.

[60] The United Kingdom has adopted the Communities' external tariff and its agricultural policy which involves imposing import levies. The United Kingdom government both collects money as an agent for the Community and arranges that its payments to the Community are charged on the Consolidated Fund. Under the European Communities Act 1972 rates of customs duties and agricultural levies can be varied directly by community regulation.

[61] *Associative Democracy: New Forms of Economic and Social Governance* (1994) at p. 8.

[62] See further, for example, Pinkney, "British Political Parties and the European Community", (1991) 6 *Public Policy and Administration* 30; Radice, *Offshore: Britain and the European Community* (1992).

for local authorities and regional agencies to maintain offices in Brussels. In doing so they "europeanise" what might seem to be their very local interests by directly lobbying for financial support and at the same time give a practical endorsement of the idea of there being a unit below that of the nation state. More diverse interest groups, which previously organised on a national basis, are increasingly operating within European confederations.[63] This is the case too with international institutions. A forum such as the United Nations has become a site for lobbying by a wide range of interests and bodies who will maintain structures to facilitate their mission of providing strategic influence. In some contexts Non Governmental Organisations (NGOs), such as Oxfam or Amnesty International, can be highly influential in determining the policy of the international community. At the same time this encourages a resetting of the compass of domestic politics. The familiar domestic dichotomy between left and right is being challenged by international movements focusing on single issues such as ecology or morality. Mulgan overstates it where he talks of the creation of "a politics that is personal and global but only tangentially interested in the classic national political sphere".[64] This might be coming sometime in the future but such a nascent trend presently exists alongside more traditional political contests as well as tendencies towards fiercely reactionary politics (this latter trend is of course itself indicative of the shifting nature of the world).

Other institutions as well as more free-floating political groupings are subject to a similar globalising trend. This has two aspects: in contrast to the growth of European and worldwide international agencies and networks there is a simultaneous decline in national institutions. Mention has already been made of the globalising trends within economies. The decline of domestic financial institutions, which reduced the Treasury and the Bank of England to the status of bit players in the attack on sterling by speculators in 1992 and exposed the persistent failure of the regulatory mechanisms to deal with issues such as the collapse of the Bank of Credit and Commerce International, is matched by the degree to which national economies and financial systems are increasingly controlled by outside forces and mechanisms. Other institutions too are subject to this decline at the national level accompanied by a growth of competition at the international level. Sometimes this comes from the commercial sector as with,

[63] See further Mazey and Richardson, *Lobbying in the European Community* (1992).
[64] *op. cit.* at p. 9.

for example, the BBC which is now subject to increased competition by independents and the international Murdoch media empire. Alternatively it may originate with the movement of people and ideas which has introduced a range of global religions to challenge the Church of England as the national faith.

The examples could be multiplied to flesh out this sketch of a government structure and civil society that is becoming increasingly internationalised. Government is escaping the confines of the nation state. The sites where power is exercised and where political struggle is focused are moving away from the domestic state and its institutions. A whole range of international and transnational bodies now provide a forum for highly politicised struggle and for restructuring political action across national, regional boundaries. Simultaneously, political issues occurring at the domestic or regional level increasingly have an international dimension and expression. It is a process that is accelerating and becoming more intense and complex. Held recognises this where he concludes that

> "what is new about the modern global system is the chronic intensification of patterns of interconnectedness, mediated by such phenomenon as the modern communications industry and new information technology, and the spread of gobalization in and through new dimensions of interconnectedness: technological, organizational, administrative and legal, among others, each with its own logic and dynamic of change".[65]

This increasing deterritorialisation of human activity and matching interconnectedness at the global level undermines and challenges the capacity of traditional, national based constitutional theory and practice to realise democratic aims and values at the points where they now matter. It is a challenge which most of the reformers of the British constitution have scarcely noticed let alone begun to respond to.

II. NEW FORMS OF CIVIL SOCIETY

In just the same way as there are changes at the international level which are outstripping the capacity of the nation state to accommodate them so too there are developments at the national level which challenge the traditional idea of the state and the claim of any version of orthodox

---

[65] "Democracy and the Global System" in *Political Theory Today* (Held ed., 1991), at p. 206.

constitutionalism to control the exercise of power. In a similar way also the importance of these trends is mistaken within the traditional constitutionalism. As with the globalising movement, which is taken only as producing some problems within the orthodox doctrine of parliamentary sovereignty rather than ushering in profound contradictions, so too is the significance of the changing nature of civil society misunderstood and its effects underestimated. The idea of civil society, like the related area of political economy, has been rediscovered from its roots in the Scottish Enlightenment and is set to become increasingly an important area of study as the nature of politics continues to change and the role of the state continues to mutate and diminish. Soon even constitutionalists will have to appreciate that there are changes occurring here which profoundly affect the subject matter of their study by altering the scope and nature of government and by producing a whole layer of intermediate groups and networks below the level of the state.

There is a widespread feeling that the programmatic, transformative politics of modernity have run out of steam. The whole project of using the state to transform economies and social structures has been overwhelmed. The disillusionment with politics and with state structures which is felt in the West is counterpointed by the demise of collectivist systems of state socialism in the East. We seem to have reached the end of what Lyotard describes as the "grand narratives" of progress, development, enlightenment, truth and rationality which until recently provided the anchor point for Western politics and philosophy.[66] The demise of the modernist project of government has brought with it decentralisation, confusion and diversity. Dichotomies such as individualist and collectivist, right and left, state and market, public and private no longer have the power that they once did to capture and explain the world. The horizons of government are shrinking and the project of governing is becoming more modest. Not only is there a disillusionment with the potential of the state to engineer a better society, but now governments find it increasingly difficult to increase rates of taxation with the result that their capacity to achieve very much along a Kenysian, welfarist agenda is limited. At the same time the established electoral politics now appears more like formalised disempowerment and the focus of political activity is changing. In particular the system whereby political parties provide the mechanism to control the state is under threat. For a whole era, beginning perhaps at the

---

[66] *The Post-Modern Condition: A Report of Knowledge* (1984).

end of the nineteenth century and ending in the 1960s, the political party may have been a natural expression of how a newly enfranchised class gained access to power through the state. Politics was about a competitive struggle between two class blocs each represented by parties who battled via a sharply polarised electoral and constitutional system for the commanding heights of the state. (From 1945 to 1970, the combined Labour and Conservative vote almost always exceeded 90 per cent.) Now, however, the party is in decline. (In 1979 the proportion of the total electorate who did not vote for either major party was just short of 40 per cent.) As Benton sees it,

> "the political party as we have known it is an anachronism. Out of all the tasks it is set there are only two it can carry out with any adequacy: it can contest elections and it can produce a caste of professional politician to take part in the ritual of public affairs."[67]

As these rituals of formal party politics go on, the traditional loyalties to occupational and functional groups are increasingly being superseded by new forms and groupings from a richer and more diverse civil society. There has been what Marquand terms "a complex cultural mutation".[68] He argues that the fault lines of class as represented by party and union have splintered and the individualism of people, as evidenced by the diversity of their consumer and lifestyle choices, shows a particularism and diversity that is "hard to reconcile with oligarchic pre-suppositions of the Westminster Model at its parliamentary height".[69]

This does not mean that there has been a depoliticisation of society or the issues of government. There is rather a politicisation along different lines. There may be a weakening of older collective solidarities as expressed in political parties, trades unions, etc. but there is a greater

---

[67] "The Decline of the Party" in *New Times: The Changing Face of Politics in the 1990s* (S. Hall and M. Jacques ed., 1989) p. 333. Smith offers some evidence from a variety of opinion polls suggesting the demise of the party and the reduction of confidence in traditional political structures. See "Post-Modern Politics and the Case for Constitutional Renewal" (1994) 65 *Political Quarterly* 128.

[68] *The Unprincipled Society: New Demands and Old Politics* (1988) at p. 201.

[69] *ibid* p. 202. Hutton argues too that changes in society have outstripped the capacity of the state to accommodate them. He argues that only 40 per cent of society has sufficiently secure income and employment prospects to provide for their own health, housing and education. There is a further 30 per cent who are marginalised and insecure, while a bottom 30 per cent is permanently disadvantaged. See *The State We're in* (1995) p. 105.

fragmentisation and pluralism. Increasingly the politics that now commands enthusiasm and involvement is not the old game of parties and elections but movements centred on general or even global themes such as the environment or the spread of AIDS or on particular issues such as development in a neighbourhood or national legislation to curtail the freedom to use public space. This is pressure-group politics rather than the sort of mass politics which has universal goals and open membership. Class movements and traditional political parties are increasingly being superseded by a whole variety of bodies and groups which reflect better the kaleidoscope of identities now replacing the hierarchies of traditional politics. There is a multiplicity of interests here but two forces are particularly important. Feminism and sex based politics, taking in issues of sexual identity, reproductive morality, and the gendered division of work and exploitation provide a major challenge to orthodox political groupings. Secondly there is the concentration on cultural identity or ethnicity which has produced, as Stuart Hall puts it,

"an astonishing return to the political agenda of all those points of attachment which give the individual some sense of 'place' and position in the world, whether these be in relation to particular communities, localities, territories, languages, religions or cultures".[70]

These may feed into and shape existing political parties but it does not correspond to their main thrust and is not adequately expressed by their activities. As Mulgan comments,

"while the parties and parliaments went on talking, what had previously been non-political issues became the great matters of life, the real issues by which people defined their position in the world."[71]

---

[70] "The Meaning of New Times" in *New Times: The Changing Face of Politics in the 1990s* (Hall and Jacques ed., 1989), at p. 133. Antony Giddens is aware of this process whereby politics is increasingly developing around particular issues such as health, education, sexuality or community development which directly affects people in their everyday lives. Giddens refers to what he calls the greater "reflexivity" in society, whereby people are less willing to trust either tradition or experts in matters which effect their "localised" politics. See further, *Beyond Left and Right: The Future of Radical Politics* (1994) p. 80–87.

[71] *Op. cit.*, p. 19. While Mulgan does capture something of the change occurring he is also representative of the trend to overstate the present extent of developments. For example, in a latter passage he refers rather excitedly to "the influence of Taoism, Buddhism and Hinuism, and of the deep ecology movements ... [which] has brought a new equation between the wider imbalances of society and personal, psychic imbalances" (p. 70). The sort of changes that we are referring to are more deep rooted and systemic if less fashionable.

Traditional politics is increasingly finding itself stranded between the macrocosmic and the microcosmic issues that now concern people. The position is captured well in the paradoxical words of Ulrich Beck who observes that "political modernisation disempowers and unbinds politics and politicises society".[72]

This fragmentation and pluralism has many causes and effects. The development of communication and social networks provided by technology and mass transport has the effect that people are not so tied to neighbourhood but freer to chose from a host of overlapping identities. There is an international dimension too in so far as modern experience cuts across boundaries of geography, class, religion and ideology and, while it does not destroy them altogether, it does weaken their ability to provide us with a social identity. Old allegiances and ties may be fragmenting but people's identities and roles are expanding. Groupings and organisations spring up to meet this. While the state itself appears less and less as the desirable prize for political activity there is an explosion in the growth in those mediating groups and networks—what ex-President Bush called "the thousand points of light"—existing below the level of the state and increasingly providing the focus for individuals' political engagement. These are spontaneous and self-sustaining groups with varying degrees of formal engagement with the state. Some are locally based community groups with little formal connection with the traditional organs of government. Others are more structured and interact with the state in a variety of ways—lobbying and shaping policy, providing expertise and legitimacy, and sometimes even performing functions that the state no longer wishes to, or is able to, perform. Increasingly the state is funding in part some of the 170,000 charities registered in Great Britain to resume the traditional roles that they played before the welfare state. Indeed, we see the voluntary sector and charities (the third sector as it is known) as particularly important here. They are increasingly becoming part of the mechanism of government within a new configuration of the state. Here politics is about renewing grants and funding as much as it is about parties sending representatives to parliament, and power is concerned with enabling and facilitating as much as it is with straightforwardly passing legislation in parliament.

---

[72] Quoted by Mulgan, *ibid.*, p. 19.

The ways in which these developments in civil society are impacting on the process of government is little understood within orthodox constitutionalism. Of course it is happening in a very informal and unstructured way. However, there seems to be no appreciation whatever within orthodox constitutionalism of these developments or of the requirement that a modern version of constitutionalism should encompass such a complex and important exercise of power.

III. GOVERNMENT AT A DISTANCE

There is a continuing revolution in the way that government is being conducted and this has major implications for our understanding of constitutional law. It is most obvious in relation to the delivery of public services by markets or quasi-markets. Here there is a whole range of ways in which what government does is profoundly changing.[73] The phenomenon is a complex one involving more than just withdrawal by the state from activities which then fall to the private sector, as with privatisation in its strictest sense.[74] Now there are a whole range of alternatives, often premised on ideas of efficiency instead of increased taxation, individual choice rather than state monopoly and the state acting as an agent to empower a range of smaller providers to compete and innovate rather than itself taking on all the details of guaranteeing and actually providing the whole range of services. This is producing profound changes in the nature of government and, although many of the basic issues of accountability and control remain, they now appear in new forms and with added complications.

What is happening is that instead of taking on the tasks that became its traditional role during the height of the welfare state, the state is now seeking to reduce its involvement. It can achieve this straightforwardly by transferring a given function to the private sector and merely arranging for its regulation. Alternatively, it may make a distinction between responsibility for providing a function and responsibility for performing that function. Nominally the function remains within the public sector, but the

---

[73] The extent of this change is well-documented in Dynes and Walker, *The Times Guide to the New British State: The Government Machine in the 1990s* (1995) which details exhaustively the range of local, national and European bodies and agencies now involved in government.

[74] See Gamble, "Privatisation, Thatcherism and the British State" (1989) 16 *Journal of Law and Society* 1 for a discussion of the range of alternative forms of privatisation.

state now organises multiple providers to actually perform the function. These are drawn from the both the private and public sectors, from a third group in the new civil society made up of religious and charitable associations as well as various public and private partnerships. Increasingly then the state reduces its involvement and responsibility by restricting its role to providing for the regulation of privatised activities and to setting the policies, mission statements and framework documents with which it hopes to exercise some measure of control.

Of course this separation of provider from purchaser and policy-maker from manager is accompanied by a whole rhetoric of choice and competition and a notion of citizenship in relation to the consumption of public services. This is a coherent and far-reaching programme. Lewis is one of the few commentators to recognise what is both a philosophy of government and a means of government. He points out that

> "the Citizen's Charter is now enmeshed with the Next Steps programme, the continued commitment to privatisation and competition (with, at least temporary, regulatory features), the marketisation of public services and the withdrawal of government to an empowering fortification".[75]

While this "potentially amounts to a new political settlement" there is a marked absence of any 'accompanying constitutional settlement".[76]

The Regulatory State. The 1980s and 1990s have seen major changes in the role of the state and ought to have seen a similar shift within constitutional doctrine as it goes about the task of identifying where power is now located and how it should be controlled. However, with consequences apparently almost unnoticed by the constitutional mainstream, there has been a move away from the welfare state involved with redistribution and a shift from the Keynsian state concerned with macroeconomic management. The emphasis now is on markets and the values of cost-cutting and efficiency that competition is supposed to bring. At the extreme edge of this policy there is the privatisation programme which has

---

[75] "The Citizen's Charter and Next Steps: A New Way of Governing?" (1993) 64 *Political Quarterly* 316. See also Birkenshaw, Harden and Lewis, *Government by Moonlight: The Hidden Parts of the State* (1990). In a very recent textbook, McEldowney *op. cit.*, commendably includes aspects of this process (see especially chapters 10 and 13). However, surprisingly, his account manages to see such developments as being largely accommodated within the existing constitutional framework and the traditional textbook format.

[76] *Op. cit.* at p. 324.

sought to ensure that activities and functions once carried out as the responsibility of the state are now conducted directly by the private sector.[77] While this ought to mean less government it has, in fact, not produced this result. In some ways the free market thrust has brought more government. Privatised utilities such as gas, telephone and water, because of the costs of their infrastructure, have the potential to remain monopolies in perpetuity and so will continue to require regulation.[78] Meanwhile the interests of competition require government to invade newly de-regulated businesses more and more to keep the playing fields level. The result is a regulatory state where the amount of government activity is perhaps no less and certainly of a qualitatively different order.

The response of government to the issue of regulation generally has been to set up a variety of regulatory bodies operating with a high level of discretion within a statutory framework.[79] They are characterised by the looseness of their remit and by the personal style of their operation. They function within a model where generally they see themselves as techno-cratic only, operating outside the political arena. The regulators, bodies such as Ofwat, Ofgas and, most recently, Oflot, style themselves as referees standing above the players in the game. Of course this is not the case in reality. The regulators are clearly involved in the game. This is not a world where technical issues prevail and politics does not raise its head. The scale of the privatisation means that perhaps up to 20 per cent of the economy is now in the hands of enterprises that were formerly state owned and run. The regulators exercise power over a whole range of highly political matters. Often they must balance the interests of customers, shareholders, employees, environmentalists and, indeed, future generations as well as the national interest, particularly if the company competes abroad. The basic utilities of gas, water and electricity are not only economically important but are linked to ideas of basic citizenship, as the public obligation aspect that has always been present in arrangements for their distribution suggests. There are all sorts of choices to be made and this surely is the very basis of politics. For example, powers to price cap have clear political significance. If prices are low it is good for consumers but if they are high it benefits

---

[77] See Vickers and Yarrow, *Privatisation: An Economic Analysis* (1988) and, more generally, Graham and Prosser, *Privatising Public Enterprises: Constitutions, the State and Regulation in Comparative Perspective* (1991)

[78] See Foster, *Privatisation, Public Ownership and the Regulation of Natural Monopoly* (1992).

[79] See further Baldwin and McCrudden (ed.) *Regulation and Public Law* (1987); Craig, *Administrative Law* (3rd ed., 1994), chap. 6 and more generally, Moran and Prosser (ed.) *Privatisation and Regulatory Change in Europe* (1994).

company shareholders and employees, especially top management. These are the sort of political decisions that were traditionally the preserve of central government. Decisions about raising prices on basic utilities are indeed tantamount to raising taxation, especially if the money generated is to go into plant and infrastructure. Even decisions about energy efficiency targets and environmental goals may be viewed as indirect ways of levying taxation for political ends. Such matters may have been handed over to regulators but they remain matters of government and politics and are not somehow magically transformed into merely technical questions or issues which the market can by itself automatically resolve in a value free way.

The present, "aconstitutional" arrangements however do seem to suggest that this is not government at all. In the United Kingdom the personal style of regulators and the absence of detailed rules, and even of much of an opportunity for judicial review to find a point of purchase, seems to deny that what is happening here is political or the stuff of government no matter how far removed it appears from the traditional institutions. There has been some limited recognition of this manifested in criticisms that the personnel selected as regulators are committed to free market ideals and in anxieties expressed about what might happen should a future Labour government introduce their personnel who might be committed to a more social outlook. However, there have not been any serious attempts to structure this exercise of government within any constitutional framework beyond the very limited channels of account-ability to parliament that presently exist. This is in contrast to the United States where a much longer history of regulation has resulted in a system that is closely integrated to political and legal structures and where the courts act as an anchor on regulators and industries by requiring informa-tion about what is happening and reasons for it. In the United Kingdom there is not even the sort of Conseil d'Etat jurisdiction which could serve as a focus for ministers and regulators to be held to account. Indeed, almost any theory within modern management would stress the need for multiple levels of control and hierarchies of accountability with mission statements, corporate plans and any social objectives therein all freely available. However, in the United Kingdom this is not the case. There the fiction that we have arm's length administrators and that government at one remove is somehow not government at all, continues with even constitu-tional reformers seeming to accept it.

The Rise of the Quango.   Closely related to the structures spawned by the regulatory state there is the more general quango body through which government is conducted at a distance. Such bodies (which include regulatory agencies but go much wider too) are one of the chief sites to which public power has been steadily moving throughout the 1980s and 1990s. Although the incoming Conservative government in 1979 promised a cull of quangos most survived the Pliatzky report largely untouched.[80] In the second half of the 1980s their numbers, powers and budgets increased once again. In 1994 one estimate put the number of quangos at 5,521 and claimed that they were responsible for over 30 per cent of public expenditure.[81] It has been forecast that there will be 7,700 quangos by 1996.[82] Such estimates are, however, dependent on how a quango is defined (if indeed quango is a useful term at all). Whitehall has always preferred reference to "Non Departmental Public Bodies", although more recently this has mutated into "Public Bodies". In 1994 the government admitted to 1,389 of these spending some £60 billion.[83] Critics argue, however, that this excludes some which were public bodies even on the government's own criteria (including eight in Northern Ireland omitted because they "fulfil functions carried out by local authorities in Great Britain") and defines many others out of existence. The latter category included formally private bodies carrying out public functions and many recently created local bodies, such as Grant Maintained Schools and Training and Enterprise Councils. In their study for the Democratic Audit, Weir and Hall prefer the term "Extra Governmental Organisations". In this they include all bodies carrying out executive functions but excluded advisory bodies, tribunals and executive agencies. Since our concern is less with charting and cataloguing the rise of such bodies than with recognising the moving of power away from formally representative institutions, we retain the use of the broad term "quango". By this we mean to signify all those bodies outside central and local government departments which are appointed or funded by central government to carry out public functions. In particular advisory, service delivery or regulatory functions (we therefore exclude the courts). We also treat the creation of "Next Steps" Agencies separately as an example of a specific and declared strategy to create government at one remove.

---

[80] *Report on Non Departmental Bodies*, Cmnd. 7797 (1980).
[81] See Hall and Weir (ed.) *Ego Trip: Extra Governmental Organisations in the United Kingdom and their Accountability* (1994) pp. 9–10.
[82] According to Lord Bonham-Carter opening a debate on quangos in the House of Lords. (*Hansard*, H.L. No. 1585, col. 611, January 19, 1994.)
[83] *The Times* October 27, 1994.

Such a working definition still leaves a large numbers of bodies which differ significantly in terms of legal powers, staff, resources and potential impact. They range from powerful executive bodies such as Regional Health Authorities and NHS Trusts (which may employ thousands of staff and spend millions of pounds) down to the boards of individual Grant Maintained Schools. Other quangos may carry out significant regulatory functions, such as the Equal Opportunities Commission or the Mental Health Commission, or provide government with independent advice, such as the Law Commission. The main growth in the 1980s has been in bodies which have taken over what were once functions of local government. Examples of this include Housing Associations, Housing Action Trusts, Urban Development Corporations, Health Trusts, the Funding Agency for Schools, the Boards of Grant Maintained Schools and Training and Enterprise Councils.[84] While some of bodies have the legal status of private companies all operate within a network of central government directives and resource allocation. The relationship of quangos to central government is a shadowy but complex one. While quangos are established as autonomous organisations the fact that they spend public money is usually deemed to require a link to a sponsoring department and hence to a minister who can be responsible to parliament. However such ministerial scrutiny often proves to be less than exacting, at least where the quango is following the broad outlines of government policy.

What can not be disputed though is that the decisions taken by quangos such as Urban Development Corporations, Ofwat, the Higher Education Funding Council or Health Service Trusts may have a major impact on significant sections of society. In many ways this is truly the new despotism. The quango system of government operates at a profoundly constitutional level to simultaneously distance central government (and

---

[84] One of the most startling examples arises from the replacement of elected government in London following the abolition of the GLC in 1985. Now a whole range of unelected bodies, including London Regional Transport Authority, London Docklands Corporation, the London Residuary Body, the London Arts Board, the London Tourist Board, the London training and enterprise councils, the Housing Corporation, London health authorities, the London City challenge boards as well as purely private organisations like London First, fill in for a London wide authority. According to Baroness Hollis, these such bodies together spend some £7.5 billion without the benefit of any electoral check. (See Hansard, H.L. No. 1585, col. 640, January 9, 1994.) This is not unique to the capital. For example, Labour's Jack Straw claims that in the West Midlands there are now at least 35 regional bodies through which central government influences public services and the regional economy. He argues that control over the annual spend of £24 billion has effectively passed from elected councils to the new quangos. (See The Times, November 6, 1993.)

the potentially inconvenient links to representativeness and accountability that this might suggest) and to allow it to exert broad control—particularly where this is in line with a market oriented philosophy. In many ways it is a new form of government rather than simply a mutation or slimming down of existing forms. It provides a self-justifying alternative to the existing imperfectly democratic institutions. Tony Wright, commenting on the general process whereby government is distanced from ideas of political accountability, writes of the "audacity of the enterprise" whereby political control is superseded by some form of market control as supervised by a quango.[85] He suggests that the corollary of the removal of public activities and services from collective public accountability is the removal of the need for those mechanisms and sites through which political decision-making takes place. Thus, he concludes,

> "in terms of its own brutal logic . . . once local government (to take the leading example) is stripped of its traditional service functions as these are put out to the market, it is but a short step to suggest that only an attenuated and depoliticized structure need remain".[86]

Quangos thus exist as both as powerful, autonomous bodies outside the existing constitutional framework and the pawns of an overbearing central government operating in a democratic vacuum.[87]

By the mid 1990s the growth of quangos has become a matter of public concern. However, much of this concern has concentrated on issues of patronage and waste. There are between 40,000 and 70,000 current members of quangos (depending on which figures are accepted) and around 10,000 appointments a year to be made.[88] This raises significant issues about who is to be appointed and how. Yet in 1992 the government acknowledged that only 24 of these 10,000 positions had been advertised

---

[85] *Citizens and Subjects* (1994) at p. 122.

[86] *supra* at p. 123.

[87] The recent example of the policy decision by the York based Funding Agency for Schools to expand grant maintained schools in the London borough of Hillingdon against the wishes of the Labour controlled council (reported in *The Times* October 26, 1994), provides an excellent example of how existing political mechanisms can be marginalised by a quango pursuing central government inspired policy.

[88] The first paper from the Nolan Inquiry, *Issues and Questions*, published in December 1994 put the number of appointments to quangos and public bodies at in excess of 42,000. The report of the Nolan Committee has certainly put the issue of appointments into sharp focus with its recommendation for a Public Appointments Commissioner to oversee membership of quangos. See *Standards in Public Life*. First Report of the Committee on Standards in Public Life, Vol. 1. (1995).

in that year. Most posts are filled from a list centrally maintained by a public appointments unit of the Cabinet Office, with the more important jobs going to the candidates of ministers or senior civil servants. The announcement by a former Health minister, Baroness Denton, that she had never knowingly appointed a Labour Party supporter to any body within her remit,[89] and a plethora of anecdotal accounts suggesting a preponderance of Conservative supporters on quango boards,[90] fuelled accusations that the government was seeking to use what are formally independent bodies to pursue its political agenda. Even if direct political bias was not at the root of appointments some accounts of how people came to be on quangos undercut the claim that they are composed of people selected for their expertise and particular skills. As a former chair of the Countryside Commission wrote in 1991,

"I became chairman . . . as a consequence of sharing a cab with a stranger. Another quango chairman was appointed following a pheasant shoot at which the secretary of state was a fellow gun; the subsequent chairman of a water authority bumped into a cabinet minister while birding on a Greek island".

Detailed examination of the membership of individual quangos (when such information is available) also reveals people sitting on several bodies simultaneously, or regularly moving from one appointment to another. Such an informal approach may be at the root of many of the rising concerns over waste and financial mismanagement that attend the operation of quangos. Quango boards do not maintain a register of members interests and studies have shown that it is not unusual for business people on such bodies to award contracts to their own companies. On a more spectacular scale, there have been a series of accusations levelled at the Welsh Development Agency (WDA) and its chair resigned in 1993 shortly

---

[89] *Independent on Sunday* March 28, 1994. Labour spokesperson Margaret Beckett has accused Baroness Denton's successor, Virginia Bottomley, of being the "Madam Mao" of the health service because of her role in packing NHS trust boards with conservative party supports. (See *The Times* November 26, 1994.)

[90] See, for example, *Hansard* H.C. No. 1645 col. 459–560 (February 24, 1994), *The Economist* August 6, 1994 at p. 20 and *The Observer* November 6, 1994. Away from the more obvious political partisanship there is evidence of other ways in which quangos are staffed from a homogeneous group. A *Financial Times* survey of 40 of the largest quangos found that 38 of the 40 people who chaired them were men and that 36 of the 40 had attended public school. (Quoted in *Hansard* H.L. No. 1585, col. 640 (January 19, 1994.) *The Observer*, May 14, 1995 claimed that three out of every five top-ranking civil servants receive jobs on quangos after retiring from service.

before the appearance of a Parliamentary Accounts Committee report criticising financial irregularities in the WDA.

Such concerns over what is sometimes called "the patronage state" are no doubt valid. However there are deeper questions here too and these are more pertinent to our interest in the drift of public power away from representative institutions. There is the issue of the accountability of quangos. Most accounts still seek to tie accountability to a responsible minister and thence to parliament. However, as we have seen, ministerial responsibility is now stretched fairly thinly as regards those areas for which ministers have direct responsibility, let alone for those bodies acting at one or several removes from the traditional site of the traditional doctrine. Select committees have sought to exercise some control over quangos but this may have the effect of driving them closer to the minister, with all the problems this brings.[91] Some quangos come under the jurisdiction of the National Audit Office and the Audit Commission, but many do not.[92] Some come under the jurisdiction of the Ombudsman but there are those that do not.[93] The real extent of parliament's power to control what quangos do is often rather minimal. Clearly there is here an exercise of public power which has escaped the institutions to which many reformers look.

Overall this is not particularly surprising or likely to be easily reversed. Many of the functions which quangos have been established to carry out are complex ones for which neither central or local government may be ideally suited. After all, the origin of the quango was as a small advisory body appointed by a Minister often in areas of technical specialism where the civil service could not be expected to maintain expertise, or in sensitive areas such as broadcasting or the Arts where government was to be kept out. Drawn from the "great and the good", operating on a small budget and claiming only expenses actually incurred, the original quangos brought to bear expertise on such diverse areas as the safety of medicines and the acquisition policy of museums and galleries. As the nature of government has changed and, in particular as an increased number of

[91] See Wilding "A triangular affair: quangos, Ministers and MPs" in Barker (ed.) *Quangos in Britain* (1982) 34, 42.
[92] See *The Economist* September 10, 1994 at p. 31. The Nolan Committee (*op. cit.* n. 88), noting that up to one-third of quangos do not have their accounts inspected by the National Audit Office, has called for all such public expenditure to be subject to National Audit Office scrutiny.
[93] See Hall and Weir (ed.) *op. cit.* at pp. 23–24

functions have been privatised, the quango has evolved to operate in what is now an increased range of areas where central or local government seems no longer to be suited. Given this, it seems right that the original expert role be augmented by input from a range of other quarters. In particular it is vital to ensure that now the increased numbers of those likely to be affected by the wider range of decisions have an opportunity to participate in them. Unfortunately, however, quangos have not evolved in this direction. Few quangos are required to allow the public to attend meetings or even to publish minutes. "Open Government" codes have not been applied to quangos and even discovering the names of those who sit on quangos can prove to be a difficult task. As many commentators have observed, quangos have emerged in a piecemeal way, enjoying a variety of means of creation—ranging from express statutory authority to a Treasury minute—and there is no developed legal code for such bodies to fit into.[94] Given this there is no coherent account of the quango's responsibilities to parliament, to the users of its services or to the general public.[95] In view of the current, and likely continuing, absence of any effective parliamentary oversight, mechanisms which entitle user groups and the public to participate more fully in decision-taking may prove to be a more effective way of checking the exercise of public power and the deployment of resources by such bodies. Certainly there is a need for those interested by the idea of constitutional change to take seriously the questions posed by the development of quangos. As we have observed elsewhere in this book, calls for greater parliamentary oversight may not be sufficient to capture the extent to which the exercise of public power has moved on.

[94] See, for example, Johnson "Accountability, control and complexity: moving beyond ministerial responsibility" in Barker (ed.) *Quangos in Britain* (1982) p. 206. Among the 55 recommendations of the Nolan Committee (*op. cit.*) there is a call for a government review to produce a more consistent legal framework for quangos.

[95] At the time of writing the Commons Treasury and Civil Service Committee is calling for a code of conduct to be introduced for civil servants and those working for bodies such as quangos which derived their income from public funds. See further Radice, the committee chair, writing in *The Times*, August 11, 1994. (A similar proposal is offered by the Association of Metropolitan Authorities, *Changing the Face of Quangos* (1995.) While the Scott Report and the Lord Nolan's Committee on standards in public life may well force the introduction of such a code in addition to the existing and more modest Treasury *Code of Best Practice for Board Members of Public Bodies*, it is unlikely that such measures with their main focus firmly on financial propriety would by themselves be enough to control all aspects of the diverse operation of existing quangos.

The New Public Management. The Civil Service has been subject to significant change this century and to revolution within the last decade or so.[96] Although almost one million public sector jobs have been transferred to the private sector since 1979, the more direct forms of privatisation have impacted on public utilities more than on the civil service. While certain developments, such as market testing, may herald a move in the future to privatisation of a sort, the focus in the last decade or so has been mainly on how to re-order the civil service and expose it to market forces rather than simply giving up particular functions as such and leaving them to private sector to take on. The phrase "New Public Management is a shorthand term for a set of broadly similar administrative doctrines that have dominated the bureaucratic reform agenda in many of the OECD group of countries since the 1970s.[97] Certainly the British experience mirrors quite closely changes occurring in the United States, Canada, Australia and most of all New Zealand.[98]

The major way in which the New Public Management has manifested itself is through the recasting of the civil service from its Northcote-Trevelyan model of a unified public service to a more market oriented affair. It was felt that traditionally the civil service was interested in, and skilled at, policy-making, political management and presentation of government policies and not in the efficient delivery of services, although on some estimates this accounted for up to 95 per cent of civil service activity.[99] Civil service efficiency could be improved and, no less importantly, public spending could be controlled and reduced, by a re-structuring of the public sector involving the assignment of a function or activity to a distinct unit of management which could then be regarded as being accountable for the efficient performance of that function or activity. Although there have been a number of different reform programmes the most significant overall thrust is the separation of policy

---

[96] See further Drewry and Butcher, *The Civil Service Today* (2nd ed., 1991); Butler, "The Evolution of the Civil Service—A Progress Report" (1993) 71 *Public Administration* 395 and Craig, *Administrative Law* (3rd ed., 1994) chap. 3.

[97] See further Hood, "A Public Management for all Seasons" (1991) 69 *Public Administration* 3 for an account of the origins and development of the cluster of ideas that constitute the New Public Management in the United Kingdom and elsewhere. See also Rhodes "The Hollowing Out of the State: The Changing Nature of Public Service in Britain", (1994) 65 *Political Quarterly* 138.

[98] See, for example, Wistrich, "Restructuring Government New Zealand Style" (1992) 70 *Public Administration* 119 and Greer, *Transforming Central Government: The Next Steps Initiative* (1994) chap. 8.

[99] Mayne, "Public Power Outside Government" (1993) 64 *Political Quarterly* at p. 327.

functions from operational functions. Increasingly government was to be directly involved in policy rather than service delivery, steering rather than rowing. Basically this involves identifying and retaining a number of "core" functions of government and setting the rest at one remove. This process commenced with the Fulton Report[1] and its ideas of increased efficiency and "hiving off". Although initially the suggestions for reform were not linked with any particular party political philosophy they were given particular impetus by Mrs Thatcher and linked with her more general themes of privatisation and competition as the engines of efficiency and effectiveness. Mrs Thatcher's Efficiency Unit, chaired by Lord Rayner from Marks and Spencer, introduced a variety of mechanisms to aid management. Initially these were primarily efficiency scrutinies directed towards establishing administrative structures such as the Management Information System for Ministers (MINIS) used by Michael Heseltine from 1979 in the Department of Environment and then in the Ministry of Defence. Then in 1982 the Financial Management Initiative (FMI) was introduced to define objectives and lines of responsibility as well as examine the costs required in exercising government responsibilities effectively. Building on this the Efficiency Unit then moved on to look at what would be gained by separating policy making from service delivery and, under the chairmanship of Sir Robin Ibbs, produced the Next Steps initiative.[2] This states as a goal that civil service should be reduced to "a relatively small core" engaged in the function of servicing ministers and managing departments, who will be the "sponsors" of particular government policies and services".[3] Everything else will be hived off into executive or Next Steps Agencies. As outlined at the end of chapter one, these are constituted by framework documents which detail the goals and objectives of the agency and, in particular, set out the responsibilities of agency chief executives who are to kept away from "policy" issues and instead concentrate on financial planning and control in relation to predetermined performance targets. While framework documents are not of course contracts as such, the language of contract and its sense of a relationship between two parties—a department and an

---

[1] *Report of the Committee on the Civil Service 1966–68* Cmnd. 3638 (1968).
[2] *Improving Management: The Next Steps* (1988). See also Goldsworthy, *Setting Up Next Steps: A Short Account of the Origins, Launch and Implementation of the Next Steps Project in the British Civil Service* (1991) and Greer *Transforming Central Government: The Next Steps Initiative* (1994).
[3] *supra*, para. 44.

agency—reflects the more commercial (and therefore impliedly more efficient) new basis of government.

By Autumn 1993 there were 93 agencies employing over 260,000 civil servants. This amounts to some 45 per cent of the establishment and there are plans for 15 more agencies to take the total to 50 per cent with a stated goal to have over 90 per cent of the civil service in agencies by end of 1995. This is a major change in the way government is conducted in this country. While the aim of the programme may have been efficiency it has had significant impact on other aspects not least accountability. From the inception of the programme, government made it clear that it did "not envisage that setting up Executive Agencies within Departments will result in changes to the existing constitutional arrangements".[4] As we noted in chapter one it has been left largely to parliament which has had particular difficulty in applying its existing mechanisms in relation to the artificial distinction between operational and policy issues on which the whole edifice of Next Steps is built.[5] Oliver attempts to fit executive agencies into the existing structures, even referring to the Osmotherly Rules which underwrite the political neutrality of the civil servants, but eventually her conclusion is that "the Next Steps both exacerbate and highlight the deficiencies in the system and the need for measures to deal with them".[6] Lewis is more direct. He says that the "agencies simply identify as nothing else could how sterile the orthodoxy really is".[7]

The problems relating to accountability in parliament are not improved by the most recent trends within the Public Management Strategy. These are towards further privatisation through market testing and contracting out. Such ideas have been present within the general scheme for some time. In 1991, for example, there was an effort to introduce to central government the policy of market testing or compulsory competitive tendering which had been imposed on local government through the Local Government Act 1988. The Competing for Quality initiative

---

[4] The government reply to the *Eighth Report from the Treasury and Civil Service Committee 1988* (quoted in Greer *op. cit.* p. 82).

[5] See Greer *op. cit.* chap. 6 for an account of parliament's role and, in particular, for an outline of how even the National Audit Office which serves and produces value for money reports to the Public Accounts Committee is hampered by the necessity of now having to go through the lengthy and costly procedure of agreeing the factual matters in its reports with both the department and the agency.

[6] *Government in the United Kingdom* (1991) at p. 68.

[7] "Reviewing Change in Government: New Public Management and Next Steps" (1994) *Public Law* at p. 107.

requires departments and agencies to open up many of their functions to competition from the private sector or other public sector contractors.[8] This operates to develop the process of agentisation as all manner of government functions are market tested in order to see if they could not be more effectively carried out in the private sector. Indeed, in some ways the Next Steps process can be seen as simply a staging post. There is the impetus from the Citizen's Charter movement which from its first report has stressed consumer choice, a preference for markets and the private sector with regulation only second best and called for a re-examination of what is to be left as the "core" of the public sector.[9] There is the Prior Options Review which offers a number of tests to be passed before the creation of a new agency and contains a strong bias towards activities being handed over to the private sector. A Next Steps Briefing Note issued in June 1993 requires that privatisation must be considered as an option in the review of framework agreements every three years. In addition there have been a number of significant personnel and establishment changes.[10] For example, there is now a special section of the Cabinet Office called the Office of Public Service and Science with a full cabinet Minister established to look after the Citizen's Charter, executive agencies and market testing. There is the move to resource-based accrual accounting introduced in the November 1993 budget to replace traditional civil service cash accounting and to enable better comparison with costs in the private sector. This has the effect that now public sector costings have to take into account the expenses of land and buildings with the result that pressures towards contracting out will generally seem inevitable. In addition, the civil service pay and staffing structure is being prepared for a new method of operation among those that remain.[11] This is a revolution that is far from over.

This change in the nature of government is a fundamental one and unlikely to go away. Much of the New Public Management is regarded as "transferable technology" available for governments of any party. Labour's

---

[8] See further, HM Treasury *Competing for Quality—Buying Better Public Services* CM 1730 (1991).
[9] See *The Citizen's Charter—First Report* (1992) Cm 2101; *The Citizen's Charter—Second Report* (1994) Cm 2540. See also Drewry, "Mr Major's Charter: Empowering the Consumer" (1993) *Public Law* 248 where the connections are examined.
[10] See further Willman, "The Civil Service" in *The Major Effect"* (Kavanagh and Seldon ed. 1994).

[11] See, for example, the Civil Service (Management Functions) Act 1992 which is designed to facilitate more individualised pay and grading structures.

chief spokesperson on the Civil Service has commented that, given the scale and pace of the government's plans for privatising and setting up new agencies it is likely that an in-coming labour government would

"inherit a civil service consisting of a mere 25 rump departments with perhaps only 2,000 officials in each—50,000 people compared with 730,000 in 1979 together with 300 or more executive agencies, more than 4000 quangos and an inventory of thousands of rolling contracts with service suppliers".[12]

Maybe this estimate is even too generous. The cut back of one-third of the senior policy making posts in Treasury announced in the autumn of 1994 and occasioned by the reduction in Treasury's role as scrutineer of public spending following the privatisation and contracting out of public services marks the beginning of what is widely expected to be a very considerable cut back in the traditional establishment occasioned by a revolution in the way government sees itself. This has two major implications.

First, there is the change in civil service ethos which traditionally was associated with political neutrality and was thought to act as an influence against radical reform. Now it is possible to make senior appointments from outside the ranks of the civil service on a contract basis.[13] And this has brought fears of a political civil service, influenced by performance bonuses within short term contracts rather than national pay agreements and career progression. It is believed that the new generation of public officials might be concerned to demonstrate loyalty to a particular minister rather than civil service traditions. While much of this may sound like protests from the last bastion of the middle classes now coming under attack, there are grounds for believing that the nature of public service is fundamentally changing. Such changes may well lead to the erosion of informal ideas of public interest which have sustained the operation of the traditional civil service and there is little evidence of any new formal structures or values being introduced to replace these. Moreover the managerialist ethos of the new civil service, with its focus narrowly on results and their measurement, may actually undermine any attempts at other, more co-operative strategies of intergovernmental management designed to facilitate networks aimed at more general problem-solving and

---

[12] *The Times*, October 6, 1994.
[13] According to Sir Robin Butler, Head of the Home Civil Service, between 60 and 70 per cent of Agency Chief Executives in post at the end of 1993 were appointed following open competition and about 35 per cent are from outside the civil service. (Butler *op. cit.* p. 400.)

negotiation.[14] Indeed, there must be doubts if the civil service will in future sustain an establishment capable of implementing the policies of an incoming administration that takes a different, more active view of its role in public administration.

Secondly, and even more importantly, there is a fundamental change in how government is to be controlled. Here the Civil Service has moved even further away from its Northcote-Trevelyan traditions where officials were organised into departments with ministerial heads and generally understood lines of demarcation and responsibility. The notion of managing by the use of "contracts" is at its heart as is the objective of devolving financial and managerial responsibility for service delivery away from central government. This is genuinely new and alternative to all that has gone before. As Greer concludes, "Next Steps is about the move to management by contract and has now, with the introduction of the Market Testing initiative, also come to be about the move to management of contract".[15] This is increasingly how government will be done. Markets (or rather quasi-markets) and contracts with a variety of bodies are replacing the lines of control based on the traditional law and custom relating to an establishment of civil servants. Of course the actual private law of contract has a very limited range of application to the relationship between a public body and a service provider. For example, the framework documents of Executive Agencies are not private law contracts as the agencies do not have a legal personality separate from the Crown who cannot contract with itself. As Harden argues, using the language of contract seems to invoke something of a "moral promise". It seems to speak to values of individual autonomy, freedom to choose, and consumer sovereignty, and thus even democratic equality in economic decision making.[16] However, the reality is that contract does not provide a ready made set of solutions to the problems of organising public services. All the familiar, basic constitutional questions about controlling discretion and

---

[14] See further Rhodes, *The New Governance: Governing with Government* (1995) which provides a report of his "State of Britain" ESRC seminar outlining the contradictions between the New Public Management and newer, alternative ideas of managing departments to create a more organic, holistic approach to government.
[15] *op. cit.* p. 127.
[16] *The Contracting State* (1992), chap. 1. See also Vincent-Jones, "The Limits of Contractual Order in Public Sector Transacting" (1994) 14 *Legal Studies* 364.

ensuring accountability re-emerge—albeit in a slightly less familiar context. In addition there are new problems too. For example, there are
tensions between the values of flexibility and accountability. The agency
or supplier must be free standing and flexible but it must remain in the
control of, and accountable to, its sponsoring department. This has
required new mechanisms a long way away from traditional lines of
ministerial control and civil service independence. As Carter and Greer
point out, the result is to make mechanisms such as performance indicators
very significant in as much as they act as "highly political instruments
mediating the delicate relationship between Department and Agency".[17]
Market research studies and customer surveys, information rights and
Charter Marks are the new tools for holding administrations to account.
Lewis is close to describing this where he attempts a distinction between
traditional "government" and new forms of "governance" which involves
empowering a myriad of providers to innovate within the limits set by
policy and contained within mission statements.[18] Unfortunately most
public lawyers, including those who would offer recommendations for
constitutional reform, have failed to notice the changing environment
which renders much of their well-intentioned advice irrelevant.

Throughout this section we have been arguing that power has shifted
from its traditional sites within the nation state as described by orthodox
constitutionalism. There are globalising developments producing changes
and structures above the level of the state as well as developments,
including new forms of civil society and the influence of markets, producing changes below the level of the nation state. The pattern produced by
these ongoing changes is not yet clear. There are contradictory and
complex forces at work. We can point to general trends but, as Mann
points out, "societies are much messier than our theories of them".[19] We
do not attempt to deny the richness and complexity of what is occurring
but we do wonder at those reformers who, no less than those within
orthodox constitutionalism, seem to have failed to notice that their whole
enterprise has changed.

---

[17] "Evaluating Agencies: Next Steps and Performance Indicators" (1993) 71 *Public Administration* at p. 414.
[18] "The Citizen's Charter and Next Steps: A New Way of Governing?" *op. cit.* p. 317.
[19] *The Sources of Power*, Vol. 1 (1986) at p. 3.

The Changing Nature of Power and Law

Most of what we have said in this chapter is pushing towards the conclusion that the very processes of governance seem to be escaping the categories of the nation state. The idea of a political system that uses the state to turn the preferences of voters into policies solely and effectively via the domestic institutions of parliament and the executive is increasingly unsatisfactory. The traditional constitutionalism that supports and under-writes such views is not credible at all and attempts by reformers to reinvigorate it are generally nowhere near ambitious enough in their remit. We have argued that the locus of power in the United Kingdom has moved, and is moving, to transnational and subnational levels beyond the national state and the parliament and central government on which most constitutional reformers continue to pin their hopes. It is necessary now to outline in a little more detail what we mean by the concept of power, how it has changed and how the related idea of law needs to be re-conceptualised.

Power is one of political sociology's most difficult terms.[20] Sociologists have disputed over issues of whether power must be coercive or whether it can be exercised with the consent of the governed, over issues of whether power is a matter of intention or effects and over questions about how power is exercised. For our purposes however certain broad distinctions are helpful. The first is that between the idea of power as *capacity* and that of power as *effect*. The former captures the idea of someone having the capacity, whether in law or fact, to alter another's behaviour even if they choose not to exercise it at this time. The latter is more concerned with how such alterations are actually brought about, with the mechanisms actually involved. The second distinction is between the idea of power as an explicit direction which can overcome resistance to alter behaviour, and the idea of power as the production of behaviour. Whereas in the former power produces effects intentionally, often contrary to the desires of those it impacts on, in the latter it shapes the desires and goals of those agents so that they see no conflict between their own goals and those of power.

A vision of power as capacity and power as direction dominate constitu-tional outlooks from the eighteenth century onwards. Such viewpoints see

---

[20] For an overview see Lukes (ed.) *Power* (1986).

the state as the supreme site of power, possessing the ability to affect any aspect of society and doing so through the explicit directions of laws— laws which could be backed up by military force if they were disobeyed. Modern constitutionalism is thus the liberal seizure of legal power. But the absoluteness of this power creates an imperative for its restriction. This restriction is to be achieved through an injunction that the state act only through laws and then by restricting the ability of the state to make laws, whether through procedural techniques or substantive guarantees. It is in this way that constitutional reformers, even today, hope to distinguish between and control legitimate uses of state power in the public interest and illegitimate uses to advance the claims of one particular group in society.

Though self-proclaimedly modernist, this approach to the issue of political power can be seen as not departing too far from pre-modern concerns about limiting the power of kings. Foucault especially has argued that although the King may be dead, constitutional struggles continue to identify actual power with the notion of legal sovereignty and endlessly debate the limits to this sovereignty. As Foucault observes "whether the jurists were the King's henchmen or his adversaries, it is of royal power that we are speaking of in every case when we speak of these grandiose edifices of legal thought and knowledge".[21] While such a vision sat easily with nineteenth century traditions of *laissez-faire* it has always failed to capture the reality of the ways in which power is exercised.

This is so because the state has always exercised power and used law in ways other than making straightforward legislation. As one of us has argued elsewhere,[22] states have always made contracts, provided subsidies, granted licences or delivered services and law operates as much indirectly— by facilitating, restructuring and enabling—as it does directly by issuing simple commands backed by sanctions. Indeed, the indirect actions of state activities may have a much more direct impact on peoples' lives than the dictates of legislation. Moreover, legal directives have often met resistances which blunt their effects. Turning the aspirations of law into reality of effects has often proved a more complex task than might first

---

[21] Quoted in Lukes (ed.) *Power* (1986) at p. 231.
[22] Morison, "How To Change Things with Rules" in *Law, Society and Change* (Livingstone and Morison eds., 1990), p. 5.

appear. Much of the sociology of law, generally ignored by constitutional-ists, has been concerned with issues of legal effectiveness and the social factors which may blunt such effectiveness.[23]

There has always been a need for a more pluralist vision of public power than appears in many constitutional textbooks. It is important to conceive of power as a result of all the plural relations within the social sphere. Power exists in competition and in conflict and, indeed, in all the interstices of social relationships. There is a need to look beyond the processes of law making in the individual state and examine the variety of ways in which a variety of emanations of the state actually effect the lives of citizens. Indeed, we would argue, this need is becoming increasingly urgent for at least three reasons. First, as has been discussed above, even the formal sovereignty of parliament is now being increasingly curbed by the impact of Europe. Parliament no longer possesses even the legal capacity to alter some aspects of the lives of its citizens. For example, a parliament that sought to legalise wage differentials between men and women or provide extensive subsidies to certain employers as part of a strategy for combating male unemployment would find its way blocked by European Union legislation. Secondly the extent of resistances to the exercise of state power have grown. The constant fear of capital flight at the push of a few computer keys is only one example of how governments may find their legislative directives turning to sand in their hands. Nearly all western governments now find that bringing government's will to bear on an issue is more a matter of indirect influence than of making a law on an issue. The third constraint is that as governments have intervened in an increasingly wide range of social activities the complexity of the tasks involved has largely outstripped the existing mechanisms of government. Neither parliament nor the cabinet has changed much in its composition since the late nineteenth century. Yet what government does, those aspects of its citizens' public and private lives that it involves itself in, has altered dramatically. Small wonder therefore that dealing with these tasks has increasingly been hived off to that broad "penumbra" of government which includes quangos, executive agencies and partnerships between the public and private sector. Without such a downward dispersal of the process of governing it is unlikely that government would possess the organisational capacity to exercise influence in all the areas that it lays claim to. Yet, as social complexity is likely to increase rather than diminish, this

---

[23] See Morison *op. cit.* pp. 5–13 for a brief review of this.

is unlikely to be a temporary phenomenon. The prospect is rather that the actual exercise of public power in the twenty-first century will assume an increasingly pluralist character. If constitutional reformers are to have anything useful to say they must begin to come to terms with this reality. Similarly the concept of the law that is deployed by governments will need to undergo a parallel shift. The hierarchical character of our existing concept of law which sees the sovereign expression of the domestic parliament as its highest form will need to change. As McCormick reports, "Roger Cotterrell and others have pointedly criticised mainstream jurisprudence for unreflectively privileging state-law over all other forms of law, as though really the only law that counts is that of the (presumably) sovereign and independent state."[24] McCormick complains, rightly, that "looking from this one-state point of view can be distorting".[25] In particular, we will all need to share what McCormick calls his "interim" conclusion, that

"from a jurisprudential point of view, there is no compulsion to regard 'sovereignty', or even hierarchical relationships of superordination and subordination, as necessary to our understanding of legal order in the complex interaction of overlapping legalities which characterise our contemporary Europe, especially within the European Community".[26]

Unfortunately however such an outlook is not widely shared particularly among constitutionalists. As we have noted already, they find the greatest difficulty in moving beyond the zero-sum game involved in traditional sovereignty. What is needed is a wider conception of sovereignty, one which can encompass the idea of there being an increasing number of agencies and bodies existing above and below the level of the nation state having multiple, competing sovereignty—rather like in the medieval world where papal and royal sovereignty competed and co-existed with baronial and local powers.

In many ways our conclusion here, and indeed to this whole first section of the book, is that orthodox constitutionalism has not only failed us but

---

[24] "Beyond the Sovereign State" (1993) 56 *Modern Law Review* 1. See also Cotterrell "Law's Image of Continuity and Imperium" in *Studies in Law, Politics, and Society,* A Research Annual (Silbey and Sarat ed. 1990) and *Law's Community: Legal Theory in Sociological Perspective* (1994) Ch.11.
[25] *ibid.*
[26] *Op. cit.* p. 10.

can not be revived in any effective form. The history of the constitution-alism that we are rejecting can be simplified as a development from a mechanical model through an organic phase to the present situation. The constitutionalism of Dicey, Bagehot and their natural successors can be viewed as offering us a vision of the state as like a machine with each part meshing together in a mechanical harmony. In the immediate post-war period and up until the 1970s the model was of an organic system that had grown up in the ruins of the machine. Here there was some coincidence of interest groups with political parties and sufficient give and take in the formal structures to allow government to be negotiated between the variety of groups that made up the two major class blocs and still appear as a collective choice. In the last 10 to 15 years however, such a model can no longer be distorted to fit the facts. The sorts of changes that we have been outlining in the last two chapters have produced and are producing a qualitative change that puts the situation beyond the reach of any version of traditional constitutionalism. What is required now is something like a model of constitutionalism as a *communication system* where hierarchy and structure is fluid and the focus is on values and processes rather than institutions. In the following chapters we will look at some nascent signs of such a constitutionalism before concluding the book with some remarks about how this might translate into the mainstream.

Chapter Three

The Northern Ireland Constitutional Debate: The Endgame of Westminsterism

Introduction

The preceding chapter provided a review of the failings of constitutionalism in the orthodox British sense to accommodate the new challenges to the identity of the state and the role and efficacy of government as we approach the next millennium. We argue here that the problems with this Westminster model of government are encapsulated and amplified by the constitutional crisis that has been occurring in Northern Ireland for the last 25 years and longer. On the face of it, issues in Northern Ireland of security and terrorism, nationalism and sectarianism and ethnicity and religion seem far away from the concerns of the rest of the United Kingdom. Northern Ireland may well appear as a democratically hopeless unit made up of political illiterates who are suited only to a pro-consular form of rule where self-government is restricted to very localised and tribally distinct pockets. The focus of constitutional interest in Northern Ireland may seem to be on self-determination to the exclusion of issues of self-government. However, we maintain that a careful reading of what is essentially a constitutional problem relating to government in Northern Ireland can provide an advanced view of the crisis in constitutionalism that is awaiting Great Britain. It can also provide indications about ways of resolving the crisis.

The present approach to the constitution of Northern Ireland shows the Westminster Model in its most advanced form, contorted to try to accommodate what seems to be an almost unreasonable abberation from a modern liberal society. The fact that it fails to provide a framework for government, even when twisted almost out of shape, is regarded variously, and depending on the degree of optimism of the observer, as a sign that yet more tweaking and tuning of the old contraption is needed or, more bleakly, that the historic problems of Ireland will remain beyond solution. It is almost never contemplated that the whole approach might be wrong. We have the spectacle of constitutional lawyers desperately casting about for more and more elaborate, baroque structures to accommodate the irreconcilable. Variants of Westminsterism are crossed with ideas from more consensual systems in an increasingly despairing attempt to square the political circle and render into constitutional form any political deal that might be struck. At the time of writing there is again one of the periodic opportunities when political talks have primacy over violence. Now constitutionalists are thinking about ways in which they could help to ensnare those involved in the political talks into a peace process of such byzantine procedural complexity that it will be difficult for them to drop out—as is the usual practice when it becomes apparent that the opposing positions remain irreconcilable. Rather than providing a "solution", the objective for constitutionalists is beginning to move more modestly to providing structures which will simply bring everyone together. It is felt that the engine of government in Northern Ireland will only run when everybody is on board and instead of final solutions constitutionalists are encouraged to think about the first objective of getting everyone to talk to each other.

The reality is that the application of the British constitutional tradition to Northern Ireland has effectively disabled traditional constitutional lawyers from contributing usefully to the resolution of, or even debate on, the Northern Ireland issue. The slavish followings of a British paradigm of constitutionalism that no longer fits either the situation it was designed for or the circumstances of Northern Ireland can not but expect failure. In Northern Ireland (probably always), as in Great Britain (certainly now), the situation is radically different from that envisaged by traditional constitutionalism. The problems with this general approach can be seen most graphically in the Northern Ireland context, where its failure is expressed conspicuously in continuing conflict with or without associated political violence, rather than more negatively, as in Great Britain where accusations of poor government, little accountability and alienation from the processes of government have produced the rash of critiques, audits of democracy and blueprints for change reviewed above.

At the same time as highlighting the failings of the British system as applied to Britain, the Northern Ireland constitutional problem also presents an opportunity to see what happens to the processes of government when the Westminster structure, with parliament at its apex controlling responsible government exercised in the public interest, can no longer claim either legitimating power or any remote connection with the everyday reality of government. In Northern Ireland it can be seen that the business of government must, can and does go on. The present arrangements are hedged about with declarations that they are temporary but they are in place and they are working. Furthermore, beyond the expediency of simply continuing, there is a barely detectable process of developing strategies of government that, of necessity, achieve the business of government more effectively (and, it will be argued, potentially more democratically). These strategies can not be said to be planned, coherent or sustained, but they can be regarded as together making up the beginning of a "New Constitutionalism". Such a New Constitutionalism, developing out of the endgame of Westministerism that is being played out in Northern Ireland, can invigorate the placid, and increasingly irrelevant, Westminster model that still provides the theoretical paradigm for British constitutionalism. We are thus arguing that Northern Ireland provides a stark and advanced example of the demise of the British approach to government and an opportunity for a new departure, a way of investing the tired structures of British constitutionalism with a new vitality to accommodate the challenges which Northern Ireland exemplifies in a more exaggerated way.

This chapter will look first briefly at the traditional way of seeing the Northern Ireland problem and the unsatisfactory attempts at solutions which all carry with them the imprint of modified Westminsterism. It will then attempt to re-cast the problem by looking at the need to move beyond the limited range of options yielded by traditional constitutional thinking. The project of getting the business of government done within all the constraints provided by political and security issues, economic and community factors, the domestic and international agenda produces a nascent form of New Constitutionalism that operates at both the traditional public macro level and a new private, micro level. The idea of this New Constitutionalism will be reviewed at the end of this chapter before its components are enlarged upon in the following chapters where the "real" constitution of Northern Ireland is examined. It is not until the final chapter of the book that the details of the connection between this real constitution and the moribund constitutionalism in Great Britain are fully brought out.

Defining the Problem

Traditionally Northern Ireland is seen as a difficult problem. In part this results from the gravity of the situation[1] but also from the narrowness of the impact of terrorism.[2] The conflict there is deep-seated and, although serious, it does not escalate to unmanageable proportions. It remains instead at a level where the stakes never become quite high enough to compel a resolution. While particular terrorist outrages may from time to time seem to force some sort of decisive action, generally the conflict remains easier to manage than to attempt to resolve. Although there are international implications to the problem (and with the attempts to contain it) it does not often climb up sufficiently high on the international agenda to demand solution. At home it is handled as a series of crises to be managed in the short term while their resolution remains a long-term objective. The initiative by John Major and former Taoiseach Albert Reynolds which resulted in the ceasefires announced in the autumn of 1994 and the new set of talks, is a rare as well as courageous effort to push the problem up the political agenda.[3] The active management of change occurs only rarely in a scenario where generally the conflict is only passively managed. The ceasefires, however, change everything and nothing. It raises many questions. At the time of writing there are fears about it holding, anxieties that fringe groups might perceive themselves as provoked into violence, misgivings about whether militant republicanism can

---

[1] In the 25 years of conflict before the ceasefire in the autumn of 1994, there have been 3,169 people killed (with one further fatality since then). 38,680 injuries and over 10,000 bombing incidents. To take one example, Fermanagh, a county in the far west of the province 60 per cent surrounded by the Republic of Ireland, has a population of 55,000. Casualties there have included 83 members of the security forces, 6 Provisional Irish Republic Army (PIRA) members and 45 civilians. If such figures were scaled up for a typical English county with a population of one million the total deaths might amount to around 1,500.

[2] As Boyle and Hadden point out, the level of deaths and serious injuries in Northern Ireland from the conflict is about half the level of death and serious injury from traffic accidents and life in Northern Ireland is generally considerably safer than in many other places in Europe and North America. *Northern Ireland: The Choice* (1994) pp. 104–107.

[3] It is interesting that sources as diverse as the economic commentator Will Hutton (in the Sixth Sir Charles Carter Lecture, Belfast June 1994) and Sinn Fein Chair, Mitchell McLaughlin (*Irish News* September 2, 1994) suggest that the financial burden of public funding and security expenditure in Northern Ireland was the chief reason for the Northern Ireland peace process moving to the top of the British political agenda.

become absorbed into the mainstream constitutional politics or whether it will begin some sort of *intifada* below the level of the military campaign sustained previously. In particular, however, there still remains the problem of producing a government structure out of the unpromising political situation of which the violence was only a reflection. The cycle of failure of successive constitutional initiatives aimed at this long-term objective reinforces the idea that there is a degree of difficulty to the problem of governing Northern Ireland that is out of all proportion to its size and strategic or economic influence. John Whyte's survey of the literature on Northern Ireland identifies a range of 10 approaches. These move from the optimistic integrated education approach through a variety of suggestions for repackaging Northern Ireland in different ways and with various degrees of compulsion to a bleaker, "no hope analysis".[4] For an increasing number of observers the issue now seems so complex that it appears most realistic to say, along with Richard Rose, that "the problem is that there is no solution".[5]

In private the British government may have come close to this view: Sir Frank Cooper is reported to have said how in cabinet Northern Ireland got into the "too difficult" category whereupon it was put "on the long finger" and rarely discussed in cabinet.[6] Publicly, however, such negative thinking is not apparent. Since the establishment of "direct rule" in 1972 it has remained the stated objective of government and of all political parties to seek a "political solution". For most this is a constitutional compromise that will end the alienation of the minority, marginalise the terrorists and restore a representative and democratic form of government to the North of Ireland. Direct rule is stated to be a "temporary solution" and each Secretary of State is given an opportunity to organise a negotiation process to yield acceptable suggestions for ending this temporary arrangement. The thinking behind the framework document issued in the spring of 1995, with its proposals for a devolved assembly which will have its legislative and administrative powers circumscribed by a variety of anti-majoritarian features and will operate in conjunction with representation from the Republic of Ireland in a North/South body, is simply the latest

---

[4] *Interpreting Northern Ireland* (1991), pp. 209–243.
[5] Rose, *Northern Ireland: A time of Choice* (1976), p. 139.
[6] Hennessy, *Cabinet* (1986) at p. 168.

development in this approach. The search for that elusive will-o'-the-wisp, a political solution, remains the chief strategy no matter how many blind alleys that hunt has been led up in the past. It is perhaps a measure of the limited success of such an endeavour that the phrase "peace process" is often now more current than any idea of "talks" or an agreement being reached.

The highly politicised nature of Northern Ireland society ensures that old quarrels persist and, indeed, old solutions and past compromises remain to reinforce ancient divisions for new generations. The present situation has an intimate connection with the past and this must be understood. (A brief constitutional chronology is offered in appendix one.) Notwithstanding its role in the past, the British government is now tied into providing financial and security support while it continues to hunt on the rather unpromising ground of local politics for the big fix, the constitutional compromise that will take Northern Ireland off the British political agenda. Whenever this search seems most fruitless there is a willingness to go beyond local politicians and discuss the issues within a British—Irish dimension. In such a context there are additional sensitivities. The constitutional status of Northern Ireland, the issue of what the appropriate democratic polity *is*, must be navigated. While for some of the partners in such talks, including the United Kingdom government the polity remains the population of Northern Ireland, for others, including at least notionally the government of the Republic still bound by its constitutional claim over the whole of the territory of Ireland, the appropriate polity is the whole of Ireland. These difficulties are evaded in a whole series of accommodations which can be seen most clearly by the frantic attempts to establish a politically neutral language in which to discuss "the totality of relations between these islands" and work towards "an agreed Ireland" where there is "parity of esteem". Notwithstanding such refinements of language the essential project is the same. There is still a belief that some sort of *deal* can be put together. In this context, as in the restricted local one, the deal generally is envisaged in terms of an arrangement for institutions of government. A devolved administration is the most widely preferred medium to long term option but in the literature as well as among the politicians there is support for a whole range of mechanisms, structures and solutions. These seem to increase in sophistication and complexity as the prospect of any relatively simple political accommodation recedes and the chance to snatch any fleeting moment of political progress and cast it into constitutional form occurs with decreasing frequency.

THE SOLUTIONS

There are a whole range of solutions offered by those who are involved in the conflict, those who look in it on from a variety of academic and political viewpoints as well as, more infrequently, those who suffer it. The enormous range and variety of proposals offered to the Opshal Commission, a rare and well- intentioned attempt to canvass the views of the latter group, suggest the diversity of views.[7] Notwithstanding this richness of opinion[8] there are really only about seven sorts of political solution on offer. The variety, and indeed conflict, between different versions may well be intense. Essentially however, although there may be many different shades there are only seven primary colours on the palate.[9] Much of the difference comes down to the method that is recommended to achieve the proposed result.

1. United Ireland. A unitary state within the island of Ireland is the main proposal here but the idea can encompass a variety of regional assemblies and councils although plenary power is to be based in Ireland. Constitutionally this idea is relatively simple to realise although politically it is much more problematic. Protestants traditionally fear for their religious and political freedoms within such a context and the task of devising effective legal guarantees would be only a little easier than selling them politically or ensuring that material standards would not fall in Northern Ireland.

Britain has no longer any strategic, economic or other interest in remaining in Northern Ireland and all the main parties if in government would go if they decently could. The status quo, enshrined in the so-called

[7] See *A Citizens' Inquiry: The Opsahl Report on Northern Ireland* (Pollock ed. 1993). See also Boyle and Hadden *op. cit.* chaps 6 and 7.

[8] In 1983 Rolston, O'Dowd, Millar and Smyth, suggested in their *Social Science Bibliography of Northern Ireland 1945–1983* that there were some 5000 publications about the Northern Ireland situation. In 1990 Whyte estimated the total to have reached 7000 (*Interpreting Northern Ireland*, 1990). The rate of increase has certainly not slowed up much since then and, although not all publications offer a "solution" as such, there is almost inevitably some sort of political resolution lurking somewhere in the background. See also the overview provided by Cox, 44 *Parliamentary Affairs* (1991).

[9] The literature would suggest many more. However, it seems to us while there may be differences in the degree of force permitted in achieving preferred solutions, alternative means recommended, and different partners involved, basically there are only seven scenarios for a macro level solution. For alternative accounts see, for example, New Ireland Forum Report (1984); Boyle and Hadden, *Ireland: A Positive Proposal* (1985); McGarry and O'Leary (ed.) *The Future of Northern Ireland*, (1990) and O'Leary and McGarry *The Politics of Antagonism: Understanding Northern Ireland* (1993), Chap. 8.

"constitutional guarantee" of section 1 of the Northern Ireland Constitution Act 1973, provides that Northern Ireland shall not cease to be a part of the United Kingdom without the consent of the majority of the people in Northern Ireland. Political demography is a highly contested science in this context as is the pepsology surrounding voting straightforwardly on religious divisions but it is likely to be a long rather than medium term possibility that catholic voters favouring reunification will outnumber protestant voters opposed to it.

From the standpoint of the Republic of Ireland unification remains a major political aspiration. Articles two and three of the constitution can be read as making a claim for the territory of Ireland to include the whole of the island. They are, of course, less securely in place in the present atmosphere of Anglo-Irish unanimity about the need for the agreement of the people of Northern Ireland. However the very considerable political and constitutional obstacles involved in amending the constitution of the Republic of Ireland have yet to be overcome. As it stands, articles two and three have had a special role in sheltering the nationalist conscience of the Republic of Ireland which may consider, along with some of the catholic middle classes in the North, that Northern Ireland and its recalcitrant protestant population are likely to be a costly and troublesome addition to the polity if this aspiration were to be realised.[10]

A united Ireland is of course the main objective of one strand of local politics in Northern Ireland with the chief difference between the two main versions espousing this solution lying in the validity (and feasability) also of using violence to bring it about. The other strand inside local politics is too centred around the idea of a united Ireland, although from the very different perspective of opposing it, with the main distinction also perhaps lying with the degree to which violence is considered as a legitimate way of opposing this aspiration.

2. *Repartition.*   The idea of re-drawing the border has been considered from time to time since the partition first came into existence in 1920. Demographic changes have resulted in majority catholic populations in

---

[10] The economic claim has often been asserted rather than argued. However, the burden of proof does seem to lie with those who claim that unity would be affordable. For example, a recent submission to the Dublin Forum for Peace and Reconciliation from two economists asserted that, notwithstanding the hopes that many have of funds from the United States and the European Union, there is no conceivable source of funds which could make good the revenues now supplied by the British taxpayer. (See *The Newsletter* December 20, 1994.)

some areas particularly in the west of the Province with protestant majorities concentrated in the east. There are several variations in proposals for re-dividing Northern Ireland but basically problematic border territories in Fermanagh and Tyrone would be handed over to the Republic of Ireland along with the city of Londonderry. This would leave a concentration of protestants in a new Northern Ireland although certain areas, notably west Belfast, would remain nationalist—although supposedly tamed by their isolation.

There may be a certain intellectual attraction to an idea which reflects shifts in the population. Certainly there would be little difficulty in arranging a re-division of territory although policing it might well be more problematic. However there are difficulties in isolating those who find themselves on the wrong side of the border and seeking to deny, through a process of mapping, the political aspirations of those who see the border as the problem rather than the solution. Indeed repartition has not proved to be a popular option among politicians, although Margaret Thatcher admits in her memoirs to have considered the idea. Generally though it has, as O'Leary and McGarry point out "been canvassed as a solution only by academics prepared to think the unthinkable"[11] and it looks likely to remain unworkable.

3. *Independence.*   This is another solution that appeals more in theory than in practice. The idea of an independent Ulster, perhaps with an elected assembly with some degree of power-sharing and most certainly within the framework of the European Union, might resolve certain aspects of the problem. It would offer unionists self-determination and the removal of the threat of a united Ireland while Nationalists would sever the link with Britain. However both parties would lose their preferred option with Unionists no longer being British and Nationalists isolated as a minority population within a potentially hostile state. As with the United Ireland option, guarantees for the minority population would occupy constitutional lawyers more than the mechanics of effecting the change although it remains uncertain if any reassurances could be politically convincing. Beyond the difficulty of ensuring that any new state would be politically stable there is the issue of whether it would be economically viable. Even with heavy subsidy from Britain or the European Union it is unlikely that

---

[11] O'Leary and McGarry, *The Politics of Antagonism: Understanding Northern Ireland* (1993) at p. 286. See also Kennedy, *The Two Ulsters* (1986) and Boyle and Hadden, *Northern Ireland: A Positive Proposal* (1985) pp. 9–10.

it could survive. These problems have made this option an unpopular one among political parties in Northern Ireland while the governments of the United Kingdom and the Republic of Ireland appear to have ruled it out through article one of the Anglo-Irish Agreement and paragraph 17 of the *New Framework for Agreement* document which stress the requirement of the consent of the majority but limits this to either remaining with the status quo or unification with the Republic. This suggests that only some form of unilateral declaration of independence could bring this scenario about and perhaps indicates the origins of this proposal in more extreme loyalist politics while revealing why it is unlikely to secure widespread support in the community.

4. Integration. This solution involves Northern Ireland being completely absorbed into the United Kingdom with no sort of government on a regional basis above the level of local councils. At first sight this might appear as a recognition of the present situation of direct rule with only the "temporary" element removed. However it involves much more, and would require much more to bring it into effect. Presently the direct rule mechanism does not involve treating Northern Ireland like any other region of the United Kingdom in legislative or executive terms. It rather puts in, as an alternative to the Parliament of Northern Ireland, a slimmed down version of Westminster in the legislative role and a government department with associated public and quasi-public bodies in the executive role. Integration requires a centralisation of government (rather in the face of movements in other regions towards a level of devolution). This would require a re-working of the legal system and its relationship to that of England and Wales and Scotland, re-structuring the civil service, empowering local government to take on, along with trusts and other bodies, the tasks of housing, education and health and indeed a fundamental re-arrangement of the constitutional basis of what has been formally and is in reality a very different state.

While such an arrangement might demonstrate how fundamentally non-British Northern Ireland really is, it is not without support in some Unionist circles. Whatever incongruities the arrangements for integration might reveal, if it were successfully achieved it would reinforce the Unionist view of Northern Ireland being, in Mrs Thatcher's words, "as British as Finchley" while at the same time returning it back to the pre-Stormont days before 1921. It also has the attraction of putting Unionists in the political mainstream and perhaps providing an anchor and a counter-weight to Anglo-Irish overtures. Nationalists do not support such an idea: it closes off the opportunity for self-determination and locks a significant section of the Irish people within a British state. From a less sectarian outlook, this option might suggest an electoral as well as an administrative integration with mainstream political parties organising in Northern Ireland followed by breaking down the tribal nature of local politics. If this were to occur it would certainly provide an element of basic democracy to the voters of Northern Ireland who could be given the fundamental right of voting for their government. However there is no reason to believe that British parties will organise successfully in Northern Ireland or that the demise of sectarian politics would follow this, and little evidence to suggest that it might.[12] The creation of a Select Committee for Northern Ireland, granted to Unionists after supporting the Conservative government over Maastricht debates, might suggest a creeping integration but it remains unlikely that this suggestion will gain sufficient momentum to become a political runner.

5. *Federalism.* The variety of proposals covered under this heading all share the idea that the conflict will in some way be diluted if the polity is broken up and its constituent parts re-ordered in their relationships with one another. If, it is believed, a more modern Northern Ireland could be created beyond the old bonds that divide, then the institutions of that state would have a new identity and might acquire a legitimacy and acceptability that is currently withheld.

The details take several forms suggesting a variety of constituent parts to any federation or confederation and admitting a range of partners in any possible government institutions. At one extreme there is the idea simply of a federation of the United Kingdom. This might attract Unionists especially if it offered majority control of (or possibly even power sharing in) a regional government of Northern Ireland. A federation or confederation of Ireland based on two or more newly created regions within a new

---

[12] The Conservative party in Great Britain was correctly termed, until relatively recently, "The Conservative and Unionist Party" indicating the close links that existed until direct rule was imposed in 1972. The moderately nationalist Social Democratic and Labour Party and the centrist Alliance Party maintain parliamentary links with the Labour Party and the Liberal Party / Liberal Democrats. A Campaign for Equal Citizenship has recently persuaded the Conservative Party to recognise candidates fielded by local constituency parties. In the 1992 general election the 11 conservative candidates in Northern Ireland secured 5.7 per cent of the votes. In the May 1993 local election the Conservative's share of the vote fell to 1.4 per cent. The other major British parties remain unwilling to test the voters in Northern Ireland.

political unit might appeal to Nationalists. However, neither arrangement has more than very limited appeal to the other grouping. Other proposals, notably from constitutional idealists who have looked at the seven or so federations that survive in long-term liberal democracies, suggest slightly more radical versions. These range from suggestions that Britain and Ireland both relinquish their claims to sovereignty in Northern Ireland and create a federation or confederation of the British Isles or of the islands of the Celtic sea, and, through ideas of Euro-federalism or a Europe of the Regions, to more modest notions of cantonisation. All of these suggestions have varying, although limited, support among the political parties in Northern Ireland, the Republic of Ireland, Great Britain and indeed Europe. Ideas about cantons suffer from the demographical fact that the population in Northern Ireland is not conveniently divided for these purposes. Federations or confederations within a European context at least have the merit of noticing changes to the role of the state generally, but would depend on those living in Northern Ireland somehow transcending their local communities, and on an enthusiasm that does not appear to be present currently in the European Union. The idea of a new federation of the British Isles, the Iona variation, might seem to offer something to everyone by giving no one what they want but is unlikely to appeal beyond this sort of abstract level.

6. Joint Authority.   This is a constitutionally and politically radical sugges- tion. (The term joint authority is preferred to joint sovereignty as it has the advantage of suggesting that formal constitutional obstacles can be avoided.) Rather like federalism its appeal perhaps lies with the idea of defusing the conflict by re-drawing old lines. The origins of this sugges- tion, as a third preference of the nationalist viewpoints assembled by the New Ireland Forum in 1983–84,[13] perhaps shows its weakness and its strengths. Its basic drawback is that no-one at the local or Anglo-Irish level actively wishes for joint authority as an end in itself. Its strength is that it gives no party all that it wants but goes some way to doing so.

Joint authority offers a direct role for the Irish Government and, although falling far short of the nationalist aspiration for a unitary Irish state, it does offer a dimension of Irish involvement and a recognition of

---

[13] New Ireland Forum, *Report*, (1984), s. 8.

Irish identity that is fundamental to nationalist sentiments.[14] For unionists
any change along these lines is abhorrent even when, as with the much
more modest enhanced consultative role given to the government of the
Republic of Ireland in the Anglo-Irish Agreement of 1985 and suggested
in the *New Framework for Agreement* document of 1995, it is accompanied
by a reinforcement of the consent requirement for any change in the
constitutional status of Northern Ireland. However, it is better for unionists than the worst case scenario of a united Ireland and it might be possible
to strengthen further the constitutional guarantee of consent to a change in
the status of the Province.[15] For the government of the Republic of Ireland
joint authority is economically demanding while remaining politically
unsatisfying. For the government of the United Kingdom it is politically
hazardous and it remains to be seen if a problem shared would really be a
problem halved. Even if other participants could be found, as with the
suggestion from the local Social Democratic and Labour Party (SDLP) for
a six person Commission including EU members, the joint authority
solution of giving no one what they really want suffers from the consequence that no one therefore has the incentive to pursue it.

7. *Devolution*.   This solution remains the one that the British government
is committed to, at least in the medium term. It is the preferred option not
least because it is the least objectionable to most parties. It has the
advantage of having worked for the 50 years that the Stormont Parliament
survived and the track record that comes both from nearly succeeding in

---

[14] It has been thought in recent years that the Irish government might require some diluted
version of joint authority as the price of its assistance in the present peace initiative or accept
it as a quid pro quo for abandoning articles 2 and 3 of the Irish constitution and any territorial
claim over the north that they might suggest. Indeed the then Taoiseach, Albert Reynolds,
maintained shortly after the Downing Street Declaration that "institutional links between
North and South will have executive powers: that's the overall framework we are looking
to" (*The Irish Times*, January 21, 1994). The *New Framework for Agreement* document of 1995
does seem, however, to rule out explicitly any formal sharing of sovereignty. The appointment to quangos of members suggested by the government of the Republic of Ireland might
provide a very reduced version of influence at executive level. See further chap. 4 below.
[15] The Labour Party are currently interested in this idea and in a publication from a group of
sympathetic academics the notion of a 3/4 majority to change the constitutional status of
Northern Ireland has been proposed as a carrot to accompany the stick that simply "the
fairness of shared authority be made apparent to unionists". (O'Leary, Lyne, Marshall and
Rowthorn, *Northern Ireland: Sharing Authority* (1993). This sort of suggestion illustrates well
the point that any such arrangement offers something to everyone while refusing them what
they really want. Here nationalists are denied legitimate self-determination for the whole
cake of unification because they would have the half cake of joint authority and Unionists
find their fears being met but at what might be unacceptable price.

1974 when an Assembly was in existence for four months, and almost getting started in the years between 1982 and 1984 when an assembly was in place waiting to take on governmental functions under the rolling devolution package.

It can come in several variations but the feature that makes it distinct from any form of federalism is that it does not alter fundamentally the relationship between Northern Ireland and Great Britain.

A devolved Northern Ireland may have a degree of self-determination but *plenary* power remains at Westminster. Unlike in a federal or confederal system where power is distributed on a geographical basis, a devolved Northern Ireland is hierarchically inferior to the United Kingdom which is an entity greater than its constituent parts. This of course means that there can be no fudging the issue that the Union is preserved, the constitutional guarantee honoured, and Nationalist aspirations limited in a situation where the Republic of Ireland retains the status of a foreign government.

The effect of this is that Unionists are generally fairly comfortable with this direction and feel unease only when the issue of power-sharing is put high up the agenda and the question of an all Ireland dimension is raised. Of course Nationalists are less happy with devolution and, fearing a repeat of the protestant domination that marked the 50 year period of the last devolution exercise, insist upon a degree of power sharing as well as some element of North-South association. Thus it is that devolution plans generally avoid the unvarnished majoritarian model of straightforward Westminsterism and contain varying degrees of adjustment and accommodation. At the academic end this is often associated with the idea of consocialism as developed by Arendt Lijphart.[16] Basically this argues that consocialism has a proven record for dealing with ethnic, linguistic and religious conflicts in bi-cultural and multi-cultural societies. The idea has four fundamental features: there must be a power sharing coalition of government; proportional representation and proportional allocation rules for those in public sector offices; community autonomy norms allowing rival groups control over their own affairs wherever possible; and, finally, constitutional safeguards and veto rights for minorities. While such notions are alien to the Westminster approach, and Northern Ireland would seem to lack the cross community links that consocialism requires,

---

[16] See, in particular, *Democracies in Plural Societies* (1977) and *Democracies and Consensus Government in 21 Countries*, (1984).

there is a belief in some quarters that the mechanisms can in some way be bolted on to existing structures to deliver an agreed settlement.

While some academics and politicians construct ever more elaborate variations on these themes, suggesting ways to lure and then snare the politicians, government is involved in a more elemental process. It must try to keep the air clear of security or political crises and seek to steer and bully all the politicians and reformed paramilitaries to come together. Threats and inducements are offered for, it is believed, only if everyone is in place can a process take place that will somehow reconcile all the irreconcilable views there present. Government's role here is akin to that of a starter at a race meeting who must coax, cajole and push the runners into some semblance of order before choosing the optimum moment to set them off. As we shall develop shortly, most of the political animals in Northern Ireland are extremely unwilling to commit themselves to this particular race and they all seek to run in different directions.

The Need to Re-Define the Problem

The fact that there is a problem in need of re-definition needs no emphasis. Not only is there a conflict which has lasted in its most recent manifestation for 25 years and taken the lives of more than 3000 people but there is a set of proposed solutions which seem to promise very little success in the long-term. These seven alternatives provide the sum of mainstream thinking on the political solution for Northern Ireland's problems. There are different *methods* of engineering particular outcomes and these range from violence, argument, referendums, preferendums, personal initiative by the Prime Minister, Taoiseach or United States peace envoy, to Anglo-Irish initiatives and United Nations' monitoring or peace keeping forces. However the range of solutions to be delivered by these various means remains limited. We do not see it a virtue or in any way as evidence of our perspicacity that, although at the time of writing hopes are high that the Major government may manage some sort of historic settlement, we are proceeding in terms of describing the conflict as being without immediate solution at this macro level. There is no reason realistically to think that any new initiative, mechanism or personal intervention will bring success in providing a durable, grand level constitutional settlement. Even if, and it remains highly unlikely, that the agreement at inter-governmental level could be translated into some form of words that could be agreed upon locally, this would not in any way magically guarantee satisfactory structures that could resolve all the devils in the details of government in a contested and highly politicised situation. A historic deal solving all Ireland's problems at a stroke is simply not there to be struck. The peace process that began officially with the Downing Street Declaration in 1993, brought about a ceasefire by all sides and continued into talks about the constitutional future, is at best only the start of a very long process which has only a limited chance of finding consensus which can be sustained into a continuing process of government. A more pessimistic view is that although the violence is currently suspended the problems that underlie it remain no nearer solution. As Sean MacStiofain, a senior IRA figure involved in negotiations following the ceasefires of 1972, has put it, "British political initiatives only make Irish disasters".[17] The problem is not that governments, constitutionalists or even politicians have failed to give sufficient attention to providing over-arching frameworks for government. It is rather that a large scale solution that will resolve all the problems is not available in terms that are readily acceptable, and there is insufficient pressure and incentive to persuade the parties to alter their fundamental positions as they impact on all the detailed, and inevitably contested, issues of government.

The history of the various initiatives which have attempted to find the illusive "political solution" that has been absent since (at least) the imposition of direct rule in 1972 reinforces this pessimistic view. As appendix one illustrates, the main initiative in the last 20 or so years has been directed towards achieving an acceptable version of devolved government. The British government have seen their role as playing variations on this same theme and attempting to bring the parties together so that a moment, however fleeting, of political agreement can be caught and then translated into institutions of government. To this end various offers are made to each of the opposing factions to bring them into this pre-governmental process. As the political tide ebbs and flows so certain elements aimed at particular factions are stressed or played down as necessary to attract that party or their opponents into an institutional framework from which can emerge an agreed system of government. The relative emphasis given to any one element at any particular time depends variously on particular local political and security conditions although

---

[17] *The Guardian* August 30, 1994.

now, and to an increasing extent, the dimension of Anglo-Irish relations too comes into play. Also, from time to time European and international pressure may play a part in how the issues are ranked. We argue that basically there are four items on the political agenda. Within the current approach of searching for a macro level, agreed political solution (whether in terms of devolution or something similar), these four areas have formed and will form the basic elements around which must be oriented the talks and the institutions that it is hoped will result from them. They are:

1. *Northern Ireland is to remain a part of the United Kingdom.* This is a basic and immutable demand in the protestant, Unionist community. It provides the minimum requirement, a *sine qua non*, of Unionist participation in any scheme for government. It has been reinforced repeatedly as part of a backdrop to ensure Unionist involvement. The "constitutional guarantee", presently expressed in section 1 of the Northern Ireland Constitution Act 1973, declaring and affirming the need for consent to any change in the status of Northern Ireland, has much more political significance than legal effect. (Indeed, its efficacy in law is at the very least questionable offering, as it purports to, a fetter on the power of parliament to exercise its sovereignty without legislating in compliance with the "manner and form restriction" of needing to ballot the population of Northern Ireland.) This star is the most firmly fixed in the Unionist constellation. It has appeared necessary to restate this commitment at almost every turn. Even in the Northern Ireland (Temporary Provisions) Act 1972, introducing direct rule, the opportunity is taken in section 2 to make the assurance that "nothing in this Act shall derogate or authorise anything to be done in derogation from the status of Northern Ireland as part of the United Kingdom." Certainly when any emphasis is given to another item on the agenda—that relating to the all-Ireland dimension—it has appeared vital (although largely ineffective) to re-assure Unionists of their constitutional future in the United Kingdom. The Sunningdale Agreement of 1973, although directed to setting up an all Ireland Council, still found it necessary to reiterate the constitutional position in Article 5. Likewise the Anglo-Irish Agreement, while directed largely at a very different audience, sought to ameliorate its unattractiveness to Unionists by giving to the "constitutional guarantee" the status of international law by re-stating it in Article 1. The initiative begun by the Downing Street declaration and carried through to the Framework Documents, also seeks to reassure Unionists on this point while directing itself mainly to the next, very different item.

2. An All-Ireland dimension.   This aspect occurs as part of the Nationalist agenda and is deployed variously to entice Nationalists into accepting the basic status quo while retaining the hope of developing a pan-Irish approach. Again each initiative has made some reference to this element although often in a rather muted form. It is of course inconsistent with the direction referred to above and its presence causes particular difficulties to Unionists. The devolved administration which flowered briefly under the Northern Ireland Constitution Act 1973 was cut down by Unionist opposition to the North-South co-operation proposed in the Sunningdale initiative. Nevertheless it is an important element in securing co-operation from Nationalists. Its presence at this level in whatever form reinforces the legitimacy of Nationalist aspirations while directing them into constitutional channels and protecting the parties of constitutional nationalism against the electoral advance of Sinn Fein.

At a minimum there is provision for consultation with the government of the Republic. This is inevitably present even when, as with the 1973 Act setting up a devolved assembly, the programme is aimed in a very different direction. That framework contained provisions in section 12 of the act for consultation and co-operation with the government of the Republic of Ireland. From this relatively low point this agenda item has developed significantly in importance. There was of course, even in 1973, the associated inter-governmental agreement signed at Sunningdale. In 1981, by executive decision of both the Dublin and London governments, an Anglo-Irish Inter-Governmental Council was formed to discuss matters of common interest and concern. The rolling devolution scheme contained in the Northern Ireland Act 1982 revived the consultation and co-operation provisions of the devolutionary scheme from nearly a decade before. The White Paper preceding that act contained the idea that the parliaments in London and Dublin might consider if governmental meetings of the Council should be complemented by an Anglo-Irish body at parliamentary level.[18] This idea finally mutated into the Anglo-Irish Agreement of 1985 where the government of the Republic of Ireland was given a role that was famously described by the then Taoiseach, Garret Fitzgerald, as "more than consultative but short of executive". The Downing Street Declaration of 1993, in its attempt to undermine the strategy of the violence of the Provisional IRA, gives further recognition

---

[18] *Northern Ireland: A Framework for Devolution* (Cmnd 8541).

to the legitimacy and validity of Nationalist aspirations. The *New Framework for Agreement* document of 1995, setting out the combined positions of the British and Irish governments, takes this to its furthest expression. Despite the assertion in the preface by Prime Minister Major about "cherishing" the place of Northern Ireland within the Union, the emphasis there is on self-determination towards an all Ireland scenario, with only the notion of Unionist consent holding up the process.

The relative importance of this Nationalist side to the equation that must be balanced in order to yield satisfactory arrangements for government is as significant as the rival and diametrically opposed Unionist position on the broader constitutional status quo. It must be present: constitutional Nationalism must be seen as achieving something towards Nationalist aspirations or else support might, so it is thought, leach away towards the less acceptable face of Nationalism that is Sinn Fein, and from there back to violence. At the same time if in their negotiations government were to steer too strongly by this star the whole vessel could be capsized by Unionist opposition.

3. Devolved government as the preferred method of rule. The restoration of devolved government has been the aim of every initiative since the collapse of the devolutionary system set up in 1920. The system of direct rule in Northern Ireland, whereby legislation is made in Westminster and the executive function is carried out largely by the Northern Ireland departments and their related quangos, is invariably described as "temporary". This not only excuses the structures being somewhat rough and ready in democratic terms but also suggests that although direct rule may have continued almost uninterrupted for 20 years it is only a stop gap until devolved local government is restored. The establishment of a devolved local administration remains the favoured immediate or medium term objective. Although representation at Westminster should continue, law-making and government functions ideally should be locally based with Westminster acting only in "excepted matters" of national importance.[19] Apart from a short period of a few months in 1974, when an assembly

---

[19] The Northern Ireland Constitution Act 1973 developed the classification of legislative competence contained in the Government of Ireland Act 1920 so that the local assembly should have unrestricted power over "transferred" matters, power to legislate but only with the Secretary of State's permission over "reserved" matters such as policing and law and order but no substantial power to legislate in "excepted" matters relating to the Crown, the armed forces, foreign relations, etc. Such a classification is likely to remain for any future devolved system.

created under the Northern Ireland Constitution Act 1973 was held together long enough to pass four pieces of legislation, this has remained an aspiration rather than a reality.

It has always been present however. Thus, even the Northern Ireland Act 1974, which was designed "to make better temporary arrangements for the orderly government of Northern Ireland",[20] also contained provisions for restoring government to the people of Northern Ireland. This was to be delivered by a constitutional convention of 78 members who were directed to devise the system of government to supersede direct rule. The report of this convention, although unacceptable because of the unwillingness of Unionists to accept power-sharing or any institutional association with the Republic of Ireland, was agreed on recommending a devolved unicameral assembly with an executive drawn from it. Although the accent may occasionally tilt more towards North-South relations the basic strategy has remained fixed on devolution. Thus the Northern Ireland Act 1982 aimed to restart the assembly created in the early 1970s through a scheme of "rolling devolution". The assembly began life with a debating and scrutinising function and took on only such matters as it wished. The idea was that devolution could roll forward as political conditions permitted but if, as is invariably the case, a political or security storm were to blow up, it could also roll back leaving the assembly intact in its scrutiny role. However ingenious the mechanism it never overcame disagreements and boycotts to move beyond being a debating chamber and was dissolved in 1986. Even the Anglo-Irish Agreement of 1985, aimed at satisfying a very different item on the agenda, can be read as an effort to "bump start' 'a process leading to devolution, since taking this option provides the only effective way for unionists to bring the Agreement to an end. Again the Downing Street Declaration of 1993, while aimed at offering PIRA the chance to back down from its terrorist campaign, does this by giving its political wing the opportunity to join talks aimed at devolution as envisaged in the framework documents.

4. Cross community aspect.   While the restoration of devolved government remains the primary or least objectionable medium and long term goal, it is clear that there is no question of a return to an unrestrained majority rule as in the 50-year period under the 1920 devolutionary scheme. All

---

[20] In the words of the White paper, *The Northern Ireland Constitution* (Cmnd. 5675 (1974), para. 29) which preceded the 1974 act.

initiatives are designed to involve representation from both communities in the process of government. This has been achieved in a number of ways, ranging from simply introducing proportional representation for elections to the imposition of power-sharing conditions which require that any executive body should represent the sectarian composition of the community and pass tests of acceptability imposed by the Secretary of State.

Beyond this there has been a revival and intensification of anti-discrimination provisions. These have been used for some time[21] but Part Three of the Northern Ireland Constitution Act 1973 contains much more detailed and far-reaching provisions designed to ensure that any legislation or executive action should be void if it discriminates on the grounds of religious belief or political opinion. The Anglo-Irish Agreement gives expression to the idea of two legitimate identities and is designed to give the government of the Republic of Ireland a role in assuring the position of the minority population. Beyond this there is the re-organisation of local government that occurred in 1973 which had the effect of depoliticising issues of housing, education, social services, etc., by transferring them to non-departmental public bodies or quangos. This de-politicisation (or more accurately re-politicisation) will be examined in some depth later but for now can be read as a way of simply moving the allocation of public services and benefits outside of the mainstream political process in order to facilitate a less contentious and more inclusive form of government.

These four items together provide the agenda to be constantly rehearsed in any peace process seeking to strike a deal between the irreconcilable objectives held by the various factions. Apparently new initiatives, such as admitting Sinn Fein to the peace process, do not in any way guarantee that any of the parties there will take up new positions on these elemental issues that will be more acceptable to their opponents. These fundamental agenda items, meanwhile, will not go away. Unionists who remain implacably opposed to any steps towards unification with the Republic of Ireland must somehow be reconciled with Nationalists who require an all-Ireland dimension. Even if it were possible through the sort of effort of

---

[21] The unsuccessful Irish Government Bill 1886 contained in clause 4 the sort of restriction on the legislature to make law that discriminates on the ground of religion that has been in place ever since while a similar inhibition on executive power can be seen as far back as the Government of Ireland Act 1914.

political will that has rescued South Africa to produce some sort of structure purporting to contain all the differing aspirations, there still remains the problem of militant nationalist opinion. In particular there is Sinn Fein who remain dedicated to the goal of British withdrawal and Irish unity by peaceful means or violently—whichever is quicker.

Within mainstream constitutional thinking this is all that there is to work with. These agenda items must somehow be resolved. It is little wonder that finding a Westminster style solution based on building a grand structure which can accommodate everyone seems such a difficult problem. As the macro level issues relating to the distribution of legislative and executive power are viewed refracted through this agenda, the political agreement from which, it is thought, a whole system of government will follow must seem illusive or at best unstable. Nevertheless the British government continues in its attempt to find a moment of consensus as if one more patient tweak of the old machine of Westminsterism is all that is needed. It remains committed towards trying to achieve a political settlement that can then be translated into institutions of government. In the meantime there remains a crisis of varying degrees to be managed. The political brinkmanship by the various parties to talks must be read in the light of the ever-present possibility of violence re-starting. This political process occurs in a context where it can be overtaken immediately and at any time by a war between paramilitaries and a high technology security force in possession of wide-ranging legal powers. The British approach works on the belief that if violence can kept at bay, or at worst held to "acceptable levels", then it might be possible to kickstart the political discussion into life. Every partner for talks towards establishing local structures is tried: when the politicians in the North fail to agree, the emphasis is put on an east-west axis with co-operation between London and Dublin. The items on the agenda are worked and re-worked with ever more subtle shades and tones. Talks and preliminary talks at different levels and in different strands are tried. Blandishments are offered—select committees to Unionists, a further Dublin involvement to Nationalists, a place at the negotiating table to paramilitaries who seem to renounce violence— in exchange for continued co-operation. The moment of agreement seems close and then recedes and never arrives. Structures are tried but so far have not withstood the storms of a highly polarised politics which connects almost every detail of social life with wider constitutional or tribal loyalties. The inability of successive Secretaries of State to lure local politicians into a political deal which can then be tied up by constitutional lawyers into a durable solution has left Britain with a problem in Ireland that seems intractable from the perspective of traditional British constitutionalism. It may seem tempting to join those who, as we noted earlier, regard the Northern Ireland problem as simply too difficult: perhaps Northern Ireland simply demonstrates the hard truth that there are some problems for which no solution can be found. However, the reality is somewhat different, and perhaps less bleak. It is that the traditional, pragmatic, institutional-level approach that characterises current British constitutional thinking is simply exhausted.

The majority of academic writing simply reflects this approach. Constitutionalism within the mainstream of constitutional writing means structures of government that can turn a basic political preference into policies for a bureaucracy to carry out. Within such an approach Northern Ireland is anachronistic. Northern Ireland is British—nominally at least. It does not, however, seem to fit into the terms of the British approach or even the comfortable debate about reforming this. For many commentators looking at Northern Ireland from the outside it must appear as a historical throwback, an uncharacteristic instance of undemocratic, medieval rancour originating in distant historical religious and territorial disputes. However, this lack of fit does not prevent the orthodoxy applying its model of constitutionalism to the issues of Northern Ireland (any more than a similar lack of fit in Great Britain prevents this occurring). Constitutional writers seem to subscribe actively, or more usually passively, to the idea prevalent within the political approach that the flexibility and pragmatism of the British constitutionalism provides the best approach to the issues of Northern Ireland. Within the traditional British approach Westminsterism is the solution: the problem is the Irish.

One major way in which this approach manifests itself is in ignoring the questions of Northern Ireland altogether. There is a lamentable tendency in the main constitutional law textbooks to neglect Northern Ireland almost completely. For a textbook approach that prizes comprehensiveness of coverage, and even yet still devotes large sections to the Commonwealth, the minutia of parliamentary procedure and the notion of sovereignty, this is shameful. Scarcely any of the textbooks mentioned in chapter one above make more than passing mention of Northern Ireland as if it were no more constitutionally interesting than Shropshire and rather less so than arcane points about the scope of judicial review. Surely from almost any perspective the issues of Northern Ireland are among the most vital and compelling of any constitutional questions within the United Kingdom? Even the more radical, reforming tendency shares this blinkered view of its remit. To take just one example, the varied collection of 26 essays arising out of the Charter 88 sponsored "constitutional convention" contains no account whatsoever and hardly even a passing mention of the constitutional issues facing Northern Ireland.[22] The volume is billed as

> "both a comprehensive guide to the ideas and arguments which fuel ... [the constitutional] debate and an exploration of the ways in which constitutional reform would alter public (and in many instances private) life in the United Kingdom".[23]

Nevertheless, one of the most constitutionally troubled and interesting parts of the United Kingdom was totally omitted from consideration. This is by no means an isolated example. It occurs across a range of issues and the fact that a significant area of the polity differs most markedly from the rest does not often inhibit most constitutionalists from viewing their work as being about the United Kingdom as a whole.[24]

The other way in which the academic approach mirrors the wider constitutionalism is in the way that those accounts which do at least notice Northern Ireland, view it exclusively from the perspective of orthodox constitutionalism. Books which take the Northern Ireland constitution as their main subject are as guilty of this as those that simply touch upon it. Thus there is the approach of Calvert who views Northern Ireland as simply (to borrow the subtitle of his book) "A study in Regional Government".[25] This is of course very much in line with his predecessors who seemed to regard Northern Ireland as only a slight mutation of Westminsterism and one which they can call their own.[26] Other writers, most

---

[22] *Debating the Constitution: New Perspectives on Constitutional Reform* (Barnett, Ellis and Hirst ed., 1993).

[23] *Op. cit.* p. xii.

[24] Rose addresses the question of whether the United Kingdom is a state and concludes that maybe it is—if one is prepared to exclude Northern Ireland. But of course, he complains, this "exceptionalist thesis" does not make sense, it is politics with the hard bits left out. It leaves the United Kingdom either as not a proper state at all, or with an English problem (or more accurately a Great Britain problem) where there is a *de facto* state that does not have *de jure* status because it must also accept responsibility for Northern Ireland. (See "Is the United Kingdom a State? Northern Ireland as a Test Case" in *The Territorial Dimension in United Kingdom Politics* (Madgwick and Rose ed. 1982) at p. 128.)

[25] *Constitutional Law in Northern Ireland: A Study in Regional Government* (1968)

[26] See further Quekett *The Constitution of Northern Ireland* (Three Volumes 1928–1946); Mansergh, *The government of Northern Ireland: A Study of Devolution* (1936); Neill (ed.) *Devolution of Government: the Experiment in Northern Ireland* and Lawrence, *The Government of Northern Ireland: Public Finance and Public Services* (1965).

notably Hadfield, have worked within this tradition.[27] For Hadfield the mechanics of government, the nuts and bolts of its structures and institutions, is the main focus of a highly detailed description. Essentially we are offered an account that is driven by the chronology of successive government initiatives and legislative acts rather than outside events. This is an official constitutional history, an annotation of the actions of the British government. In an effort to bring detachment, there is little sense of public law having a dimension beyond the legislation setting up structures. Indeed, it is claimed "where analysis may have led into an articulation of political preferences, the analytical role has been eschewed".[28] Palley, on the other hand, is willing to explore how the social and political historical background impinges on the problem.[29] However, her focus is almost exclusively on how to secure macro level institutions from any political deal that might be struck.[30] McEldowney is one of the very few textbook writers to give any degree of attention to Northern Ireland.[31] Here again though the focus is a particularly British one, reflecting the concerns of the orthodoxy of British constitutionalism. Thus there is an account of the institutional structures aimed at providing a macro level "solution" although this is augmented by an overview of emergency powers and their effect on civil liberties. Again, however, the focus is one that reflects the concerns of mainstream constitutionalism although here transplanted to difficult circumstances at the edge of the polity. There is a struggle always to view Northern Ireland as an aberration *within* the mainstream rather than something fundamentally apart. Increased police powers, a slimmed down criminal justice system and all the other apparatus of a state in crisis are to be seen as exceptional, as if in some way it is only these and the on-going failure to secure institutions of government that distinguishes Northern Ireland from the polity as conceived within the orthodoxy of British constitutionalism.[32]

---

[27] See particularly *The Constitution of Northern Ireland* (1989).

[28] Hadfield *op. cit.* p. ix.

[29] See "The Evolution, Disintegration and Possible Reconstruction of the Northern Ireland Constitution" (1972) *Anglo American Law Review* 368.

[30] See, for example, "Constitutional Solutions to the Irish Problem" (1980) 33 *Current Legal Problems* 12 and "Ways Forward: The Constitutional Options" in *The Constitution of Northern Ireland: Problems and Prospects* (Watts ed., 1981). See also, *The United Kingdom and Human Rights* (1991).

[31] *Public Law* (1994), chap. 19.

[32] The collection of essays, *Northern Ireland: Politics and the Constitution* (Hadfield ed. 1992) is a further instance of this approach.

Boyle and Hadden do see Northern Ireland as a place apart. The starkness of "The Choice"[33] they posit between separation and sharing, between greater integration or further segregation, is striking and not something that sits easily within the orthodoxy of British constitutionalism. They are suggesting a resolution of the conflict based on an acceptance of the reality of social, religious and political life in the North of Ireland. This is something very different from the view of the polity posited in traditional constitutionalism. However, even here the main focus is on the big constitutional questions of borders and, especially, structures which can tie in and commit all parties into institutions. These institutions are not only at the macro level: there is a proper appreciation of how education, housing, employment, policing, etc., are constitutional issues. Nonetheless, there is always the underlying belief that institutions can provide solutions—if only they are worked out with sufficient sophistication. For example, Belgium figures largely in Boyle and Hadden's analysis of structures for both sharing and separation. While it is accepted that circumstances there are very different, the "highly complex arrangements in Belgium" are commended as "both workable and respectable".[34] We differ from Boyle and Hadden in so far as we do not believe that resolving the conflict is only a matter of increasing the complexity and detail of the structures. We are not persuaded by the Belgium experience. There a population of 10 million have three levels of government—federal, regional and provincial. The most recent so-called settlement, the fifth since 1970, establishes a complex structure with three socio-economic regions and a plethora of councils with jurisdictions across a whole range of matters. A massive public sector debt, exceeding 130 per cent of Gross Domestic Product, high taxes, an outmoded infrastructure and the rise of far right politics do not suggest that complicated institutions provide a full answer.

McCrudden too provides an important contribution to the public law literature on Northern Ireland.[35] While some attention is directed towards macro level settlements there is an emphasis on understanding how constitutional issues pervade a whole range of public areas and areas which elsewhere would be regarded as in the private sphere. Although for us

---

[33] *Northern Ireland: The Choice* (1994). See also Boyle and Hadden, *Ireland: A Positive Proposal* (1985).
[34] *Op. cit.* p. 201.
[35] "Northern Ireland and the British Constitution" in *The Changing Constitution* (Jowell and Oliver ed., 3rd ed., 1994).

McCrudden's focus is perhaps too much upon the role of anti-discrimination law, we accept and endorse the insight that Northern Ireland shows us the failure of a constitutional tradition based on pragmatic empiricism and the need for some reformulation to accommodate the more complex distribution of power which is presented in Northern Ireland. McCrudden's insistence on the need for constitutionalism to embrace values as well as institutions is very welcome, although for us his account underplays the role of a range of values, such as participation, dialogue and pluralism, by stressing the goal of securing equality and freedom from discrimination.

The Northern Ireland constitutional debate, even in much of its most sophisticated form, is about making Westminsterism work—albeit in a reworked form to take into account local difficulties. Thus we see that the focus is on boundaries of the state and guarantees of the status quo. Attention is directed at the big institutions of government and how to persuade dinosaur political parties to become involved in these. Concern then moves to how minorities are to be protected and involved in this government by establishing legislative limits and weighted majorities. Even where the debate moves more into the relatively sophisticated world of political science, where we encounter the language of "double minorities" and "zero-sum games", the aim is always that of classical liberalism, to curtail government. Much less effort is directed at the more difficult issue of *making government act in the ways that people might want it to*. There are however a number of important developments which begin to suggest the beginnings of a new approach.

A New Constitutionalism in Northern Ireland?

We argue that the failure of traditional British constitutionalism is even more marked in Northern Ireland than it is in Great Britain. There undemocratic mechanisms of direct rule and a whole panoply of special, "emergency" powers can be clearly seen. The whole circus of talks and talks about talks at different levels and in different strands continues rather as if, as Unger suggests, every conflict should find an institution appropriate to its level and this political side-show and all its attendant bureaucracy is appropriate here.[36] All this provides a visible sign that the

---

[36] *False Necessity: Anti-Necessitarian Social Theory in the Service of Radical Democracy* (1987) at p. 449.

degeneration of the orthodox paradigm is more advanced. In some senses the crisis in Northern Ireland has provided a breach in the continuity of government there, but in Great Britain the absence of such a challenge has allowed the constitution to atrophy. At the same time the failure to resolve the crisis demonstrates the impoverishment of the traditional British approach which largely remains wedded to ideas of pragmatic solutions at an institutional level stressing (at best a modified) majoritarian democracy, parliamentary sovereignty and the value of creating structures which give effect to the traditional values and mechanisms. Even in the unlikely event that a "solution" in these terms could be reached, the problems would be far from over. There is an enormous capacity for the detailed issues of any government structure in practice to provide problems that will assume constitutional dimensions. Northern Ireland is not now (and never really was) the sort of roughly homogeneous society where the British approach to constitutionalism reviewed earlier could be transplanted. The point of this book is that Britain no longer has, and Northern Ireland never had, the sort of civil society and state, or relationship between the two, where the traditional forms of constitutionalism could work effectively. Northern Ireland is Westminsterism's endgame. The central question is now whether there is anything of value in the experience of thinking about how to govern Northern Ireland long term, and *actually* governing it in the short term, which is of value for the future of Great Britain.

We believe that there is. The crisis in constitutionalism in Great Britain may be differently caused and less advanced but its roots in an outmoded idea of the role of the state and of the reality of government in a complex and fragmented society provide direct parallels with Northern Ireland. Just as orthodox constitutionalism seems less and less to fit the reality of government in Britain, so in Northern Ireland its redundancy is more marked but its regeneration is perhaps less distant. We argue that there are some small signs of a new constitutionalism emerging in Northern Ireland.[37]

---

[37] See also Morison, "Crisis and Control: A 'New Constitutionalism' for the United Kingdom from Northern Ireland" in *Control in Constitutional Law* (Zoethout, van der Tang and Akkermans ed., 1993; Morison, *The Micro Constitution Beyond the Politics of Consent: A Submission to the Opshal Inquiry* (1993) and Livingstone, "Using Law to Change a Society: The Case of Northern Ireland" in *Law, Society and Change* (Livingstone and Morison eds., 1990).

The failure of the large-scale, institution-oriented approach aimed at providing a macro constitutional settlement in Northern Ireland has left a problem of crisis management. At one level this has required security and legal initiatives deployed in reaction to developments in a campaign of violence and directed towards keeping disorder at 'acceptable levels'. At another level in part it has involved simply getting the business of government done. With politics at the hard, constitutional end corralled off into a "peace process" there has been the necessity and freedom to get the business of government done without even the semblance of an associated political system. This has been achieved through the direct rule mechanism whereby law-making is carried out in Westminster and the executive function is carried out by a civil service acting on behalf of ministers drawn from Westminster in association with a highly developed quango and voluntary sector. Beyond this there is some evidence of another approach to the problems of Northern Ireland. This does not form part of any strategy as such in so far as it is not organised or coherent, but rather, as with the items on the macro political agenda, it is shaped by a whole range of issues, crises and demands in the domestic and, indeed, international sphere. There are many ways in which these trends manifest themselves although always their effect appears partial and ad hoc rather than sustained and planned. In an important sense the key aspects governing the New Constitutionalism can be summarised in the phrase "security, economic support and community relations". This captures the way in which security imperatives overcome much else. It suggests the manner in which economic support has been maintained at levels far in excess of Great Britain in an effort to underwrite attempts at political reconciliation. Finally, this phrase make reference to the various initiatives designed to sustain and protect two separate religious or political identities in the north of Ireland. The variety of mechanisms and initiatives that have been developed in response to this immediate agenda suggest the very different origins of individual aspects of this new constitutionalism. It has come about in response to various, often contradictory, aspects of the security and political agenda both at home and outside. However, when viewed together, these aspects can be regarded as making up a new approach.

Although it is developing rather than developed, this new constitutionalism can be seen as having two aspects. The first relates to an *external* constitution. We are referring here to the increasing role that the European Union, other European and international institutions, other governments and non governmental organisations play in influencing the affairs of Northern Ireland. This is particularly significant in so far as

Northern Ireland demonstrates to a developed degree the importance of such external influences in the absence of a roughly homogeneous population who are orientated around, and identify themselves in relation to, a broadly defined nation state. The essentially contested nature of national identity in Northern Ireland pulls into sharp focus a whole range of ideas which challenge and explore the possibilities of external control. This aspect is examined in chapter six.

The second aspect of the new constitutionalism may be termed a *grassroots* or *interpersonal* constitution. Again, rather than focusing on trying to bring into existence satisfactory domestic institutions, this operates in a different way and at a different level. It is concerned to use values, procedures and categories to re-work issues at a very small-scale level. It seeks to use public power—economic and administrative as well as straightforwardly legal—in what is usually conceived of as being in the private rather than public sphere. Law is used in this project, along with other forces, to help reconstitute people into new structures, attitudes and behaviours. Its role is to restructure, implement and facilitate at many levels rather than simply set up and regulate institutions and mechanisms of government.

One of the chief ways in which this aspect is manifest is in the depoliticisation of government. Public administration, and to some extent the legal system,[38] take on roles that elsewhere traditionally at least might be politically driven. There is also an element of re-politicising the embryo social groupings from which it is hoped government will develop. This is apparent with the recognition (or creation) of two identities or traditions in Northern Ireland. Each of these, the protestant, unionist one defined in relation to Great Britain and the catholic, nationalist one orientated around the Republic of Ireland, are declared repeatedly now to be equally legitimate and to have parity of esteem. Increasingly it is becoming the task of government and of law to sustain and protect these two identities. This idea has been in existence for some time but it was the Anglo-Irish Agreement that gave full recognition to the notion of two cultural traditions, although this has been reinforced often subsequently and such thinking underpins the initiative that produced the joint declaration of December 1993 and now powers the present peace process. The general aim of this may well be to make each mutually hostile faction equally valid

---

[38] See further Fox and Morison, "Lawyers in a Divided Society: Legal Culture and Legal Services in Northern Ireland" (1992) 19 *Journal of Law and Society* 124.

(so long as they eschew violence) and so go some way to legitimising and demarginalising the minority community in order to assist in the process of reaching a political accommodation at the institutional level. However, outside of this, the creation and regulation of two identities has enabled government to achieve some of the aims of getting the business of government done. The two identities idea has provided an underpinning and *modus operandi* for government, quasi-government agencies and an important and highly developed voluntary sector to take out of the hands of politicised, sectarian local government politically charged issues such as housing, health, education, industrial planning, etc. Elsewhere these might well be regarded as simple "bread and butter" issues but in Northern Ireland they are "constitutional" issues and have traditionally been a site of sectarian, political struggle. At the same time this notion of identities provides a basis on which the power of public law can be used to penetrate many areas and levels that are, elsewhere in the British tradition, seen as private and so outside its preserve. Thus there are ground rules about the conduct of relations between the two communities in terms of what is permissible with regard to expression of opinion, access to public offices, public money, the media, etc. There is also regulation in terms of protecting and reinforcing the existence of two identities where groups and individuals meet and combine as fellow citizens in the public space or as employers and employees where they are restrained from discriminating against one another. The anti-discrimination industry in Northern Ireland, and the related craft of community relations, are part of a potentially important use of public power in a relatively new fashion to reconstitute and redesignate basic conditions and categories in a way that sees issues of government as occurring in important ways beyond structures and institutions.

This general argument will be developed in the next three chapters where the real constitution of Northern Ireland is explored. The final chapter follows up ideas about reinvigorating the British constitutional tradition from the experiences of having to conduct the ordinary business of government in the extraordinary context of Northern Ireland.

Conclusion

This chapter has sought to demonstrate the limited range of options open to those who would in some way seek to "solve" the problems of Northern Ireland through a political accommodation that can then be translated into an institutional settlement. It has indicated how the British tradition, with its focus on processes and structures, is unlikely to develop anything innovative or effective to deal with this most advanced breakdown of its method. We have also sought here to introduce the argument that the reality of everyday government in Northern Ireland contains some signs of a new constitutionalism which could potentially enrich and reinvigorate the moribund British tradition. Although the decline of the Westminster method is most advanced in Northern Ireland it is here that we might look for its regeneration. In an earlier project[39] we evaluated the arrangements of government in Northern Ireland according to criteria of democracy which essentially stressed ideas of popular control and political equality.[40] It might be surprising that, although we found much that was "undemocratic"—particularly with regard to the operation of direct rule, Northern Ireland was not simply a democratic black hole. Although the new constitutionalism is concerned primarily with getting the business of government done, it does carry with it a largely unfulfilled potential to enrich and democratise the processes of government both in Northern Ireland and in Great Britain. It is to this that we now turn.

---

[39] Livingstone and Morison, *An Audit of Democracy in Northern Ireland* (1995) and *From the Peace Process to Democracy* (1995).
[40] See further Beetham, *The Democratic Audit of the United Kingdom: Auditing Democracy in Britain*, 1993.

Chapter Four

The Real Constitution of Northern Ireland

Introduction

In the previous chapter we examined how the "constitutional issue" of Northern Ireland has been treated over the past 25 years. The search for a grand "constitutional solution" has been a constant preoccupation of politicans and political analysts in Northern Ireland during this time. It has also occupied a prominent place in the thoughts and deeds of those English and Irish politicans who, whether out of obligation or concern, have exhibited an interest in the affairs of Northern Ireland. Following the ceasefires declared by loyalist and republican paramilitaries in August 1994, engaging in the game of proposing constitutional settlements once again came to seem a worthwhile pursuit. However, such are the difficulties of juggling the various positions and perceptions outlined in the last chapter that it would be a brave person indeed who would predict a satisfactory settlement would eventually be found.

While everyone has been waiting and some have been working for that settlement the situation has not remained static. Indeed over the past 25 years the constitution of Northern Ireland has altered significantly. While formally Northern Ireland may have remained a part of a settled United Kingdom throughout this period the scope of public power, the objectives to which it is orientated, the means by which it is exercised and the mechanisms by which people have influence over it have changed markedly since 1968. In the next chapter we examine the institutions of governance and how they now operate in Northern Ireland. In this chapter we examine the overall constitutional design of these institutions, the objectives they are designed to fulfill and the constraints that they work within.

Our approach is primarily historical and we outline three stages of development in relation to the working constitution of Northern Ireland. The first, which lasted from 1922 to 1972 may be termed as we have described it at the end of chapter two, *mechanical constitutionalism*. In this period the Westminster model was simply transposed to Northern Ireland and its flaws exposed. Accountability to Parliament as a touchstone of constitutional legitimacy made little sense when the governing party had a permanent majority. Nevertheless that governing party did largely operate in the way nineteenth century constitutionalists envisaged, leaving most matters beyond security and taxation to the private sector, even when the limitations of that sector showed the clear need for government intervention.

The second period, from 1972 to 1985 can be seen as the period of modern constitutionalism or *organic constitutionalism*. In this period government intervened heavily in the private sphere. The deployment of large numbers of soldiers and police on the streets of Northern Ireland and the use of extensive security powers may have been the most visible manifestation of a more interventionist state, but government also intervened heavily in areas which previously were largely the concern of the market. It involved itself extensively in the housing and labour markets and sought to influence the pattern of industrial development. The ideological orientation of such intervention was reformist and neutral. It claimed that all inhabitants of Northern Ireland would be treated equally, that no particular identities would be recognised and therefore treated differently. The opportunities for citizens to challenge the ways in which such intervention took place, to assert desires or identities which went unrecognised by government, remained limited however. For while the scope of public power had increased, the mechanisms by which people could influence or challenge the exercise of this power remained, as with the rest of the United Kingdom, largely stuck in the nineteenth century Westminster model. This became of even less relevance to Northern Ireland where no one even voted for any of the M.P's who exercised any power in that system.

The third period, from 1985 to the present we style the *communicative constitutionalism*. In this period government has sought to withdraw from the task of directly organising many areas of social and economic life. Instead government has handed over the delivery of services it used to provide directly to a variety of quasi-governmental bodies, many of which operate within some type of market regime. In some cases the service has been directly delegated to the market. "Softer" techniques of regulation and influence are also utilised more than direct service delivery or legal prohibition. While government has been seeking to disengage from some areas of social involvement it has also found itself increasingly subject to some form of regulation as to its policy objectives and the mechanisms by which it seeks to achieve them. Much of the pressure for this type of regulation has come from what we refer to in chapter six as "external influences", notably the influence of Europe. Utilisation of such "external influences" has offered some groups, largely blocked out of domestic channels of influence, a way of asserting their aspirations. This withdrawal from direct service provision and a commitment to provide services does not, however, simply mark a return to the *laissez-faire* approach of the classical constitution. While the state decreases its capacity to directly control the life of its citizens through provision of a wide range of services it actually attempts to indirectly influence and regulate ever broader areas of social existence. To achieve this it begins to enter into a wide range of accommodations with different elements of civil society.

It is this emerging but confusing constitutional landscape, replete with possibilities and dangers, which we argue is the most interesting develop-ment in Northern Ireland and also the one which most significantly prefigures developments in Great Britain. It is a development which is neither clear nor consistent. Elements of what we describe as a com-municative constitution may be discerned in both the organic and mechanical periods, even if they may have played a different role at this time. The communicative constitution itself is emerging in a jagged way, with some of its elements likely to remain unclear for some time to come. However we would argue that already enough can be seen in the recent constitutional development of Northern Ireland to provide a point of departure for those constitutional lawyers who do not want to enter the twenty-first century with a set of theories that might have been redundant by the end of the nineteenth.

The Mechanical Constitution (1922–1972)

Following partition in 1922 Northern Ireland obtained a constitution which contained, by British standards, several innovative features. The Government of Ireland Act 1920 introduced a devolved form of govern-ment by granting some law making powers to the new regional Northern

Ireland parliament while retaining others for Westminster. It also included a substantive restriction on the power of that parliament. Section 5 of the Government of Ireland Act prohibited the making of laws which interfered with religious liberty or discriminated on the grounds of religion. The same Act required proportional representation for elections to the Northern Ireland parliament, an electoral process that had already been introduced for local government elections by the Local Government (Ireland) Act 1919. In addition the new government took office at a time when the extent of its territory was still under dispute, the British government and the new government of the Irish Free State having agreed to jointly establish a boundary commission to sort out the new boundary between the Free State and the United Kingdom.

Most of these innovations, however, were to be quickly removed or proved to be a dead letter. Proportional representation was to be removed for local government in 1922 and for elections to the Northern Ireland parliament in 1929. The boundary commission report in 1925 affirmed the status quo.[1] Despite section 5 of the Government of Ireland Act the Northern Ireland parliament passed legislation which helped entrench religious segregation in 1930.[2] Few legal challenges were ever to be brought under the Act and none were to prove succesful. While section 75 of that Act preserved the supremacy of the Westminster parliament the government of the United Kingdom largely left the regional administration and parliament to its own devices.[3] Except in the area of financial control Westminster and Whitehall largely rejected any more active role for central government. In particular they rejected any role of ensuring that certain national standards were maintained regardless of local sensibilities.

From the mid 1920s onwards Northern Ireland was to do its best to become a mini-Westminster where the party which won the most seats at the election obtained the right to form a government and to pass whatever sort of legislation it managed to get through parliament. The main

---

[1] For a summary of the Boundary Commission's activities see Murphy, *Ireland in the Twentieth Century* (1975), pp. 62–3.

[2] The Education Act (Northern Ireland) 1930, which even the Northern Ireland government itself had decided was unconstitutional by 1947.

[3] A telling example being its decision to grant the Royal Assent to the Bill abolishing proportional representation for local government elections despite strong opposition from the government of the Irish Free State. For a summary see Buckland, *The Factory of Grievances: Devolved Government in Northern Ireland 1921–39* (1979), pp. 267–75.

problem with this, of course, was that it was the same party that consistently won all the elections. From 1922 to 1972 the Unionist party was never to be out of power.[4] Such continuity tended to undermine the claim that the absolute power the Westminster system confers on the governing party will always be checked by that party's realisation that they may lose office if they abuse it. The claim might have been even more completely undermined if the Unionist governments of those years had made extensive use of their parliamentary power to repress the nationalist minority. Instead, with the important exception of policing and security powers, the years of Unionist power were characterised by a fairly informal style of government and the maintenance of a laissez-faire approach that was going out of fashion in Great Britain even before the First World War. Thus while central and local government in Britain came increasingly to see the provision of services such as housing, education and health as part of their public duty from the 1920s onwards, in Northern Ireland such matters were still largely being left to the control of the private sector until well after the Second World War. Thus early efforts in education by the new Minister of Education, Lord Londonderry, to establish non-denominational state schools ran into fierce resistance from both the Protestant and Catholic churches. Neither were prepared to transfer their schools to the Ministry of Education. By the time of the Education Act (Northern Ireland) 1930 these efforts had largely been abandoned. That statute made Bible instruction by teachers mandatory, something which the Catholic church strongly opposed, and restored the power of appointment of teachers to school management committees, most of which were composed of local churchmen. Thereafter Protestant schools increasingly transfered to the jurisdiction of the Ministry. Since the Act required half of the school management committee to be appointed by the transferors the Protestant clergy effectively maintained their control of them. Catholic schools largely remained outside the system. Although changes in the 1940s brought the organisation of education in Northern Ireland closer to that which prevailed in Great Britain, a largely segregated school system, with a prominent role for the Protestant clergy in state schools and a large voluntary Catholic sector, remained in place right until the 1980s. The grammar school sector remained strong and there was never the support for comprehensive education that existed in Britain in the 1960s and

---

[4] In 12 elections to the Northern Ireland parliament Unionists never won less than 34 out of the 52 seats and only in 1962 did their share of the vote fall below 50 per cent.

1970s.[5] In the field of housing Northern Ireland's local authorities were to gain an international reputation for sectarian allocation, a reputation which was to prove one of the factors leading to the growth of the civil rights movement in the late 1960s. However it was not until the 1960s that they actually took the provision of public housing seriously. Throughout most of the history of the state, the building of houses by the public sector lagged well behind the rest of the United Kingdom and most local authorities built very few houses.[6] The introduction of the National Health Service to Northern Ireland, via an Act of the Northern Ireland parliament in 1948, occurred only with certain modifications "more in keeping with Unionist principles than the system adopted across the water".[7] Northern Ireland was also slow to develop any kind of industrial policy, with the result that its weak economy lagged further behind Great Britain, particularly in the inter-war years.[8]

Some change in these areas of public policy did begin to occur by the 1950s and early 1960s. The government commissioned a number of studies on the economy and began to develop a more aggressive industrial policy, aimed in particular at attracting inward investment.[9] The number of new houses built by the public sector rose significantly from the early 1960s onwards. The merits of comprehensive education were more openly discussed and government developed plans for a second university in Northern Ireland. Ironically, in a manner familiar to many historians of revolutions, it was exactly at this point of greater government inter-vention, of the Northern Ireland state beginning to intervene more extensively in society, of it, indeed, beginning to act like a modern welfare state, that issues of the legitimacy of the state began to be more sharply posed. Elements of the Civil Rights movement of the mid and late 1960s posed questions about the way this intervention was taking place and of why it was that most of the new industrial investment, public housing and the siting of the new university all went to predominantly protestant areas.

---

[5] See Cave and Dallat, "Education: Step by Step or Out-of-Step" in *Public Policy in Northern Ireland: Adoption or Adaption* (Connolly and Loughlin, ed., 1990), pp. 303–322.

[6] See Murie, *Housing Policy in Northern Ireland: A Review* (1992), p. 7.

[7] Quoted in Ditch, *Social Policy in Northern Ireland 1939–1950* (1988), p. 99. These related especially to the decision not to automatically include all voluntary hospitals, as had been done in Great Britain. As a result the main Catholic hospital, the Mater in Belfast, remained outside the scheme.

[8] For discussion of the limited efforts at industrial policy see Buckland, *A History of Northern Ireland* (1981), p. 74.

[9] See Buckland, *op. cit.* pp. 110–113.

They also posed questions about impartiality in the one area in which the state had been consistently prepared to intervene since 1922, that of law enforcement. The first legislative act of the new Northern Ireland parliament was to pass the Civil Authorities (Special Powers) Act 1922, which essentially continued war time defence regulations and endowed the state with broad powers of arrest, search and detention.[10] The Act was regularly renewed until 1933 whereafter, to avoid an annual parliamentary wrangle with nationalist representatives, it was made permanent. Its powers to detain without trial, carry out arrests and ban demonstrations were regularly resorted to, especially in times of political tension. To implement the law the government relied on the Royal Ulster Constabulary (RUC), most of whose members were drawn from the protestant community and which was supplemented by locally recruited reserve forces (The "A", "B" and "C" Special Constabulary). The Special Constabulary in particular was seen by many catholics as a biased force and little more than another name for the paramilitary Ulster Volunteer Force (UVF) from which the Specials had drawn much of their original membership in the 1920s.

Policing and law enforcement are very much staple elements of what a nineteenth-century vision of the constitution sees the state as being responsible for, even if the partial character of its operation in Northern Ireland departed from liberal constitutional ideals. Within such a vision the state enforces contracts and the civil peace but leaves most matters of social organisation and resource provision to private society and the market. The role of the law is simply to prohibit certain forms of conduct and to offer a mechanism to resolve the conflicts of the market. In a twentieth-century welfare state both law and state go much further than this. The state takes on the task of ensuring that many key services are provided and the law becomes one of its agents for the achievement of this. Northern Ireland was clearly never a pure nineteenth-century liberal state: government always did play a role in regulating the economy and in providing health, education and housing. However neither was it clearly a modern welfare state, at least not until the early 1960s. Moreover, whatever the historical merits of the nineteenth-century liberal vision, it based its claims to legitimacy on the idea that a free market allowed all an equal opportunity to contract to achieve their own ends. Inequalities in power and wealth

---

[10] For a discussion of the origin and content of the Special Powers Act see Campbell, *Emergency Law in Ireland 1918–25* (1994).

rendered this claim dubious in most societies but in Northern Ireland widespread segregation on religious grounds strained its credibility even more. The private sector was not a zone of free contracting but rather a highly stratified society where conflicts of identity served as a bar on contracting, notably with regard to employment. Organisations such as the churches and the Orange Order played as significant a role as the market in the organisation of society and the allocation of resources. Moreover segregation was not on an equal basis but rather took the form of an unequal distribution of wealth and power between protestants and catholics (though neither were monolithic blocks, both contained their wealthy and poor). The real constitutional arrangements of Northern Ireland between 1922 and 1972 did nothing to change this and in a number of ways the actions of the state notably at local government level exacerbated it.

The Organic Constitution (1972–1985)

The removal of the Stormont government and the introduction of direct rule from Westminster in 1972 did not produce as much change in the constitutional arrangements of Northern Ireland as might have been expected. This is largely because the objective of the British government was to maintain most of the existing structures in place pending the working out of a new constitutional settlement. Apart from some elements in the Ulster Unionist party and in the Conservative party, direct rule has been seen by all as an interim solution at best. Therefore the Secretary of State largely took over the executive functions of the government of Northern Ireland, while the making of legislation for Northern Ireland was moved to Westminster. Apart from a brief experiment with a regional assembly in 1973, which was to operate alongside cross-border institutions as envisaged by the Sunningdale Agreement of 1974, "direct rule" from Westminster has continued without interruption for more than 20 years.[11] Although, as we noted in chapter three, the focus has largely been on finding grand level solutions, there are at present some features which break up the starkness of the status quo of direct rule. In particular, there are the anti-discrimination measures in Part Three of the Northern Ireland

---

[11] For further details of this, and an assessment of the democratic costs of this system, see Livingstone and Morison, *An Audit of Democracy in Northern Ireland* (1995). See also Appendix One below for an overview of constitutional developments.

Constitution Act 1973 which apply to law-making and the exercise of executive power both by direct rule bodies and local councils and the reintroduction of proportional representation for local council elections. These amendments did not, however, produce a set of constitutional arrangements that deviated sharply from the Westminster model. All power remained in the hands of the governing party, though that party was now located in Westminster rather than Belfast. The attempt to devolve power back to the power sharing executive and the Northern Ireland Assembly under the Constitution Act of 1973 ended after six months in the Ulster Workers Council strike of 1974. In 1982 another assembly was established under Secretary of State Jim Prior's model of "rolling devolution", whereby legislative powers would progressively be returned as the Northern Irish political parties reached agreement on a basic constitutioal framework. The main constitutional nationalist party, the SDLP, boycotted the Assembly however, and no agreement had been reached by all parties by the time the Assembly was wound up in 1986. Despite the removal of a regional tier of government the functions and powers of local government were decreased rather than increased during this period. Financial arrangements for Northern Ireland were altered to integrate Northern Ireland more fully with Great Britain. In particular the level of overall expenditure would now be detemined at Westminster. A method for calculating Northern Ireland's share of each tax was laid down and a general grant in aid to the Northern Ireland Consolidated Fund replaced the special forms of assistance and ad hoc arrangements which had previously existed.

What changed more dramatically was the scale of government activity and the way in which such activity was executed. Even before the end of the Stormont regime the delivery of important public services was transfered from regional and local government to appointed public bodies. Between 1970 and 1973 policing, public housing, health and public education were all placed under the control of nominated boards. One reason for this transfer was that the increasing complexity of delivering such services in a modern society was recognised as having outstripped the organisational capacity of Northern Ireland's highly fragmented local government system, which itself was subject to reform during this period. Another was that extensive allegations of religious and political discrimination in the delivery of such services, especially in relation to housing and policing, had undermined the case for local political control of them.

These changes brought Northern Ireland much more into line with the ideology of a modern liberal welfare state. Rather than retaining the position of a predominantly laissez-faire state, whose commitments did not extend much beyond the maintenance of social order, the state now undertook to provide a wide range of services to its citizens. Moreover it undertook to provide these equally to all citizens regardless of religion or political opinion. Changes in the strucure of public service delivery were accompanied by changes in its extent. Especially under the Labour administrations in Westminster of 1974–1979 public expenditure in Northern Ireland grew significantly. Even the Thatcher Conservatives, while committed to a reduction in the extent of state provision maintained a high level of public expenditure and public service provision in Northern Ireland.[12] Thus total public sector employment grew by 40 per cent in the period 1970–1974 and by a further 25 per cent in the 1974–79 period.[13] Although much of this increased employment was in policing and prison services there was rapid growth in health and employment also. The number of employees in the health service, for example, increased by 43 per cent in the period 1974–1987.[14] Overall public expenditure grew by 33 per cent in the years 1972–1975[15] and remained high throughout this period. Much of this expenditure was justified by the need for Northern Ireland to "catch up" with the level of public servce provision in the rest of the United Kingdom and indeed some have argued that even with such an increase in public expenditure the level of relative deprivation in Northern Ireland is such that service provision still lags behind Great Britain.[16]

However these increases in public expenditure in Northern Ireland did not derive purely from concerns as to social deprivation. They were also part of a policy designed to undercut the social and economic reasons for people turning to political violence. While the major issue of what form the state was to take in the future was put on hold, the British government sought to ensure that what the state did *currently* was untainted by sectarianism. Putting appointed bodies in charge of such services as housing, policing and education was designed to "take these issues out of

---

[12] See Gaffikin and Morrisey, *Northern Ireland: The Thatcher Years*, (1990), especially chap. 2.

[13] See Teague and Smyth, "The Public Sector and the Economy" in *The Economy of Northern Ireland*, (Teague ed. 1993), p. 121, 124.

[14] See Hewitt, "The Public Sector" in *The Northern Ireland Economy*, (Harris, Jefferson and Spencer ed., 1991), p. 353, 361.

[15] See Hewitt, n.10, at p. 366.

[16] See for example Northern Ireland Economic Council, *Economic Strategy: Overall Review*, Report No. 73, (1989).

politics" and remove the potential for conflict developing around them. If such services were delivered by appointed bodies it seemed more likely that they would be delivered according to neutral, techocratic, criteria and less likely that their provision would be swayed by sectarian political considerations. Removing direct political control over these issues made it more likely that all of Northern Ireland's citizens would have an equal say in how important public services were delivered (even if that turned out to be virtually no say at all) and more likely that all would benefit equally from them. Perhaps the clearest public commitment to a state free of sectarian influences came with the passing of the Fair Employment (Northern Ireland) Act 1976. The Act went beyond the prohibition on discriminatory actions by public authorities contained in the Constitution Act to prohibit discrimination on the grounds of religion or political opinion by *all* employers. The Act also created a Fair Employment Agency to investigate complaints of discrimination and to conduct investigations into the extent of equality of opportunity. Employers were also encouraged to subscribe to a Declaration of Principle and Intent, upon signing which they would be certified as equal opportunity employers.[17] The Fair Employment Act, unthinkable under the Stormont system, was the clearest public declaration that the values of the state were antithetical to discrimination on religious grounds. Instead all citizens of Northern Ireland were to be afforded equal treatment regardless of their religious affiliation. This was clearly a long way from ideas of a "Protestant Parliament and a Protestant State", as set out by Northern Ireland's first Prime Minister Lord Craigavon.[18]

Although the restoration of devolved government remained the declared objective of British policy, what effectively occured during this period was a greater alignment of Northern Ireland with British public policy and public institutions, at least as they existed prior to 1979.[19] The British government appeared to be answering a consistent call of many reformers throughout the 1960s that they become more involved in the affairs of Northern Ireland and ensure that standards for the conduct of

---

[17] For a discussion of the development of anti discrimination policy see McCrudden, "Northern Ireland and the British Constitution" in *The Changing Constitution*, (Jowell and Oliver ed., 3rd ed. 1994), pp. 344–6.

[18] See Wilson, *Ulster: Conflict and Consent*, (1989) at p. 73 for further discussion of the background to this notorious remark.

[19] See Loughlin, "Administering Policy in Northern Ireland" in *Northern Ireland: Politics and the Constitution*, (Hadfield, ed., 1992), pp. 70–72.

public policy that applied in Great Britain also apply in Northern Ireland. These reformers argued that if the British government had taken such action then there would have been little basis for discontent and Northern Ireland would not have become a "constitutional problem" at all. Whatever validity such arguments might have had if action had been taken prior to 1969, instituting such reforms after 1973 did not produce constitutional stability. Though many factors may explain this two at least are worth highlighting.

First, although Northern Ireland may have become "more like Britain" in respect of things like public housing and health in the 1972–85 period it was clearly very different as regards policing and law enforcement. Changes were made in this area. The Royal Ulster Constabulary (RUC) was reorganised and removed from direct political control. Efforts were made to improve the quality of its training and recruits. It was encouraged to develop a more professional attitude to policing and to see its task as being to serve all citizens of Northern Ireland, regardless of religion or political persuasion. The B Specials were disbanded and replaced by the Ulster Defence Regiment (UDR), a locally recruited regiment of the British army, in the hope that the sectarian character of the local militia might be diluted.[20] The overall orientation of security policy also changed in the mid 1970s from the use of detention without trial and the primacy of the army, a strategy which contained echos of martial law and the quelling of a rebellion, to police primacy and the use of the criminal law against those seeking political change by military means.[21] However, the continued use of special courts and emergency powers of arrest, detention and trial, plus the continuing deployment of troops and a heavily armed police force gave the lie to any idea that Northern Ireland was just like the rest of the United Kingdom, only with a little more crime. Constant allegations of security force harassment, mistreatment of suspects and unlawful killings, much of which was supported by outside observers[22] and which the courts seemed powerless to prevent or redress, fuelled the sense that Northern Ireland was not yet a liberal democratic state where the rule

---

[20] See Brewer, Guelke, Hume, Moxon-Browne and Wilford *The Police, Public Order and the State*, (1988), pp. 51–53 on these developments.
[21] See Hillyard, "Law and Order" in *Northern Ireland: Background to the Conflict*, (Darby ed., 1983), pp. 43–53.
[22] See, for example, Amnesty International *Report of a Mission to Northern Ireland* (1978), heavily critical of interrogation procedures in Castlereagh police station.

of law prevailed.[23] The fact that the overwhelming majority of these allegations came from the catholic community also undermined claims that impartiality in law enforcement had been achieved. By the mid 1980s the UDR had largely been discredited by the illegal sectarian actions of some of its members while the success of the RUC in blocking the Stalker investigation (discussed in more detail in chapter five) seemed to indicate that it remained a force above the law.

A second factor was that sectarianism turned out to be much more deeply rooted than the government appeared to believe. Or rather that it turned out not to be based simply on ignorance and the views of a minority of bigoted individuals, but rather to be a reflection of deep seated social and economic divisions in Northern Ireland. This was demonstrated by the emergence of data in the mid-1980s which showed that 10 years after the adoption of fair employment legislation there remained substantial inequalites in the employment of protestants and catholics.[24] Male catholics were shown to be two-and-a-half times more likely to be unemployed than protestants, a ratio that appeared to have widened since 1971. Moreover, investigations undertaken by the Fair Employment Agency in the early 1980s displayed significant failure to ensure equality of opportunity in public sector areas such as health, higher education and the Northern Ireland civil service.[25] Yet these were exactly the areas where the government had greatest influence and where it might have been expected that a new ideology of impartial and neutral treatment would have taken deepest root. The emergence of this information threw into doubt the whole approach of the Fair Employment Act and the work of the Fair Employment Agency. This had relied heavily on education and persuasion, resorting to legal sanctions only against the worst offenders. Such an approach might have been adequate if discrimination was simply aberrational activity founded on ignorance and prejudice. The findings of the early and mid-1980s indicated, however, that the problem went much deeper than this and that it was embedded in practices by which people conducted their everyday lives in Northern Ireland. Making an impact on

---

[23] See, generally, Boyle, Hadden and Hillyard, *Ten Years On in Northern Ireland* (1981).

[24] Notably the 1981 census, the 1985 Continuous Household Survey and a series of reports commissioned by the Standing Advisory Commission on Human Rights from the Policy Studies Institute which were published in 1987. See Standing Advisory Commission on Human Rights *Religious and Political Discrimination and Equality of Opportunity in Northern Ireland* Cm 237, (1987).

[25] For a discussion and criticism of such investigations see Standing Advisory Commission on Human Rights, *op. cit.*, n.24, at pp. 112–32.

those practices would require rather more radical measures and a rather different philosophy than that contained in the 1976 Fair Employment Act.[26]

Even before the fair employment figures of the 1980s appeared an event had taken place which demonstrated graphically that seeking to depoliticise the Northern Ireland problem was not producing widespread support for the prevailing constitutional arrangements. This was the hunger strikes of 1980–81 in which 10 convicted republican prisoners starved themselves to death in a protest over the failure of the prison service to grant five demands which would have clearly marked their differention from "ordinary criminal" prisoners.[27] The hunger strikes convulsed Northern Ireland as no event had since the Ulster Workers Council strike of 1974, leading to a significant rise in the number of riots and disturbances. They also led to the electoral rise of Sinn Fein, which had played a major role in organising public support for the hunger strikers case and which clearly rejected any notion of solving the Northern Ireland problem by the application of "British standards".[28] The hunger strikes, and in particular the considerable public support they received,[29] clearly mystified the British government and large sections of the protestant population of Northern Ireland.[30] They were unable to see why, despite the reforms that had taken place, such a large section of the catholic population in Northern Ireland would lend support to a collection of convicted terrorists. Even the SDLP, with a strong base of support in the catholic middle classes, and a proven record of opposition to political violence, felt unable

---

[26] For a strong criticism of the situation in the mid 1980s see McCrudden "The Experience of Legal Enforcement of the Fair Employment (Northern Ireland) Act 1976" in *Religion, Education and Employment: Aspects of Equal Opportunity in Northern Ireland,* (Cormack and Osborne ed., 1983), pp. 201–221.

[27] The five demands were to wear their own clothes, to refuse prison work, to receive one parcel a week, to associate freely with one another and to get back remission lost as a result of their protest. Granting of the demands would basically have put politically motivated prisoners back in the position they were in prior to 1976 when "special category status" granted to internees had been extended to those convicted of terrorist offences. The phasing out of special category status was recommended by the Gardiner report and led to a series of protests which culminated in the hunger strikes. After the hunger strikes came to an end many of the demands were granted in the 1982 revision of the Northern Ireland Prison Rules and were extended to all prisoners.

[28] On the rise of Sinn Fein see Clarke, *Broadening the Battlefield: The Hunger Strikes and the Rise of Sinn Fein,* (1987).

[29] Most independent estimates put the turn out for the funeral of Bobby Sands, the first hunger striker to die, in excess of 100,000.

[30] For the best analysis of this mutual incomprehension see O'Malley, *Biting at the Grave* (1990).

to field a candidate against the lead hunger striker Bobby Sands in the Fermanagh by-election. Nor would they even field a candidate against Sands' election agent Owen Carron, who won the seat after Sands's death. Unlike the early stages of the civil rights movement of the 1960s there was little cross-community support for the hunger strike. The episode demonstrated how deeply divided Northern Ireland remained, how indeed 10 years of violence had deepened such divisions and how large sections of the catholic population remained substantially alienated from the institutions of the state.

The hunger strike also refocused the attention of the world's media on Northern Ireland and brought into play again the international dimension that began to have an influence during this period. The riots of 1968 and 1969 were shown on television throughout the world and brought the conflict in Northern Ireland to international attention. One part of the world where interest had always existed was the United States. With its large population of Irish immigrants, many of them originally from the six north eastern counties, many American politicians had reason to show interest in Irish affairs. Especially after the deployment of British troops in 1969 and the introduction of internment in 1971 some Irish-American politicians, such as Senator Edward Kennedy, began to talk of Northern Ireland as "Britain's Vietnam" and sought American political support for British withdrawal. However, the strong support of the Republican administrations of Nixon and Ford for the United Kingdom in its fight against terrorism meant that such demands made little headway until President Carter came to power in 1976. By then, under the influence of SDLP leader John Hume, Kennedy's stance had moderated somewhat and his main stress was on the need for an agreed settlement and dealing with human rights abuses. Joining with a number of other prominent Irish-American politicians he encouraged President Carter to issue a statement on Northern Ireland in 1977 which encouraged the British government to work with the Irish government in seeking a solution to Northern Ireland's problems. The Carter administration's stress on human rights issues in its foreign policy also led to a more critical approach to Northern Ireland and concerns as to mistreatment of suspects in Castlereagh police station was to lead to a State Department decision to suspend arms sales to the RUC in 1979.[31] In the long run however, the main influence of Irish

---

[31] For a summary of American involvement in this period see Guelke, *Northern Ireland: The International Perspective* (1988) pp. 128–148.

lobbying in the United States was to strengthen the view of American politicians that a role for the Irish government was a key to any political settlement relating to Northern Ireland.

Britain and Ireland were already increasingly linked after 1973 when both joined what was then the European Economic Community. The Community however was to show little appetite for dealing with an internal political conflict of a Member State until the hunger strike of 1981. Thereafter the European Parliament debated both the hunger strike and the use of plastic bullets, passing a resolution against the use of the latter in 1982. Its Political Affairs Committee also commissioned a report into the political and economic problems of Northern Ireland in 1983. Although the subsequent Haagerup Report, which the European Parliament approved by 124 votes to 3 with 63 abstentions in 1984, was very moderate and cautious in its content it did refer to Northern Ireland as a "constitutional oddity" and recommended the establishment of joint British-Irish responsibilities in a number of fields.[32]

The Irish government did not directly challenge the United Kingdom's handling of the Northern Ireland situation within the forums of the European Community. It did however, utilise another European institution, the Council of Europe's European Convention on Human Rights, to challenge the security policies which Britain had adopted in Northern Ireland. Following extensive allegations of mistreatment of those interned in 1971 the Irish government instituted an action against the United Kingdom under Articles 3 and 5 of the Convention, claiming both that internment was unnecessary and that internees had been subjected to torture. Ultimately the European Court was to find internment justified but also concluded that the interrogation techniques used against internees amounted to "inhuman and degrading treatment" in violation of Article 3 of the Convention.[33] While this was a less severe rebuke than that from the Commission, which concluded that the techniques amounted to torture, it remained a major embarassment for the United Kingdom. This was especially so as two government appointed committees had approved the use of these techniques, though the government had discontinued them in

---

[32] See *Report drawn up on behalf of the Political Affairs Committee on the situation in Northern Ireland*, European Parliament Working Documents 1983–4, Document 1-1526/83, (1984).
[33] Series A. No.25 *Ireland v. United Kingdom* (1978) 1 E.H.R.R 25.

1972.[34] Although not a part of domestic law the Convention did provide an opportunity for individuals who felt aggrieved by the law or its operation in Northern Ireland to take their challenge beyond the limitations of the domestic system. Most of these challenges failed but there were successes, notably in the *Dudgeon*[35] case which led to the decriminalisation of homosexuality in Northern Ireland, 15 years after the rest of the United Kingdom. Even failures brought criticism of government policy. A challenge to prison policies adopted prior to the 1981 hunger strike failed at the Commission stage in the *McFeeley* case.[36] However the Commission did condemn the "inflexibility" with which the British government had handled the situation. While an overall assessment of the impact of the Convention on the protection of the rights of citizens in Northern Ireland must await chapter six, it was already clear in this period that the Convention might operate as a more significant constraint on security policy than the domestic legal system.

While the attention given to the Northern Ireland conflict by Europe in this period was limited, attempts to raise the issue in the United Nations met with even less success. The Irish government had made a brief attempt to call for the sending of a peacekeeping force to Northern Ireland in August 1969. This however, was quickly dropped after the British made it clear that they regarded it as interfering in their internal affairs, and the Security Council showed little interest in the proposal.[37] Thereafter, although United Nations human rights monitoring bodies continued to have some interest in Northern Ireland, arguments that extreme measures were necessary to deal with terrorism were largely accepted.

Although the Irish government had little success at the UN the main impact of "internationalisation" of the Northern Ireland issue, both in Europe and the United States, was to provide greater legitimacy for the Irish Republic having a role in its resolution. By the mid-1980s it was clear that international opinion would be reluctant to endorse any constitutional

---

[34] See *Report of the Inquiry into allegations against the security forces of physical brutality in Northern Ireland arising out of the events of 1971*, Cmnd 4823, (1971) and *Report of a committee of Privy Counsellors appointed to consider authorised procedures for the interrogation of persons suspected of terrorism*, Cmnd 4901, (1972).

[35] Series A. No. 45 *Dudgeon v. United Kingdom*, (1982) 4 E.H.R.R. 149.

[36] *McFeeley v. United Kingdom*, (1981) 3 E.H.R.R. 161.

[37] Boyd, *Fifteen Men on a Powder Keg*, (1971), p. 328, indicates that the Irish government were neither surprised nor disturbed by this outcome and had made the proposal mainly for domestic consumption.

settlement in Northern Ireland which was not approved by Dublin. Events within Northern Ireland in the 1980s also pointed the need for some sort of "external dimension" to any fresh set of constitutional proposals.

The Communicative Constitution 1985–95

In Northern Ireland since 1985, as with the rest of the United Kingdom since 1979, there has been a retreat from Keynsian economics and the idea that the state has an obligation to provide a wide range of services to its citizens. The level of new public house building in Northern Ireland has dropped sharply since 1987. With the selling off of two major industrial employers (the Harland and Wolff shipyard and the aircraft factory Short Bros) and a greater stress on competitiveness in industrial policy, especially since 1990,[38] government has moved away from the idea that it has a role in safeguarding jobs regardless of cost. The electricity service has been privatised, trust status introduced for hospitals and personal social services (the latter an area where Northern Ireland is ahead of Great Britain), some moves have been taken towards allowing schools to opt out and Compulsory Competitve Tendering (CCT) has been introduced for a number of local council services. While the level of government spending remains much higher than in the rest of the United Kingdom[39] the impression given by government statements and action is that, as in Great Britain, the state is seeking to withdraw from several areas of service provision. At best it seeks now to act as a regulatory body, at worst it seems to return some activities entirely to the market or to voluntary sector activity.

What makes Northern Ireland especially interesting is that these developments occur at the same time as the state declares its commitment to respect principles of equal treatment in the formulation and execution of policy. The emergence of a notion of "two traditions" in Northern

---

[38] See Department of Economic Development, *Competing in the 1990s*, (1990). This document stressed "backing winners" as a key element of future economic policy.

[39] In 1990–1, for example, public spending in Northern Ireland per capita was at a value of 143 against a United Kingdom average of 100. Quoted in Smyth, "The Public Sector" in *The Economy of Northern Ireland: Perspectives for Structural Change* (1993), p. 128.

Ireland, as opposed to attempts to play down cultural differences in the 1970s and much of the 1980s, and the need to respect them equally has given a different slant to government policy since 1985. In many ways this meshes well with notions of the state divesting itself of public service delivery functions. Since the minority community, in particular, has not always seen itself as adequately represented in the institutions of the state it has developed a range of community and voluntary organisations to replace or supplement the provision of state services.[40] Turning the resources to deliver such services over to these community and voluntary sector organisations fits both the rhetoric of respecting the minority and that of giving consumers greater choice and control over service delivery. Because of this sense of distance from the state, community organisations have also sought to gain assistance and resources from groups and institutions outside the United Kingdom, though this often proves a difficult task.[41] It is this intersection of the privatising and downsizing of government with the greater stress on the normative regulation of government policy, a normative regulation which has both internal and external dimensions, that gives events in Northern Ireland a particular constitutional significance and makes them suggestive of potential constitutional ideas.

In many ways the key constitutional provision of this period is the Anglo-Irish Agreement of 1985. This gave formal recognition to what had long become evident on the international plane (and had long been an objective of SDLP leader John Hume), that any constitutional settlement relating to Northern Ireland would have to win the approval of the Irish government and hence that the Irish government should have a clearly recognised role in the achievement of that settlement. Although Mrs Thatcher might still claim that Northern Ireland was "as British as Finchley" it clearly was not. Or rather it was not if being "as British as Finchley" meant that in seeking to advance any political project in relation to Northern Ireland one looked only to British institutions and British voters. The Anglo-Irish Agreement suggested that the United Kingdom

---

[40] See Oliver, *The Role of Non Profit Organisations in a Divided Society: The Case of Northern Ireland* (1990), p. 8–10.
[41] See Doogan, *EEC Funding in Northern Ireland* (1988), pp. 2–3 observing that direct applications from the voluntary sector were allocated only 1.6 per cent of the total ESF funding of Northern Ireland in 1987.

government recognised that there was an "external dimension" to constitutional developments in Northern Ireland and that to make any progress it would have to satisfy other governments and international institutions of the fairness of its actions. That both the British and Irish governments quickly sought approval for both the Anglo-Irish Agreement and the 1993 Downing Street Declaration in the United States and the European Community showed how well this lesson had been learned. However if this is what being "as British as Finchley" means then, as we have been suggesting throughout this book, perhaps Britain is not as British as Finchley any more.

However, the Anglo-Irish Agreement had an internal as well as an external dimension. This was that the Irish government was recognised as having a legitimate interest in the internal politics of Northern Ireland, notably in relation to such central issues of state activity as policing and the criminal justice system. It was recognised as having this interest because many nationalists within Northern Ireland looked to it for protection. The formal acknowledgement by the British government of the Irish government having this role carried within it an implicit concession that the United Kingdom state did not adequately encompass the identities of all its citizens in Northern Ireland. It was an implicit acknowledgment of the idea that Northern Ireland was composed of "two communities", only one of which saw itself as represented fully in the state. Although the Agreement stopped short of giving the Irish government any executive powers or a veto over decision-making, it did allow it to make recommendations over a wide range of policy functions, including suggesting people for nomination to a number of quangos.

Recognising the existence of "two communities" in Northern Ireland also implied that they should be treated equally, or at least that the majority community should not be allowed to oppress the minority. This recognition altered the view of what "discrimination" amounted to and enouraged policy makers to see it less as individual acts of bigotry in a generally tolerant society and more as evidence of deeply entrenched social patterns. Prodded notably by campaigns in the United States around religious discrimination in Northern Ireland's workforce, government introduced a new and considerably strengthened Fair Employment law in 1989. While falling short of the demands of many on the nationalist side, the Fair Employment (Northern Ireland) Act 1989 did significantly strengthen the rights of those who claimed that they had been discriminated against on grounds of religion or political opinion, as well as the remedies available to them if their claims were found to have been vindicated.[42] It also introduced the notion of "indirect discrimination"[43] into religious discrimination law (which had rather surprisingly been left out in 1976, despite being already established in race and sex discrimination law). Further it required employers to monitor their workforce and entitled them to take limited forms of affirmative action if the workforce does not display "fair participation" by members of each community in Northern Ireland.[44] The Fair Employment Commission (FEC) may also require employers to take such action if a review of monitoring returns reveals a lack of fair participation. These measures clearly reflect a view of discrimination as a structural phenomena, which is in need of broad based rather than purely individualised remedies. They also indicate a move away from education as the paradigm approach to dealing with problems of discrimination towards an approach which seeks to require employers to consider what barriers in their selection, training and promotion practices might inhibit one community from participation. This shift was not achieved without a struggle. Regular government assertions that the new legislation would not interefere with the principle that jobs are awarded on merit and the rejection of more radical solutions—such as quotas or compulsory affirmative action plans to attain government grants or contracts—testify to the hold that individualised notions of discrimination have. However, the legislation clearly moves a long way down the road of recognition that differential access to economic resources has been a central feature of life in Northern Ireland.

At the time that the Fair Employment legislation was passed some, including SACHR whose 1987 report on Fair Employment had a considerable influence,[45] expressed the view that action on employment was

---

[42] For example by allowing individuals to bring their claims before a Fair Employment Tribunal (FET) as opposed to having them considered in a non adversary way by the Fair Employment Agency. The Agency, now renamed the Fair Employment Commission, was given greater resources and one of its new tasks was to assist individuals in bringing complaints before the FET. The damages available for findings of discrimination were also set at up to £30,000, at that time higher than could be awarded for a finding of race or sex discrimination in the United Kingdom.

[43] This prohibits requirements or conditions which are such that a substantial number of one community cannot comply with them, that act to the detriment of members of that community and which cannot be justified by the requirements of the employer's business.

[44] For a discussion of this term, which is left undefined by section 31 of the Act, see McCrudden, "Affirmative Action and Fair Participation: Interpreting the Fair Employment Act 1989", (1993) 21 *Industrial Law Journal* 170.

[45] Standing Advisory Commission on Human Rights, *Religious and Political Discrimination and Equality of Opportunity in Northern Ireland: Report on Fair Employment*, Cm 237, (1987).

not enough. Instead they argued that government must incorporate equality considerations into all aspects of public decision making. Since government had long been the most significant economic player in Northern Ireland[46], it was argued that only such comprehensive action by government could produce equal opportunities for all. In the early 1990s the government began to respond to these calls with the publication of guidelines on Policy Appraisal and Fair Treatment (PAFT). These guidelines were issued to all government departments and encouraged them to review all present and future policy initiatives to examine whether they afforded equality of opportunity. Although the guidelines encouraged departments to consider equality relevant to a number of characteristics (including sex, race, disability and sexual orientation), it was clear that fair treatment on the grounds of religion or political opinion was likely to attract the most attention. In addition to PAFT the government also announced the policy of Targeting Social Need (TSN) in 1992. A TSN component was announced as being part of every government department's actions. Departments were instructed to compile "need indexes" and to make use of these in deciding upon projects and spending priorities. Though TSN was not exclusively concerned with ensuring more equal treatment of the catholic community, the Secretary of State announced when introducing the policy that as majority catholic areas of Northern Ireland had relatively greater need it was likely that they would be the major beneficiaries from this policy.[47] The next chapter will examine the extent to which the rhetorical commitments of PAFT and TSN have been translated into actual practices. At an ideological level, however, they clearly mark a further development of the idea that there are "two communities" in Northern Ireland and that the state must respect both of them in the way that it conducts its business.

In addition to PAFT and TSN government has adopted a range of initiatives to encourage the recognition and reconciliation of the two communities. These include the creation of the Community Relations Council (CRC), of funding for community relations programmes by local government, greater public support for the Irish language and funding for

---

[46] Public Expenditure is equivalent to around 60 per cent of GDP and the public sector accounts for over 40 per cent of all employment in Northern Ireland. See Northern Ireland Economic Research Centre *The Northern Ireland Economy: Review and Forecasts to 1995* (1990) pp. 3–4.
[47] Secretary of State to the Standing Advisory Commission on Human Rights, March 10, 1992.

cross-community contact schemes for schools.[48] Whereas in the 1970s governments sought to win the "hearts and minds" struggle for political legitimacy by extensive public expenditure programmes, the policies of the 1990s have been more directly targeted on recognised community divisions but have also been substantially cheaper. The Community Relations budget, for example, does not currently exceed £7 million.

Seeking to reduce government spending while making policies more responsive to community divisions has also led government into more extensive partnership with voluntary organisations in Northern Ireland. Since the 1970s there has been a significant growth in the number and scope of voluntary organisations in Northern Ireland, especially in predominantly nationalist areas. In 1978 the first major study of voluntary sector organisations in Northern Ireland identified 700 voluntary organisations and estimated that there was in excess of 1000 voluntary welfare organisations.[49] Over 60 per cent of these voluntary organisations dated their creation after 1960. Although no comparable study has produced contemporary figures, estimates put the current number of voluntary organisations in excess of 3000. While this total includes some large organisations with several hundred staff most are small community organisations, many of which have arisen directly as a result of the political conflict.[50] In addition to direct service provision such organisations have played a significant advocacy role, especially on social and economic issues, where they often have specialist expertise and where politicans have lacked either the forum or the interest to be involved. Government departments and quangos have increasingly been drawn into consultative relationships with such organisations, though often on terms which voluntary organisations feel are not to their advantage.[51] As elsewhere in

---

[48] For a summary see Knox and Hughes *Equality and Equity: An emerging government policy in Northern Ireland* (1993) pp. 3–10.

[49] Griffiths, Nic Gioll a Choile and Robinson, *Yesterday's Heritage or Tomorrow's Resource? A Study of Voluntary Organisations Providing Social Services in Northern Ireland* (1978).

[50] See Williamson "Yesterday's Heritage or Tomorrow's Resource" in *The Voluntary Sector in Northern Ireland*, ed. (Acheson and Williamson Forthcoming 1995), who quotes one estimate that over 500 community action groups have arisen directly because of the partial breakdown in the social fabric of Northern Ireland after 1969.

[51] One large voluntary organisation of which we have knowledge keeps an up to date diagram showing the changing structure and politics of the Northern Ireland Office, which provides most of its funding. Also with any individual project there is often concern about the extent to which the aims of the sponsoring department are dictating those of the voluntary organisation. The phrase which is used as a touchstone, "How far up the hosepipe does this take us?", captures this concern.

the United Kingdom, government has also sought to involve some of these organisations in taking on the delivery of what were formerly public services, such as community care or the care of the elderly, and has increased the proportion of government funding to the voluntary sector. In Northern Ireland this now exceeds £100 million per annum, close to the total budget of local authorities. The government's concern for further partnership with the voluntary sector was demonstrated by the publication, in February 1993, of the *Strategy for the Support of the Voluntary Sector and for Community Development in Northern Ireland*. The *Strategy* document broke new ground by stressing government's commitment to work with community groups and the voluntary sector as well as setting out principles and guidelines for how government departments would interact with this sector. It also indicated that such groups should be involved in the formulation of departmental policy, thus indicating a willingness to deal with the lack of consultation by departments and quangos that has long been a source of frustration for many in the voluntary sector. A Voluntary Activity Unit was also established to co-ordinate government activity with respect to the voluntary sector, ensure that government policy took account of the likely affect on the voluntary sector and improve communication between government departments and the voluntary sector.

The *Strategy* document significantly links voluntary sector activity with community development activity and recognises the particular role that voluntary sector organisations play as regards the public life of Northern Ireland. It states

> "Government Departments in Northern Ireland acknowledge the intrinsic value of the voluntary sector and its capacity to generate and harness goodwill and motivation and to translate these into action in response to a wide range of needs. They also recognise the important role played by the voluntary sector in the social and economic life of the Province where, in the context of Northern Ireland's special circumstances, it provides a forum for reflecting the views and concerns of individuals and communities to government."[52]

One example of this recognition was the involvement of the voluntary sector in the preparation of the *Northern Ireland Structural Funds Plan 1994–1999*, which was submitted to the European Commission in November 1993. The European Affairs Committee of the Northern

---

[52] Department of Health and Social Services *Strategy for the Support of the Voluntary Sector and Community Development in Northern Ireland* (1993) para. 6.

Ireland Council for Voluntary Action (NICVA) co-ordinated opinions, formulated proposals and suggested recommendations from the voluntary sector throughout the process. The final document clearly shows the effect of its impact, with a much greater stress on ideas of promoting social cohesion and dealing with socio-economic differentials between Northern Ireland's communities than was evident in the 1989–93 version. The plan also calls for the creation of a monitoring body, The Northern Ireland Community Support Framework Monitoring Committee, to oversee the operation of community support projects undertaken with Structural Fund assistance. Both government departments and the voluntary sector are represented on this body but, unlike the situation for most of the rest of Europe, there is no role for elected representatives. Major domestic social policy initiatives, such as "Making Belfast Work",[53] or the "Londonderry Project" have also been undertaken with a considerable role for the voluntary sector, as well as for private, commercial concerns.

Involvement with the voluntary sector, especially the community development aspects of it, creates certain tensions for government. The most significant of these is that between effective service provision, which might require partnership with a group which is "closest" to the community, and the conferral of legitimacy on either the policy or the group providing it, which might be thought to require a more selective approach. The most obvious battleground of this conflict has been over Action for Community Employment (ACE) funding. ACE, a wage subsidy scheme aimed at providing short term employment for people unemployed for six months or longer, has had a major impact on the voluntary sector. With more than 100,000 places at a cost of over £50 million a year it has enabled many community development groups to fund the employment of staff and hence expand their activities. However, since 1985 ACE funding has been made subject to criteria set out in a written parliamentary answer by then Northern Ireland Secretary Douglas Hurd. The most important of these "Hurd criteria" are that government will not grant aid organisations which had

> "sufficiently close links with paramilitary organisations to give rise to a grave risk that to give support to these groups would have the effect of improving the standing or furthering the aims of a paramilitary organisation, whether directly or indirectly".

---

[53] See Birrell and Wilson "Making Belfast Work: An Evaluation of an Urban Strategy" (1993) 41 *Administration* 40.

Around 30 organisations have had their funding cut as a result of the operation of these criteria, most of them in predominantly catholic areas of Northern Ireland. No reasons are normally provided for the decision and those who have suffered vetting have frequently alleged that government disfavour with their political activities (or with the political activities of some of the group members) rather than links with paramilitary groups have been at the root of such decisions. Legal challenges to denial of funding, often based on religious discrimination grounds, have foundered on the rock of state pleas of national security,[54] although some groups have had their funding restored after taking unsuccessful legal action.

The ACE funding experience demonstrates that although government may show greater openness in dealing with the community representatives of the recognised communities it still retains both the desire and the capacity to invoke notions of state security to exclude certain groups from this process. It is a warning against too easily asserting that values of community involvement and welfare pluralism have become pre-eminent in the constitutional structure and indicates that government can still exert control at arms length. However the involvement with the voluntary sector in Northern Ireland does show one of the outlines of what a post-modern constitutionalism might be like. Instead of dealing with politicians and political parties as community representatives for a whole range of social and economic issues, the state increasingly interacts with more specific community representatives who lobby on a range of more specific issues. It may even turn over aspects of state social and economic activity to those groups. This scenario raises a whole new range of questions about the legitimacy and accountability of such groups, the relationship of citizens to them, the terms on which they interact with the state and what role this leaves for formal political institutions. Legal and constitutional analysis have hardly begun to engage with such themes as yet.

The role of NICVA's European Affairs Unit in making recommendations as to the Structural Funds plan was only one example of another trend that has developed during this period, the attempt by citizens and groups within Northern Ireland to bypass the domestic state structure and make use of the "external constitution" to realise their political and social projects. NICVA also participates in a European Poverty Network and has sought to establish good contacts with Commission officials in order to influence European Union policy and funding in respect of voluntary

---

[54] *Re Glor na nGael* [1991] Northern Ireland Reports 117.

organisations in Northern Ireland. The use of international human rights bodies by groups and individuals in Northern Ireland is a further example of seeking to bring the "external constitution" to bear on domestic law and policy. The volume of applications to the European Commission of Human Rights rose during this period and although the Strasbourg organs continued to exhibit an overall endorsement for the government's anti-terrorist policy,[55] there were some notable successes.[56] There were certainly more successes than before the House of Lords, which continued to exhibit a largely deferential stance towards security measures taken in Northern Ireland during this period.[57] Human rights organisations also sought to make greater use of United Nations human rights monitoring mechanisms during this period. After a report by the United Nations Committee Against Torture in 1991 which was critical of the safeguards against mistreatment of detainees in Castlereagh police station, following a hearing heavily lobbied by human rights groups, allegations of mistreatment declined sharply. Another source of non-governmental inspired external pressure was the McBride campaign for Fair Employment in the United States. Although bitterly resisted by the United Kingdom government the campaign was very succesful in getting American state and city governments, as well as private companies, to agree to invest in Northern Ireland only in concerns which respected the McBride standards. The campaign undoubtedly played a major role in encouraging government to rethink its policy on religious discrimination and provided an important litmus test for the content of the 1989 Fair Employment law.

At the more formal political level the stress on Anglo-Irish co-operation, signalled by the 1985 Agreement, continued with only minor hiccups over the past decade. The Downing Street Declaration of 1993 and the ongoing "peace process" have raised that co-operation to new levels and even all but the most die-hard Unionists have come to recognise

[55] Notably by upholding the United Kingdom's derogation from the Convention in respect of Prevention of Terrorism Act arrest powers in Series A. No. 258-B *Brannigan and McBride v. United Kingdom* (1994) 17 E.H.R.R.

[56] Notably in *Brogan v. United Kingdom* (1989) 11 E.H.R.R. 117 (power to detain for seven days in police custody without charge in violation of Article 5(3)), *Fox, Campbell and Hartley v. United Kingdom* (1990) 13 E.H.R.R. 157 (power to arrest on suspicion of being a terrorist in violation of Article 5(1)), *John Murray v. United Kingdom*, Application No. 18731/91 Report of the Commission, June 27, 1994 (denial of access to a solicitor for 48 hours coupled with inferences drawn from defendant's silence in police custody in violation of Article 6 of the Convention).

[57] See Livingstone, "The House of Lords and the Northern Ireland Conflict" (1994) 57 *Modern Law Review* 333.

that what they might see as a "foreign power" now has a central role in any constitutional developments regarding Northern Ireland. The peace process has also shown the role that other governments, notably the United States, may play in the affairs of Northern Ireland. In contrast to the very low key role of previous American administrations that of President Clinton has been much more prominent and the decision to grant Sinn Fein leader Gerry Adams a visa to visit the United States in early 1994 was quickly seen as a significant step in bringing Sinn Fein in from the cold and creating the conditions for a republican ceasefire. Where Adams went other politicians from Ireland, North and South, followed. All were apparently convinced of the need to influence American public and political opinion if the British and Irish governments were to be influenced in turn. The two governments have also sought the approval of the European Union, with an eye to financial support for any period of reconstruction in Northern Ireland, and Europe has responded with a guarantee of a financial package in excess of £200 million to support the peace process. The Framework Document, published by the British and Irish governments in February 1995, envisages that a new body composed of political representatives from the North and South of Ireland could make joint proposals to Brussels and oversee joint implementation of E.C. projects. Such a development could move towards the idea of Ireland being treated as one region in the European Union for all practical, as opposed to political, purposes.

Conclusion

The developments which have occured in these last 10 years most clearly resemble, and indeed amplify, changes we have detailed in earlier chapters as happening elsewhere in the United Kingdom. Public power, certainly as represented by the delivery of public services, has moved further away from the direct control of elected politicians to quangos and community representatives. Policy making in relation to the exercise of public power has become increasingly fragmented, with representative politicians losing their pre-eminent status and becoming only one of a number of groups which interacts with state agencies. Government has sought to contract (in both senses of the word) its responsibilities for public service delivery but also to influence an increasing range of what might previously have been seen as private activities through communications mechanisms such as community relations programmes or anti-discrimination laws. It has also, perhaps uniquely in Northern Ireland, subjected itself to normative limitations in the form of equality norms and an emphasis on respecting the "two traditions". Though not all areas of governmental activity have been affected by these changes, policing and law enforcement especially has remained stubbornly resistant, new relationships and opportunities have been opened up.

The other way in which Northern Ireland reflects and amplifies change is in the greater role for the external dimension of its constitution. Whether this be international human rights bodies, European Union finance, citizen lobbies abroad or the role of the Irish and American governments, it is clear that what people do in counties outside the United Kingdom can have a significant impact on what happens in this part of the United Kingdom. Moreover this is a fact not lost on many within Northern Ireland, who have sought to utilise these external influences to bring about domestic change.

The picture which emerges is complex and confusing. It is also one which neither constitutional scholarship nor constitutional law has caught up with. In the next two chapters we seek to map out the current landscape in more detail, first in relation to domestic developments, then to look at the external dimension. One thing that is clear is that these developments take us a long way from the premises of old style parliamentary democracy. Whether Northern Ireland's emerging constitutional process can afford to ignore these developments and simply seek to restore a modified form of parliamentary democracy, is something we return to in our final chapter.

Chapter Five

Getting The Business of Government Done

Introduction

As we sketched out in chapter four, the past 22 years have seen significant shifts in how Northern Ireland is governed. These shifts have largely been aimed at getting the business of government done, with ensuring that laws are enforced and public services delivered. It is a business which has to be carried on against a background of constant social, economic and political change from which Northern Ireland has not been immune. Government has sought to devise institutions that ensure the business of government gets done, institutions whose shape responds to pressures from within Northern Ireland, from political developments in the rest of the United Kingdom and (as we shall see in chapter six) from pressures outside the United Kingdom.

Moreover, as we have seen in chapter four, matters of law making, law enforcement and public service delivery are not entirely divorced from the broader "constitutional question". Conflict originally flared in Northern Ireland over specific issues of government action; such as housing allocation, industrial location and the disposition of policing. There has been a generally unspoken view since the onset of direct rule that unless some of these issues can be depoliticised the conflict will become impossible to manage. As we saw in chapter four there is now a growing view that repoliticising some of them in a managed way can be a way forward to dealing with the conflict. Whereas that chapter sought to give an overview of the development of what we have called the real constitutional arrangements of Northern Ireland this chapter focuses more on the institutions that have been produced by those developments. It examines how those institutions have come about, what functions they play and to what extent they realise constitutional principles in theory or practice. This chapter aims to produce a map of the current constitutional landscape, a map that has already been redrawn several times and is likely to experience further revision.

Law Making

As was mentioned in chapter four, the method of enacting legislation for Northern Ireland depends on what sort of law is being made. The Northern Ireland Constitution Act 1973 provides a three part classification. If the subject matter of the law comes within the scope of excepted matters, legislation can only be by way of an Act of Parliament. If the subject matter of the law falls within the definition of reserved matters or transferred matters legislation may be made by way of Order of Council. In practice the use of the Order in Council has predominated since 1973, to the dismay of most orthodox constitutional lawyers.[1] Indeed they note that even legislation which falls within the excepted matters category, such as anti-terrorism legislation, often receives a very limited amount of parliamentary consideration despite its impact on citizens' rights. Even the Prevention of Terrorism Act 1989 (which although a United Kingdom wide statute has its most extensive effects in Northern Ireland) was subject to the guillotine. Although there are exceptions, such as the Fair Employment Act 1989,[2] where genuine parliamentary discussion does take place on Northern Ireland related statutes, most legislation on excepted matters is produced after fairly perfunctory discussion of the government's proposals.

Such criticism is even more extensive, from politicians as well as constitutional lawyers, in relation to orders in council, which have covered a very wide range of matters including education, policing,

---

[1] See, for example. Hadfield "Legislating for Northern Ireland: Options for Reform" in *Eighteenth Report of the Standing Advisory Commission on Human Rights* Cm 739 (1993) pp. 111–128.

[2] See McCrudden "The Evolution of the Fair Employment (Northern Ireland) Act 1989 in Parliament" in *Lessons from Northern Ireland* (Hayes and O'Higgins ed. 1990) pp. 57–78. Issues of employment and religious discrimination are not excepted matters and the decision to proceed by way of a full statute seems to have been influenced by a desire to establish the legitimacy of this law.

industrial relations, sex discrimination and children's law. These are often tabled only after 10.00 p.m. when few M.P.'s are present. They cannot be amended, only approved or rejected. Often statutes made for the rest of the United Kingdom include a clause that similar measures may be introduced for Northern Ireland by way of order in council. This can then be done by a negative resolution procedure, which requires an M.P. to find parliamentary time within 40 days to introduce a prayer that the order not be enacted. To compensate for the limited opportunity to debate these orders in parliament the government normally produces a draft order and circulates this amongst parties who are thought to have an interest in the matter. However, there is no legal requirement to do this and on occasions the government has neglected to produce a draft order for consultation. Perhaps the most notorious example was the Criminal Evidence (Northern Ireland) Order 1988, which made significant inroads to the defendant's right to silence in all criminal trials. After the protests of the Standing Advisory Commission on Human Rights, the body which might be thought to have the most direct interest in the issue, the Secretary of State gave an undertaking that no such measures which could affect human rights would again be introduced without consultation.[3] Even when consultation does take place the consultation period is usually a maximum of six weeks and few changes have been made in orders as a result of this process. There is also a facility within parliament for draft orders in council to be referred to a Northern Ireland Standing Committee,[4] though this is at the discretion of the Secretary of State and to date only 11 of over 400 orders in council have been referred.[5] The Standing Committee cannot do more than make recommendations for changes in the draft order.

In orthodox constitutional terms the arrangements for law making in respect of Northern Ireland are clearly defective. It might be argued that orders which do no more than "bring Northern Ireland law into line" with that prevailing in statutes in Great Britain are the outcome of extensive discussion of their policy in Parliament, though this is something we would dispute. However the same cannot be said for those orders which have a specific impact on Northern Ireland. Provisions such as the Police (Northern Ireland) Order 1987, the Criminal Evidence (Northern

---

[3] See Hadfield, *op. cit.*, n.3 at p. 120.

[4] This is composed of all Northern Ireland members of Parliament plus not more than 25 other M.P.'s.

[5] The practice fell into disuse between 1982 and 1991, when the government declared its decision to revive it.

Ireland) Order 1988 and the Education (Northern Ireland) Order 1990 clearly fall into this category and amount to little more than executive orders on significant policy matters. However although the introduction of a Northern Ireland Select Committee shows government concern as to the absence of parliamentary scrutiny of executive decisions in Northern Ireland there is little evidence of change as regards the order in council procedure. In orthodox thinking a move away from it would probably be in the direction of putting more Northern Ireland matters into primary legislation, yet this would have the political effect of integrating Northern Ireland more clearly into the United Kingdom, something the government is obviously anxious to avoid. Even on a symbolic level there is clearly a desire to demonstrate that Northern Ireland is different by having a different procedure for making its legislation. The *Framework for Accountable Government in Northern Ireland*, published in February 1995, envisages that a regional assembly should take over some of these law making functions but would exclude powers relating to law and order. In view of the history of the Special Powers Act it is likely to be some time before authority to pass security laws is returned to a regional assembly—should one evolve. The history of such security laws, which is examined in more detail later in this chapter, shows how powerless Parliament is to protect even the most fundamental liberties once a governing party decides to remove them. Rather than displaying concern with the fact that Northern Irish orders in council are not as "democratically" made as Westminster acts constitutionalists might observe how contact with Northern Ireland shows up the limits of democracy in the Westminster process. They might also observe that opportunities for more interesting experiments have largely been wasted. The exercise of issuing a draft order in council, for example, could be developed further to allow interested parties to put forward representations, perhaps at a formal hearing. Even with full acts of parliament such representations are currently consumed by the secrecy and compromises of lobbying.

The Executive Branch

The years of direct rule have seen a significant increase in the power of the Northern Ireland government departments. Although they have had to deal with new external influences, which we discuss further in chapter six, they have largely been freed from the limits placed on their authority by the legislature or local authorities. As we have seen above, most legislation is now by way of orders in council, which are drawn up by departments themselves, although many are simply to bring Northern Ireland "into line" with policy decisions made at Westminster. The competence and budgets of local authorities in Northern Ireland have been dramatically reduced since 1972 and, although many of their functions have been handed over to quangos rather than central government departments, it is departments which set quango budgets and often issue directives to them. In formal terms this increased power has accrued to the Secretary of State for Northern Ireland and three Ministers of State who between them have responsibility for the various government departments. The Secretary of State is answerable to Parliament for these departments as well as having the task of seeking a political settlement. However regular changes in ministerial appointments and the phenomena of "helicopter rule",[6] whereby English Ministers often spend only a few days a week in Northern Ireland, has meant that in practice much of both policy-making and implementation has been ceded to officials.[7] The comparatively small number of these officials and their relative public invisibility has accentuated the idea of government by an elite, a sense captured by the notion that all important decisions in Northern Ireland are taken in "six key dining rooms in North Down".[8]

Decision-making in the key area of policing and law enforcement will be discussed separately in this chapter. Though the Secretary of State has an important role in relation to both, he must share this authority with the Police Authority on one side and the Secretary of State for Defence on the other. The Northern Ireland Office does, however, have responsibility for the running of Northern Ireland's prison system. In addition to this the Northern Ireland Office is responsible for other matters relating to law and order, such as the administration of the criminal injuries and damage compensation schemes, and for providing political advice to the Secretary

---

[6] See Oliver, *The Role of Non-Profit Organisations in a Divided Society: The Case of Northern Ireland* (1990), p. 5.
[7] However Loughlin "Administering Policy in Northern Ireland" in *Northern Ireland: Politics and the Constitution*, (Hadfield ed. 1992) p. 65, notes that as many Stormont ministers, especially before 1945, regarded government as a part time occupation, civil servants have always played an important role in policy formulation.
[8] North Down is Northern Ireland's wealthiest area and home to many leading civil servants and security force personnel.

of State. Six other government departments exist in Northern Ireland, with each minister of state normally being responsible for two of them.[9]

In terms of the policy formulated and implemented by these departments the philosophy of maintaining parity with Great Britain retains a strong ideological influence. Apart from the fact that most senior officials are from a unionist background,[10] and therefore might be expected to have a personal sympathy with such an approach, there are good institutional reasons as to why the civil service in Northern Ireland might not stray too far beyond the lines of policy set in Whitehall. One is that most civil servants' professional contacts are likely to be with their equivalents in Great Britain. Secondments and training courses in England reinforce the sense of unity and encourage the idea that Great Britain is the natural reference points for models of new development. Another is financial constraints. The budget for Northern Ireland is normally set in negotiations between the Department of Finance and Personnel (DFP) and the Treasury. It is then left up to the Secretary of State to allocate this between the various departments. However, some of this spending is fixed by national formula (as with benefits spending, which is dictated by the number of claimants) or is dependent on E.C. provisions (as with agricultural price supports). Income raised within Northern Ireland is insufficent to meet total spending in Northern Ireland.[11] Given that such a large part of Northern Ireland government income is derived from a Westminster subsidy, administrative measures that do not find a point of comparison with what is being done in the rest of the United Kingdom may prove more difficult to justify to the Treasury.[12] Many government policies in Northern Ireland, notably in fields such as health care or industrial relations, continue to seem to be largely copied from what is happening in Great Britain, often with little apparent discussion of whether they are appropriate in the conditions of Northern Ireland.

---

[9] These are the Department of Agriculture for Northern Ireland (DANI), the Department of Economic Development (DED), the Department of Education for Northern Ireland (DENI), the Department of Finance and Personnel (DFP), the Department of Health and Social Services (DHSS) and the Department of the Environment (DOE).

[10] The Fourth report of the Equal Opportunities Unit of the Civil Service (1991) put the percentage of Protestants in A and B grades at around 70 per cent, Catholics amounted for less than 20 per cent, with the remainder made up of those "not declared".

[11] For a discussion see Slattery, "Northern Ireland Central Government Spending and Income" (1993–4) 41 *Administration* 433.

[12] This has always been a consideration for public policy in Northern Ireland, see Birrell and Murie, *Policy and Government in Northern Ireland: Lessons of Devolution*, (1980), pp. 232–233, discussing constraints on social security spending in Northern Ireland.

However, as we saw in the previous chapter the 1970s did witness the achievement of a degree of autonomy from Whitehall, an autonomy which continued throughout most of the 1980s. Apart from security this was most obvious in the fields of housing and industrial development. While government spending in these areas declined in Britain, Northern Ireland witnessed spending levels that kept steady or even increased.[13] Much of this spending was channelled through quangos such as the Industrial Development Board or the Housing Executive but the impetus for the policy development came from within the government sector. As we have argued in chapter four such developments were directly influenced by the idea that poor housing and high levels of unemployment played an important role in fuelling the civil conflict. As the private sector was clearly incapable of altering this situation the government pursued a much more interventionist line than was evident in England, Scotland or Wales throughout much of the 1980s.

Such considerations still play a significant role in the formulation of government policy but as we observed towards the end of chapter four, the late 1980s and 1990s have also witnessed a shift towards government directly engaging with the divisions in Northern Ireland society. Rather than simply providing economic development programmes for Northern Ireland as a whole, in the hope that this will undercut the reasons for conflict turning violent, the government now appears to be seeking to bridge the gap between the two most visible communities in Northern Ireland. Apart from the development of a community relations programme through a quango, the Community Relations Council, and the deeper impact of fair employment laws, the most visible manifestation of this within central government has been the creation of the Central Community Relations Unit (CCRU) in 1987. The aim of the Unit is to advise the Secretary of State on all aspects of the relationship between the different parts of the Northern Ireland Community. It reports directly to the Head of the Northern Ireland Civil Service and is charged with

---

[13] Thus Hewitt observes that whereas in Northern Ireland public expenditure per head of the population stood at 90 per cent of that in England and Wales by in the late 1960s 1987 it had reached 150 per cent. Overall public expenditure GDP as a percentage of gross GDP in Northern Ireland rose from 33 per cent to 44 per cent in the period 1974–87. At the same time in the United Kingdom as a whole it rose only from 29 per cent to 34 per cent. See Hewitt, "The Public Sector" in *The Northern Ireland Economy: A Comparative Study in the Economic Development of a Peripheral Regime* (Harris, Jefferson and Spender eds. 1990), chap. 13.

formulating, reviewing and challenging policy throughout the government system, with the aim of improving community relations.[14] Initially CCRU had a substantial role as a grant making body. Much of this has now been turned over to the Community Relations Council although the Unit continues to fund District Council community relations schemes.

Increasingly CCRU's role is in formulating policy guidelines and monitoring policy performance. This has led to the development of Policy Appraisal and Fair Treatment (PAFT) guidelines in 1994 which the CCRU uses to "equality proof" government policies.[15] The guidelines extend to all public bodies directly or indirectly answerable to the Secretary of State. The guidelines are designed to encourage departments to build in notions of fair treatment from the outset of policy development and to ensure that policies do not have a differential effect on people of different religion, gender or sexual orientation. At a rhetorical level PAFT is a powerful commitment to the idea that the value of equality constrains government decision-making. Though not a legal commitment it has the potential to be a significant *constitutional* principle in the organisation of government in Northern Ireland, one that goes beyond the non-discrimination provisions of the Constitution Act. Certainly this seems set to be *the* significant idea which will underpin post-ceasefire public policy. We have heard of one senior civil servant describing it as the "perfume that now pervades everything that we do". However, as yet, the mechanisms for the implementation of this commitment, for disseminating the guidelines and monitoring compliance are still lacking in specificity. Neither is it clear as to whether the results of such monitoring (which must be presented in a report to the Secretary of State) will be made public, a development which might significantly enhance the potential of the guidelines to assume a quasi-constitutional character through public analysis and criticism.

The CCRU has also contributed to the development of the Targeting Social Need (TSN) policy developed as a public expenditure priority by government in 1990. TSN requires government departments to establish indicators of socio-economic need by which they can identify the areas of greatest need and target social policies on these. Departments are also required to monitor the impact of policies and programmes on the two main communities and to target remedial action to address any unfair

---

[14] See CCRU *Community Relations in Northern Ireland* (1991), p. 2.
[15] Central Secretariat Circular 1/93.

differential impact that policies or programmes are having. In a message to the Standing Advisory Commission in 1992 the Secretary of State indicated that while TSN is not about positive discrimination

"However since the Catholic section of the community generally suffers more extensively from the effects of social and economic disadvantage the targeting of need will have the effect of reducing existing differentials".

Like PAFT though, the implementation of TSN so far appears to fall short of the rhetoric. In 1994 only one department, the DHSS, had issued a TSN strategic statement while others were claiming that TSN considerations had been adopted into existing policies. NICVA commented that

"Unless Government establishes new ways of progressing the policy and of challenging Departments to implement it with vigour and enthusiasm it may unfortunately remain a nice idea existing in the margins of Government and the minds of a few committed individuals".[16]

Overall therefore it may be said that while government in Northern Ireland is moving towards seeing its policies as being subject to certain normative principles, with the principle of fair treatment of the two communities being the most significant one, it is still some way short of devising the institutional techniques and mechanisms to achieve this. Nevertheless it is worth while noting that these initiatives have emerged from within the bureaucracy, with only a limited input from the political process.[17]

While the development and implementation of Northern Ireland government policy can have a major effect on the lives of citizens, the opportunity for input into such decision-making from outside government circles is somewhat limited. Only in 1994 did Northern Ireland acquire a Select Committee at Westminster, which will allow M.P.s to examine the performance of Northern Ireland government departments, if within the established limits of the Select Committee process. Between 1982 and 1986 a similar function was performed by the Northern Ireland Assembly, its scrutiny of government departments generally being agreed

---

[16] Northern Ireland Council for Voluntary Action, *The Implementation of Targeting Social Need* (1994).
[17] Although some of these developments were advocated by the Standing Advisory Commission on Human Rights in their second report on *Religious and Political Discrimination and Equality of Opportunity in Northern Ireland*, Cm 1107, (1990).

to have been one of its more succesful aspects.[18] Parliamentary questions can also be addressed to the Secretary of State but this is on a rather limited basis. There is little input from anyone outside the government as regards the setting of public expenditure targets and priorities, despite the fact that few people in Northern Ireland voted for the political party which the Secretary of State represents. Individual citizens may also complain about acts of maladministration through the Ombudsman system, but this is limited to the implementation rather than formulation of policy.[19] Between the rather limited procedures at Westminster and the individual complaints mechanisms of the Ombudsman or judicial review there is a clear gap in terms of democratic accountability and the ability of government to receive feedback on the operation of its policies. As we noted in the previous chapter, this gap has been one reason why the growing NGO and voluntary sector has played an increasingly significant political role. However there are few legal obligations to consult this sector in policy formulation and the quality of consultation that does occur has often been seen as unsatisfactory by the voluntary sector.

Local Government

If the central Northern Ireland government has gained in power and autonomy since 1972 then one of the clear losers in this period has been local authorities. Reorganisation of local government in the early 1970s, mainly on efficency grounds, proved to be a prelude to a reduction in the scope of matters over which local authorities had responsibility.[20] In particular control over public housing was entirely removed from local authorities after extensive complaints of religious discrimination in its

---

[18] See O'Leary, Elliot and Wilford, *The Northern Ireland Assembly 1982–6* (1988).

[19] For a discussion of the Ombudsman's powers see Hayes, "The Ombudsman" in *Lessons from Northern Ireland* (Hayes and O'Higgins ed. 1990), pp. 31–55.

[20] These reforms followed the 1970 Macrory Report, which argued that many of the 73 local authorities existing in Northern Ireland at the time were too small to generate the financial and organisational resources to carry out their functions. As a result the Local Government (Northern Ireland) Act 1972 provided for a rationalisation into 26 district councils and removed all responsibility for housing, health, education and social services from local authorities.

allocation.[21] Now local authorities have responsibility only for street cleaning, recreation and burial, or as it has often been put colloquially "drains, bins, graves and sports centres". Even these are now in danger as a requirement of compulsory competitive tendering (CCT) has been introduced with regard to a number of local authority services, despite almost universal political opposition within Northern Ireland to the idea of CCT.[22] However Northern Ireland was spared the reorganisation of local government finance that took place in the rest of the United Kingdom in the 1980s. In a reply to a Parliamentary Question in 1991 an NIO minister tellingly observed that Northern Ireland had not experienced the problems of accountability that led to reforms of local authority finance in Great Britain.[23] In addition to their executive functions, local authorities have the right to appoint representatives to Education Boards and have the right to be consulted about planning and housing developments within their boundaries. They also have a very limited capacity to support local economic development and to grant aid voluntary organisations concerned with economic and cultural development. The total annual budget for local authorities is now around £70 million, well below that of health, education and housing services. Even the Industrial Development Board receives comparable funding. Local authority employment has fallen to around 3 per cent of total public sector employment.

Unionist politicians, in particular, have decried the lack of powers given to local authorities and have argued that as they remain the only directly elected forum within Northern Ireland that restoring more powers to them would alleviate the "democratic defecit". Nationalists remain wary of the idea, fearing a return to Unionist domination and abuse of power. This is despite the fact that electoral reform and the reintroduction of proportional representation for local authority elections has significantly reduced the number of unionist dominated councils. Also if powers were to be returned to local authorities it is likely that the exercise of them would be subject to rather more exacting legal constraints in respect of

[21] However, since 1945 the provision of public sector housing was not the exclusive province of local authorities. The Northern Ireland Housing Trust was established in 1945 but even its efforts combined with those of local authorities fell well below comparable new house starts in Great Britain in the 1945–72 period. See, generally, Murie, *Housing Policy in Northern Ireland: A Review* (1992), pp. 3–10.

[22] For a discussion see Knox, "Compulsory Competitive Tendering in Northern Ireland Local Government" (1993) 19 *Local Government Studies* 208.

[23] See Barnett and Knox, "Accountability and Local Budgetary Policy: Unitary Principles" (1992) 20 *Policy and Politics* 265.

equal treatment than prevailed before 1972. Thus far the government has shown more sympathy with the nationalist case, arguing that the use of local authorities as a vehicle of defiance to the Anglo-Irish Agreement[24] and the open expressions of sectarianism which dominate Belfast and some other District Councils[25] suggests that many councillors are more interested in political posturing than in providing services to their constituents. Recently however, there have been some changes in Northern Ireland's Councils. A number have adopted "power sharing" schemes whereby the Chair or Deputy Chair may be rotated between unionists and nationalists (though Sinn Fein has generally been excluded from such agreements).[26] Also government, via the CCRU, has sought to encourage respect for the two traditions in local government by making money available for the development of community relations programmes by local councils.[27] All councils have now joined this scheme and government has on occasion given hints that more powers might be given to those councils which "behave responsibly".

Quangos

While local authorities have lost power since the early 1970s quangos[28] have been substantial gainers. The Northern Ireland government 1922–1972 had always resorted to quangos more extensively than was the

[24] Several local authorities refused to strike a rate in protest against the Agreement.

[25] The Unionist majority on Belfast Council has tended to nominate only unionists to statutory boards, nominations which have on occasions been rejected by the Secretary of State. A significant number of findings of religious discrimination in employment have also been made in local councils since the introduction of the 1989 Fair Employment Act.

[26] In 1993 11 District Councils, six with a Unionist majority and five with a Nationalist majority, had adopted some sort of power sharing arrangement. This normally involved the rotating of the position of chair or deputy chair of the council between Unionists and Nationalists. For a discussion see Bierne, *Local Government in Northern Ireland: Cooperation Across the Communal Divide* (1993) MSC Thesis, Queens University Belfast and Grant, *Local Government in Northern Ireland* (1995) LLM Thesis, Queen's University, Belfast.

[27] For a discussion of this programme see Knox and Hughes "Equality and Equity: An Emerging Government Policy in Northern Ireland" *University of Ulster Papers in Public Policy and Management*, No. 22 (1993).

[28] We refer to the term "quangos" loosely here to indicate bodies which are appointed or directly funded by central government but which are not in themselves aspects of government departments. Therefore we will not be discussing in any depth in this chapter the powers or performance of "Next Steps" agencies, which we see as essentially remaining a part of their sponsoring department. See further Livingstone and Morison, *An Audit of Democracy in Northern Ireland* (1995) pp. 13–16.

case in Great Britain, especially as regards the delivery of public services. (Indeed for much of its relatively recent history the whole of Ireland was effectively governed by a range of quangos and boards, often with very little local input.) Whereas the provision of public housing and health care were, until recently, a responsibility of local authorities in England, Scotland and Wales, the establishment in 1948 of the Northern Ireland Hospitals Trust (with responsibility for health care provision) and the Northern Ireland Housing Trust (to supplement the work of local authorities in providing public housing) in 1945 indicated a greater role for non elected bodies in Northern Ireland. In large part this was due to the fact that many of Northern Ireland's 73 local authorities lacked the financial or organisational resources to deliver services to national standards. In the 1970 review of local government a rationalisation of local government units and the transfer of more functions to appointed bodies was advocated for similar reasons.[29] However, it was the political context of allegations of discrimination by local authorities, notably in housing allocation[30] and local authority employment, which provided the impetus for significant change in 1972. The reforms of 1971–73 saw the establishment of the Northern Ireland Housing Executive (NIHE), of the four area Health Boards and of five area Education and Library Boards.[31] Policing, which was previously the responsibity of the Northern Ireland regional government and which comes within the competence of local authorities in Great Britain, was allocated to a quango, the Police Authority for Northern Ireland, by the Police Act (Northern Ireland) 1970. To organisational rationalisation the early 1970s added the idea that it was best to remove certain services from the controversies of party politics.

Government has continued to allocate service delivery to quangos. The creation of the Industrial Development Board (IDB) in 1982 is a further example. The IBD has the role of encouraging the economic development of the private sector and attracting inward investment, primarily through financial assistance and support. In 1971 the Local Enterprise Development Unit (LEDU) had been established as a company to provide similar support to the small firm sector in Northern Ireland. Service delivery

---

[29] *Review Body on Local Government in Northern Ireland* Cmnd. 546 (1969).
[30] The Cameron Commission found evidence of discrimination in six of 60 councils it investigated.
[31] These changes were the result of the Housing Executive Act (Northern Ireland) 1971, the Health and Personal Social Services (Northern Ireland) Order 1972 and the Education and Libraries (Northern Ireland) Order 1973.

quangos are among the largest employers in Northern Ireland and spend substantial proportions of the public budget.[32] Although the "Next Steps" initiative has been introduced slowly in Northern Ireland it is clear that in years to come at least some central government services will be moved into the executive agency and contracted out sphere, if not fully into the quango sphere.[33] The period since the imposition of direct rule has also witnessed the extension of regulatory quangos, of which the Fair Employment Commmission and the Equal Opportunities Commission for Northern Ireland are perhaps the best examples. Such agencies play an important role in the development of the micro-constitution which we have discussed in chapter three. Before 1972 Northern Ireland was largely devoid of advisory bodies.[34] These too have been a growth area, with the creation of bodies such as the Standing Advisory Commission on Human Rights or the Northern Ireland Economic Council in the 1970s.

The attractions of quangos for government in Northern Ireland are clear. Quangos distance government from some key areas of decision-making in society and hence reduce the threat of a legitimacy crisis in the state. On the other hand they are unlikely to become a site of alternative political power or political conflict, always a risk with local authorities. Most quangos in Northern Ireland remain largely dependent on their sponsoring government departments, in both law and practice. The legislation which establishes bodies such as the IDB or the NIHE makes it clear that they operate within paramaters set by the Department and that the Department may give them directions as to matters which the quango can and cannot deal with. Financial control is also total. Most quangos obtain all their income from a sponsoring department and although the NIHE, for example, is allowed to borrow money it may only do so with the approval of the Department of the Environment. Studies of the operation of quangos have also suggested that they have achieved little autonomy from the Departments to which they are answerable. Connolly, for example, suggests that almost every decision taken regarding education is refered to the Department of Education.[35] Harrison argues that the IDB

---

[32] In 1993–94, for example the Health Boards employed over 46,000 people and the Education Boards in excess of 16,000. Each had a budget in excess of £1000 million.

[33] Currently seven "Next Steps" Agencies have been established in Northern Ireland, including the Compensation Agency and the Social Security Agency. Imprisonment, which was agentised in Great Britain in 1993, was agentised in Northern Ireland in 1995.

[34] See Birrell and Murie, *Policy and Government in Northern Ireland: Lessons of Devolution* (1980), pp. 138–9.

[35] Connolly, *Central—Local Relations in Northern Ireland: A Report to the ESRC* (1983).

has seen its role as purely being one of executing rather than making policy[36] while Brett commented of the Housing Executive that it enjoyed only a limited degree of independence from the Department and that in the case of a conflict it can "always be brought to heel either by a formal declaration or (less obviously) by a twitch of the purse strings".[37] The formal powers to give directions have rarely been used, although rent increases were forced on the NIHE in the early 1980s and the Eastern Health Board was directed to accept a tender from outside cleaners in respect of one hospital in 1989. In general though, the impression given by Northern Ireland's quangos is of them working in harmony with government policy, much of which is determined in Whitehall. Indeed greater autonomy appears to have been achieved when quangos and their sponsoring departments together have sought to resist policy developments emanating from London. A good example of this was the way in which government spending on public housing remained high in Northern Ireland throughout the early and mid 1980s, a time when it was declining significantly in the rest of the United Kingdom. Indeed housing remained the government's main socio-economic priority in Northern Ireland until 1987, a prioritisation no doubt considerably assisted by the fact that special assistance from the European Communities was available in this area. One set of commentators has observed that the small and tight-knit nature of the housing policy network in Northern Ireland considerably assisted the development of effective resistance to a nationwide trend.[38] By 1987 this network appeared to have unravelled as public housing slipped from the government's agenda.

In a constitutional system which formally values accountability, but generally recognises accountability only to parliament or to the law, quangos are a constitutional oddity.[39] The legal framework within which they operate generally offers them too much discretion to make them accountable to the law in any meaningful way. On the other hand one of the main reasons for allocating functions to quangos is that the task is too

---

[36] Harrison "Industrial Development in Northern Ireland: The Industrial Development Board" in *Public Policy in Northern Ireland: Adoption or Adaption?* (Connolly and Loughlin eds, 1983) pp. 149–74.
[37] Brett, "Housing in Northern Ireland" (1982) *Housing Review* 75.
[38] Connolly and Knox, "Policy Differences within the United Kingdom: The Case of Housing Policy in Northern Ireland 1979–89" (1991) 69 *Public Administration* 303, 320.
[39] For a discussion of their legal status see Lewis "Regulating Non Government Bodies: Privatization, Accountability and the Public-Private Divide" in *The Changing Constitution* (Jowell and Oliver ed., 2nd ed. 1989).

large for central government, or requires special expertise, or (a reason less
often publicly expressed) where government would like to be relieved of
responsibility. Nevertheless it is unacceptable in a democracy that a body
should be able to spend significant amounts of public money without
being accountable to someone. Three basic approaches to this problem
appear to exist, each of which has a close relationship with a particular
view of how quangos arose and what they are supposed to do. The first
concerns itself with ensuring ministerial policy and financial control over
the activities of quangos. This view tends to see quangos merely as bodies
designed to implement government policy and seeks to fit quangos back
into the chain of ministerial responsibility for policy development and
implementation. The second is concerned with increasing the representative character of quangos. This view has arisen especially in critiques of
quangos as having taken over functions from elected local authorities. It
therefore seeks to bring quangos closer to that model of representative
politics. The third approach focuses on the decision-making processes of
the quangos themselves and stresses the need for transparency in these.
This view does not see quangos as some form of a substitute for central or
local government decision making. Instead it regards them as, in some
cases, an appropriate way of making public decisions which have grown
too big for local politics but which are also too detailed or complex to be
handled by the national political system. This view sees quangos as being
one way of responding to the developing "issue" politics of the late
twentieth century, to a politics based around issues that national political
parties and institutions find difficult to accomodate. To achieve this
however quangos must be open to as wide a range of views on these issues
as is availiable.

   All three notions of quango accountabilty can be seen in Northern
Ireland. The greatest emphasis, either because of the origins of most
quangos or because the political culture remains fixated on ministerial
responsibiity, has been on the first of the three approaches. We have
already seen that ministers are empowered to give directions to many
quangos. Most are also subject to parliamentary auditing procedure, as the
IDB's predecessor, the Northern Ireland Development Agency, found out
painfully in the 1970s.[40] However concerns about quango representativeness are also addressed. Some, such as the Education and Library Boards or

---

[40] In relation to the De Loren affair, see Cunningham, *British Government Policy in Ireland
1968–89* (1991), p. 128.

(until recently) the Health Boards, have reserved slots for local councillors to represent the local constituents. Others, such as the Industrial Development Board or the Northern Ireland Economic Council, are more expert focused, with their members appointed by the relevant Minister on the basis of their economic knowledge and influence. As regards all types of quangos, but especially those which aim to have a representative character there is evidence that government seeks a balance of the "two traditions" in Northern Ireland. Unionist controlled councils have tended to nominate only unionists as council representatives to bodies such as the Housing Council, Health Boards or Education and Library Boards. As a result ministers have tended to seek representatives of the nationalist tradition, or at least people identified with the centrist Alliance Party to serve as their nominees on such Boards. Such nominees are drawn from a register of people willing to serve on public bodies which the Northern Ireland Office maintains. It regularly seeks recommendations from a wide range of voluntary bodies. Also Article 6 of the Anglo-Irish Agreement of 1985 gives the Irish government a right to be consulted over nominations to a number of quangos which are seen as having particular political significance.[41] As elsewhere in the United Kingdom it is not unusual to find people who sit on more than one quango board. This apppears to be especially true of those nominated from the local council sector.

The third approach to quango accountability, that which stresses opportunities for extensive participation in the quango's decision-making, is the least well recognised. With the exception of the Education and Library Boards none of the major quangos, and few of the minor ones,[42] allow the public to attend their meetings or publish minutes. Most publish annual reports and accounts. Although some have formal duties to consult with particular bodies (the Housing Executive must consult with a advisory council made up of local councillors and the Health Boards with an advisory council made up of professionals) others do not. The Police Authority, for example, is not required to consult with anyone before it takes any policy decision. Nor have the courts been willing to widen the net of those required to be consulted. In the 1993 case of *Re Shearer and Another's Application*[43] the High Court found that a Health Board had no

[41] These are the Standing Advisory Commission on Human Rights, the Fair Employment Commission, the Equal Opportunities Commission, The Police Authority and the Independent Commission for Police Complaints.
[42] See Northern Ireland Council for Voluntary Action *Quango Anon Directory* (1994).
[43] [1993] 2 NIJB 12.

obligation to consult with any individual or group before it took the controversial decision to establish a pregnancy advisory clinic. Aside from the formal requirements, it does not seem that a strong tradition of informal consultation has grown up between quangos and interest groups. The Northern Ireland Council for Voluntary Action undertook a project to establish a quango directory listing the functions of quangos and the names of their members precisely because many community and voluntary groups were unaware of who to deal with. The same groups have often observed that they have much better relations with government departments.

If anything the trend seems to be even more in this direction, as is evidenced by the establishment of health and social services trusts in Northern Ireland. Such trusts are providers of health services, with the health boards being reduced to the role of purchasers. While the Health and Personal Social Services (NI) Order 1994, which established the framework for trusts, provided for a wide range of organisations to be consulted before any trust was established there are no such consultation obligations in respect of the operations of a trust once established. Unlike the Boards there is no requirement for representation by local councillors on the board of the trust. Instead, accountability is to be ensured through the mechanism of contract standards and audits of performance. In the contract culture which seems set to play an increasing role in public service delivery, notions of compliance with objective standards rather than community support is likely to be deemed the most significant yardstick of success.

In many ways quangos may be seen as a successful way of getting much of the business of government done in Northern Ireland. Services have continued to be delivered and the standard of services delivered in fields such as housing, education and health have demonstrably improved since 1972. Moreover those services appear to have been delivered in a more equitable way over the past 20 years, although disparities in treatment between the two major communites continue to exist.[44] Quangos charged specifically with the task of combatting discrimination appear to be having

---

[44] The Standing Advisory Commission on Human Rights found continuing disparities in areas such as employment, income, public housing and education. See, *Religious and Political Discrimination and Equality of Opportunity in Northern Ireland* Cm 1107 (1990), pp. 9–16.

an increasingly important impact.[45] Government is also probably much better informed and advised as regards its social policies than was the case in the days of the Stormont administration. Moreover, with the exception of quangos who have policing responsibilies and (to a lesser extent) those concerned with economic development, these bodies have largely escaped public debate and censure. Even the operation of the Child Support Agency in Northern Ireland came in for much less criticism than across the Irish Sea. However arguably these appearances of success have been bought at a price. That price has been the discouragement of any public debate on social and economic policy, the sort of debate that might have redirected energies in Northern Ireland. Removing the exercise of much of public power from the sphere of formal electoral politics and political institutions need not have led to its depoliticisation. Indeed we would argue that quangos could become sites of a quite different form of debate over the use of public power, but one better suited to the developing constitutional landscape. This is an issue we return to in our final chapter.

Policing and Security

As the most visible, and arguably most controversial, exercise of public power in Northern Ireland the formulation and execution of policing policy deserves separate consideration.

Perhaps the first observation worth making in relation to the policing sphere is the growth of an extraordinary range of legal powers which infringe individual liberties. The experience of Northern Ireland has clearly put paid to any idea that a combination of parliamentary sovereignty and respect for the rule of law safeguards individual civil rights in the United Kingdom. In the past 25 years in Northern Ireland people have been detained without trial,[46] jury trial has been suspended and widespread

---

[45] See Cooper, "Concrete Floors", *Fortnight* September 1994, p. 22, discussing how recent Fair Employment Commission studies show an increasing number of Catholics in professional and managerial positions. The proportion of job applicants who were Catholic is also rising. However the unemployment differential has remained largely resistant to change.
[46] Though this power has only been utilised in the period 1971–75. For a discussion see Spujt, "Internment and Detention Without Trial in Northern Ireland 1971–5" (1986) *Modern Law Review* 38. The power however remains on the statute books and can be activated by an order of the Secretary of State for Northern Ireland.

powers of search and arrest without warrant have been given to the police and military.[47] Throughout the United Kingdom the Prevention of Terrorism Acts (first passed in 1974 as a response to IRA activity in Britain) have given the police powers to detain those they reasonably suspect of involvement in terrorism for up to seven days and to detain people at ports for similar periods in order to carry out identity checks.[48] The Home Secretary may also stop people moving from one part of the United Kingdom to another without even the need for a court hearing. All these powers have been brought into law with parliamentary approval, though parliamentary debate on many of them has been fairly slight. Some measures, such as the broadcasting restrictions[49] or the curtailment of the right of silence[50] did not even require parliament to pass an act. Other measures, such as the use of lethal force by the security forces in Northern Ireland which has resulted in over 300 deaths since 1968, did not even require a new law. Not only has parliament and the executive proved willing to enact such draconian provisions but the courts have proved less than assiduous in their dedication to the cause of protecting individual rights when interpreting them. Far from offering the narrow reading of statutes which infringe individual liberty envisaged by many constitutional law scholars[51] the House of Lords, in particular, has endorsed a broad reading of emergency powers as best suited to capture Parliament's intentions.[52]

To notice the existence of these legal powers is not necessarily to say that the United Kingdom, or at least a particular part of it, has become a

---

[47] These powers, contained currently in the Northern Ireland (Emergency Provisions) Act 1991, allow the police or army to stop people and vehicles to ascertain a person's identity and movements (sections 23(1) and 26). They may also search a house without a warrant if they have reasonable suspicion that a suspected terrorist is there or that explosives, firearms, ammunition or transmitters will be found there (sections 16 and 19). Until 1987 this power, and that to arrest someone suspected of being a terrorist could be exercised on mere, rather than reasonable, suspicion.

[48] Under section 16(2) of the Prevention of Terrorism Act 1989.

[49] These prohibited television and radio stations from broadcasting directly the voices of members of a number of organisations including the IRA, the UDA, UVF and Sinn Fein. They were introduced by an order of the Home Secretary under clause 13 (4) of the BBC licence and section 4 (1) of the Broadcasting Act 1981 and were revoked on September 16, 1994.

[50] Introduced by the Criminal Evidence (Northern Ireland) Order 1988.

[51] See, for example, Allan "Legislative Supremacy and the Rule of Law: Democracy and Constitutionalism" (1985) 44 *Cambridge Law Journal* 111.

[52] For a summary see Livingstone, "The House of Lords and the Northern Ireland Conflict" (1994) 57 *Modern Law Review* 333.

tyranny. Successive governments have argued that such powers are necessary to deal with the threat posed to life, property and democracy posed by
terrorist activity relating to Northern Ireland. It is an argument that has
consistently enjoyed overwhelming support in the United Kingdom as a
whole and even within Northern Ireland has enjoyed the support of a
majority of people. It is also an argument which has largely prevailed on
the international plane. The European Commission and Court of Human
Rights have found for the government in more cases emanating from
Northern Ireland than they have found against.[53] Most prominently they
have consistently upheld the government's right to derogate from certain
articles of the Convention on the grounds that a situation of public
emergency exists in relation to Northern Ireland such that not all the
guarantees of the Convention can be given full effect to. Human rights
concerns in relation to Northern Ireland have featured only to a limited
extent in relation to United Nations machinery and even international
human rights NGOs have been fairly circumspect in their critique of the
situation in Northern Ireland. Nevertheless the European Court of
Human Rights has found the United Kingdom to have violated rights to
liberty and to protection from inhuman and degrading treatment in
Northern Ireland. The United Nations Committee Against Torture *has*
expressed concern about the treatment of suspects in police custody in
Northern Ireland.[54] International NGOs *have* raised questions as to
whether the right to life or to free expression are adequately guaranteed in
Northern Ireland. Whether these concerns are valid or not is perhaps an
issue for another time. The important constitutional point is that at least
international human rights discourse provides a set of standards and
mechanisms to induce serious reflection on the extent to which individual
rights may be curtailed to deal with a major threat to social stability. Few
such mechanisms exist in the constitution of the United Kingdom to mark
out consideration of fundamental rights from consideration of any other
social issue. The experience of Northern Ireland shows that where
pressure to curtail fundamental rights does arise they can be fairly swiftly
done away with.[55]

---

[53] This is discussed in greater detail in chapter six.
[54] CAT/C/SR.92.
[55] The best example perhaps being the right to silence, often seen as a fundamental aspect of
British criminal justice for over 300 years, which was curtailed after two-and-a-half hours
debate on the Criminal Evidence (Northern Ireland) Order 1988.

In addition to the creation of a formidable range of legal powers
Northern Ireland has also witnessed the deployment of the military and a
significant rise in the numbers of its police after 1969. The actions of the
police and military in that period in turn have raised issues of accountability and the adequacy of complaints mechanisms. Since the disposition
of the armed forces is a prerogative matter the initial decision to deploy the
army in Northern Ireland, after a request from the Inspector General of the
RUC, did not require the approval of Parliament,[56] nor did any subsequent decision to incease or reduce troop numbers. While the Prime
Minister did announce to Parliament the deployment of the SAS in South
Armagh, this seems to have been more for political reasons than out of any
sense of constitutional propriety. Decisions as to the strength of the police
force also come within the scope of executive discretion. When the army
was first introduced into Northern Ireland, the Downing Street Declaration, between Prime Ministers Wilson and Chichester-Clark, gave it
effective control over security policy. In 1976, after the report of a
Northern Ireland Office working group, a policy of police primacy was
introduced. Neither of these policy changes was the subject of any
Parliamentary debate.

On a day to day level, security policy in Northern Ireland is determined
by a Security Policy Committee composed of the Secretary of State, the
Chief Constable of the RUC and the General Officer Commanding
military forces. This meets weekly. The extent to which it fully informs
the Secretary of State as to the actions of the police and military agencies is
open to question. A recent account of such activity noted that when
intelligence information provides the military with an opportunity to
"intercept" suspected terrorists the Secretary of State will usually be told
that there is an opportunity to deal a significant blow to the terrorists. He
will normally then tell the officer in charge that they should do what they
think is right.[57] Such "interceptions" often resulted in the death of
suspected terrorists, some of whom turned out not to have been involved
in any paramilitary activity.

The Chief Constable is apppointed by and is accountable to the Police
Authority for Northern Ireland, at least as regards those matters which the
Chief Constable decides do not raise "operational" issues. The Police

---

[56] For a discussion see Greer "Military Intervention in Civil Disturbances: The Legal Basis
Reconsidered" [1983] *Public Law* 573.
[57] See Urban, *Big Boys Rules* (1992), p. 170.

Authority is Northern Ireland's most secretive quango. In response to the killing of two of its members by the IRA in the 1970s and death threats to others only the name of its chair is made public. The Authority may seek reports from the Chief Constable but cannot give him directions. Members of the Authority are appointed by the Secretary of State who is directed by the Police Act (Northern Ireland) 1970 to ensure that "as far as is practicable" its membership is "representative of the community in Northern Ireland". The Act also makes it clear that in selecting members for the Authority the Secretary of State should consult with what appear to him to be representative organisations and that certain bodies should be represented on the Authority, including the legal profession, trade unions, business, voluntary organisations concerned with the care of young people, local authorities, universities and the Northern Ireland Office. Achieving a representative character has been rendered difficult by the refusal of the SDLP, the main nationalist party, to nominate anyone to serve on the authority.[58] Disappointed by the apparent lack of influence of the Authority the Irish Congress of Trade Unions (ICTU) has also decided not to make nominations. It considered changing this policy in 1993 but decided not to after a meeting with Chief Constable Sir Hugh Annesley wherein he indicated that he would pay as much attention to a letter in the *Irish News* (the main nationalist morning newspaper in Northern Ireland) as he would to the Police Authority.[59]

The attitude that the ICTU reported the Chief Constable displaying to them reflects the high degree of autonomy from the Authority which the RUC appear to have developed under Annesley's predecessors Sir Kenneth Newman and Sir John Hermon. Some well publicised clashes between the Chief Constable and the Authority have occurred, notably in the wake of the Stalker/Sampson report when the Authority decided by one vote not to recommend disciplinary action against Hermon and two Assistant Chief Constables. While the secrecy within which the Authority operates makes it difficult to provide any true estimate of its influence, it appears that its input on such controversial issues of policing policy as the use of plastic bullets, the interrogation of suspects and the policing of marches or paramilitary funerals is limited. The Chief Constable has been able to define many of these matters as "operational" and outside the scope

---

[58] In September 1994 the SDLP removed the party whip from a councillor in Cookstown who accepted a nomination to the Authority. See *Irish Times* September 14, 1994.
[59] Quoted in *A Citizens Inquiry: The Opsahl Report* (1993) p. 417.

of the Authority's concern. Since the Secretary of State sets force numbers, may make regulations affecting the force, sits on the Security Policy Committee and ultimately has the power to dismiss the Chief Constable it is likely that the latter sees his relationship with the Secretary of State as being rather more important than that with the Police Authority. Indeed the Secretary of State may, on the request of the Chief Constable, veto the Police Authority's request for a report from the Chief Constable, though this power has not been used. At the beginning of 1994 the Police Authority found those powers it did have under attack as the Northern Ireland Office published proposals to restructure police accountability in Northern Ireland.[60]

Police officers, including Chief Constables, often like to assert that their real accountability is to the law. Where the law contains such broad powers to arrest, detain and search as exist in Northern Ireland, citizens may be forgiven for thinking that such accountability is rather minimal. Moreover, as has been discussed earlier, the willingness of the higher judiciary to give a broad reading to such powers has diminished further the impact that the law may have on controlling police action.[61] Concern over the limited effect that the law may have as regards rendering police activity accountable is stoked by the depressing saga of complaints against the police in Northern Ireland. In response to regular allegations of police mistreatment, notably in the late 1970s, the government developed progressively more extensive mechanisms for dealing with complaints against the police, culminating in the establishment of the Independent Commission for Police Complaints (ICPC) in 1987. The Commission goes some way towards meeting calls from civil rights groups and some

---

[60] These were published in the Northern Ireland office documents on *Policing the Community*, March 30, 1994.

[61] Commentators have generally taken a more favourable view of the decisions of the courts in Northern Ireland, see Dickson "Northern Ireland's Troubles and the Judges" in *Northern Ireland: Politics and the Constitution* (Hadfield ed., 1992) p. 130 and Hill and Lee "Without Fear or Favour? Judges and Human Rights in Northern Ireland: A Subjective Essay" in *Eighteenth Report of the Standing Advisory Commission on Human Rights* (1993) H.C. 739, Appendix B. However criticism of judicial performance in Northern Ireland has come in precisely those areas—such as admissibility of confessions, arrest powers and the use of lethal force by the security forces—where judges have the greatest opportunity to regulate police action. See, for example, Walsh, *The Use and Abuse of Emergency Legislation in Northern Ireland* (1983), pp. 46–53.

politicians for a fully independent system for the investigation of complaints by providing that a member of the ICPC (who are appointed by the Secretary of State on much the same basis as the Police Authority) will supervise the police officer investigating the complaint against another officer. However, in the six years of its existence so far the ICPC has yet to sustain a single complaint of assault against a police officer. This is despite the fact that the period covered includes 1991, when the UN Committee Against Torture was to express concern about the treatment of detainees in police custody in Northern Ireland and Amnesty International was to issue its first *Urgent Action* on Northern Ireland in relation to allegations of torture resulting from the mistreatment of a suspect in Castlereagh police station.

Perhaps the episode most damaging for notions that the police in Northern Ireland are accountable to the law was the Stalker affair. In the space of several weeks in late 1982 six people were shot dead by the RUC in three incidents in south Armagh. All were unarmed although five were acknowledged members of republican paramilitary organisations. Subsequently a number of police officers stood trial for murder in relation to these killings but were all acquitted. In the course of the trial however, it emerged that the officers involved, who came from RUC Special Branch's E4A unit, had been instructed to give false information by their superiors to the CID detectives investigating the killings. In response to public concern at these revelations an inquiry was instituted under Manchester Deputy Chief Constable John Stalker in May 1984. From the start Stalker seems to have interpreted his terms of inquiry as being rather wider than the investigation of why misleading stories were given to CID. By mid 1986 he had apparently come to the conclusion that several of the killings were unlawful and that there had been a conspiracy to cover this up. Stalker was due to return to Belfast to interview the Chief Constable and several of his most senior officers under caution when he was removed from the inquiry pending investigation of his links to Kevin Taylor, a Manchester businessman who was under investigation for (subsequently unproven) criminal offences. The inquiry was taken over by Cambridgeshire Chief Constable Colin Sampson who would eventually recommend that eight officers be charged with conspiracy to pervert the course of justice. In January 1988 then Attorney-General Sir Patrick Mayhew announced that these officers would not be prosecuted on the grounds of national security. References to national security have subsequently emerged again as public interest immunity certificates have been issued to prevent the coroner having access to Stalker's report during the inquests to the 1982 shootings. These inquests have yet to conclude.[62] The removal of Stalker on dubious grounds at such a vital point of his inquiry and the decision not to proceed with prosecutions on national security grounds cast grave doubts on the idea that the security forces in Northern Ireland were ultimately accountable to the law. While speculation persists as to the reasons why the full truth has never been allowed to come out, the episode is a clear example of how malleable constitutional principles have proved to be in the context of the conflict in Northern Ireland.

The constitutional accountability of the army is even less extensive than that of the police. Individual soldiers must act within their legal powers, while broader questions of policy and discretion can be examined only through the responsible minister. However, the efficacy of the law as a means of regulating military activity in Northern Ireland is no more clear than in regard to the police. Most cases of the use of lethal force have involved soldiers yet only two military personnel have ever been convicted of murder or manslaughter arising out of these killings and the acquittal rate runs at close to 90 per cent.[63] None of these convictions have involved members of special units such as the SAS which have been involved in some of the most controversial incidents.[64] A formal complaints procedure in respect of the army was established under the Emergency Provisions Act only in 1991. Ministerial accountability to Parliament is arguably even more of a charade than we have discussed elsewhere in this book given the existence of the perogative power to withdraw questions of the disposition of the armed forces from Parliamentary discussion.

A final element in the security forces deployed in Northern Ireland is the intelligence services. MI5 in particular has played an important role in providing information on which many operations by the police and army are based. Since 1993 it has also had overall responsibility for anti-terrorist operations in Great Britain. As with the rest of the United Kingdom even the existence of the security services was not officially acknowledged until the Security Services Act of 1989. The Act requires the head of MI5 in

---

[62] At the time of writing the coroner has abandoned these inquests after his challenge to the issuing of a public interest immunity certificate in respect of parts of the Stalker/Sampson report has been rejected by the Northern Irish courts. The Northern Ireland Secretary also issued a certificate in May 1995 to prevent Stalker testifying as to certain matters in a civil action brought by Taylor against the Greater Manchester Police.

[63] For details see *Broken Covenants: Violations of International Law in Northern Ireland* (1993), p. 342.

[64] For an overview see Urban, *Big Boys Rules* (1992) pp. 69–78.

Northern Ireland, the Director and Co-ordinator of Intelligence, to report to the Secretary of State. However, little is made known publicly as to the activities of the security services in what, especially since the end of the Cold War, has been one of their most important fields of operation. Indeed the government has consistently gone to great lengths to ensure that information does not leak out. The security services were involved in the surveillance operations which led up to the killings investigated by Stalker. Part of the government's evident desire for as little as possible to be known about those incidents may stem from a concern to prevent much being revealed as to exactly what the nature of that involvement was.

In addition to demonstrating the fragility of guarantees of individual rights in the United Kingdom constitution, the experience of policing policy in Northern Ireland exhibits a strong desire to remove such issues from any form of popular accountability. Perhaps due primarily to the controversial nature of the issue and the dependency of so much security force work on intelligence information, successive governments have been persuaded that it would be best not to expose too much of the activities of the police and army to public scrutiny. While government has been willing to permit some limited experiments in other policy fields, policing remains an area where government has been reluctant to examine structures in any great depth. This may be understandable. Ultimately if the lid is to be kept on Northern Ireland and progress to be made in other aspects of social policy, the government needs to be assured that it can deal with any social disorder that may result. Retaining the support of the police is vital to ensure this. The police, in turn, have developed a formidable ideology of autonomy and professionalism. Although challenged by claims of collusion with loyalist paramilitaries, claims which appear though to have greater foundation with regard to the actions of the military, the RUC has developed a self-image of professionalism and neutrality. So much so that during the leadership of Chief Constable Hermon especially, politicians and public representatives appeared to be regarded with disdain. Although this ideology may be an improvement over one which identified the police with the maintenance of unionist hegemony—a change which was clearly marked by the refusal of police officers to join the protest against the Anglo-Irish Agreement—it also has its drawbacks. The principle of the primacy of civilian politicians over the actions of the police may be undermined and efforts to produce a more acceptable police force (notably to Northern Irish catholics who currently comprise less than 5 per cent of the Force) may meet significant internal resistance. Yet if a police force is to be devised that can police effectively through public support rather than the strength of its intelligence and hardware it is exactly these challenges which will have to be faced.

Conclusions

Perhaps the most obvious, but also the most significant, fact about getting the business of government done in Northern Ireland is that the business of government has got done. Claims from various factions that Northern Ireland would be rendered ungovernable have proved to be untrue for all but very short periods. The institutions through which the business of government has been done have tended to fragment and technicise public power. They have generally been designed and have operated in a way that precludes citizen participation and public debate but appear to have avoided rigid policies and to have responded to local pressures in a pragmatic fashion. However, enabling the business of government to get done has not conferred legitimacy on the institutions of the state. Those institutions which are least open to public influence in the name of efficiency, such as the police, are arguably those with the greatest legitimacy problems. This may lead some to the conclusion that only a political settlement may produce legitimacy and that the type of developments we have described in this chapter are only a temporary phenomenon. However, while we agree that the search for a political development is a worthwhile, and indeed inevitable, endeavour we feel that it is important to recognise that progress can be made by isolating certain social and economic issues from general political bargaining.

The way forward for this strategy may be to further explore such issues and in particular to explore the democratisation of how these policy areas are administered. The greater role for the voluntary sector, which we discussed in chapter four, is a move in this direction. However, more would need to be done to enable people in Northern Ireland to have a say in decisions which affect them immediately, while the political discussions around a long term settlement continue. Indeed, we would argue that greater involvement with such decisions might well foster alliances around new issues and facilitate movement away from the zero sum game politics which have made agreement in Northern Ireland so difficult to achieve. A clearer legal framework which guaranteed rights to information and participation in decision-making might be part of this. So too might legally established civil and political rights which could protect a space for public discussion and debate. In this respect it is disappointing to see that the

Framework document, especially that aspect of it which focuses on the future government in Northern Ireland, concentrates almost exclusively on the institutional arrangements of a new assembly and has little to say about government below that level. It is also disappointing in so far as it offers little of substance with regard to the legal protection of individual or group rights. Yet if an adequate framework is not provided in domestic law increasingly people are looking beyond the boundaries of the United Kingdom. It is this which is the subject of our next chapter.

Chapter Six

The External Dimension

Introduction

Public lawyers have traditionally divided into those concerned with domestic law and those whose primary focus is international law. Sustained by the dualist tradition in United Kingdom law— that international law only becomes enforcable in domestic courts when "incorporated" into national law, normally by act of Parliament—there has been little reason for the two to meet. Domestic constitutional lawyers have always had some interest in the legal regulation of the conduct of foreign affairs but, as this has generally been seen as a preogative power, it is a fairly limited form of regulation and hence a fairly limited interest.[1] Accession to the European Community in 1972 and the gradual acceptance by the courts of the supremacy of Community law should have produced something of a breach in this wall.[2] However, as we have seen in chapter one, within the orthodoxy, supremacy can be attributed to the the European Communities Act and the separateness of international legal regulation preserved. European law remains a matter largely for the European law specialist and at most as an "add on" to the domestic constitution, though this surely ought to be changing in the light of the Maastricht treaty debates and the *Factortame* case.[3]

---

[1] For a discussion see, for example, Wade and Bradley, *Constitutional and Administrative Law* (11th ed. 1993), pp. 324–31.
[2] For a discussion of the supremacy of Community law see Weatherill and Beaumont, *E.C. Law* (1993) pp. 317–22.
[3] *Factortame Ltd v. Secretary of State for Transport* [1989] 2 ALL E.R. 692.

In other areas of law, such as environmental law, company law or media law a transnational context is increasingly being taken for granted. Acid rain and river pollution means that preventing pollution in one country may require action in another. Multi-national corporations mean that company and tax lawyers need always to have one eye on what their counterparts are doing in other jurisdictions if they are not to see their objectives frustrated. Since television and radio signals can cross frontiers, regulatory action which stays within one set of boundaries is likely to prove of limited effectiveness. We would argue that such a sensitivity to an international dimension should increasingly characterise public law as well, if it is not to lose touch totally with the changing reality. The influence of the European Union now goes well beyond setting some product quality standards and providing agricultural price support. European Union rules on state aids, public procurement and competition policy now significantly constrain government economic policy. Virtually the whole of equal pay law and much of contemporary labour law owes its origin to European directives. Areas such as the environment and immigration will increasingly come under European influence. Although formally Parliament may still do anything, in reality significant areas of public power are already now beyond its control.

The European Union is not alone in its influence. Since 1966 the European Convention on Human Rights has played an increasing role in defining the civil and political rights of people in the United Kingdom. Although the European Convention on Human Rights has not been incorporated into domestic law (despite increased political and senior judicial support[4]) the decisions of the Commission and Court have generally been reflected in changes in United Kingdom law.[5] Prisons policy, the treatment of the mentally ill and the regulation of the media have all been significantly affected by the succesful outcome of individual applications to Strasbourg. So too has security policy in Northern Ireland, though to what extent is a matter to which we will return. It is not without credence that the European Court of Human Rights has been refered to as

---

[4] Both Labour and the Liberal Democrat parties have now declared an intention to incorporate the Convention into United Kingdom law. Lord Lester's latest Bill to do so has received support in Parliament from several Law Lords.

[5] See, generally, Churchill and Young "Compliance with Judgements of the European Court of Human Rights and Decisions of the Committee of Ministers: The Experience of the United Kingdom" (1991) 61 *British Yearbook of International Law* 283.

"Britain's constitutional court".[6] In the next few years more legislative activity in the Council of Europe may also extend the scope of rights available to people in the United Kingdom.[7]

While the influence of the United Nations has been less marked, even as regards human rights, this is also changing. The United Kingdom, like many states, is now coming under increasingly regular scrutiny by a variety of committees of experts to which it must deliver country reports in respect of a range of treaty obligations.[8] As domestic human rights groups make greater use of these forums, these committees may be able to bring a well informed critique to bear on the United Kingdom's performance and hence increase pressure for the implementation of international standards. Outside the human rights area other UN institutions and mechanisms have a significant impact on the formulation of domestic policy in areas such as refugees and military deployment.

In addition to these formal influences enshrined in international law, we noticed in chapter two that the phenomena of "globalisation", especially in finance and communications, exercises an increasing influence on the choices open to domestic polities. We are clearly a long way from global government but we are also some way from the absolute power of parliament in fact and the idea that democracy is adequately served if Ministers are accountable to a directly elected House of Commons. Sovereignty is now attenuated and shared in a variety of ways. We do not argue for a retreat from this. The interconnections of the world economy and the advent of rapid international communication makes such developments inevitable. Instead we aim to map out the types of external influences that now exist and how they exercise this influence. We also consider how domestic, political and legal activity increasingly interacts with this international dimension. We argue that already there exists a prefiguring of a new set of political and legal relationships which would re-order what citizens expect from their state and how they set about influencing the exercise of power within that state. These developments raise new questions about accountability and representation that are considered in our conclusion.

---

[6] As described in *The Guardian* ,October 1, 1993.
[7] Further Protocols to the Convention may include one on the rights of people in detention and one on minority rights.
[8] Examples in the 1990–3 period include reports under the International Covenant on Civil and Political Rights, the Convention Against Torture and the Convention on the Elimination of Religious Discrimination.

Northern Ireland is a particularly apposite arena in which to raise such questions as it has been especially susceptible to external influences for a number of reasons. First it is a disputed territory, perhaps the only really disputed territory within the European Union, whose international legitimacy is in question.[9] Opponents of Northern Ireland's present constitutional position in particular have appealed to international opinion for support. In turn the United Kingdom government has had to spend time in international forums defending the legitimacy of its position and arguing that the present situation of Northern Ireland is in conformity with prevailing legal and political norms at the international level. Secondly a history of emigration has left a large number of people of Irish descent in many different parts of the world. At various times some of these people, notably in the United States, have prevailed upon their governments to take a particular policy stance with regard to developments in Northern Ireland. Thirdly the effects of the Northern Ireland conflict have been directly visited on other governments or inter-governmental organisations. Terrorism, especially of the Irish republican variety, has extended to attacks on British military bases and personnel in Belgium, Germany and the Netherlands. This in turn has prompted governments in these countries to take at least a security interest in the Northern Ireland problem. Issues of the extent to which international standards of human rights are being protected in Northern Ireland have arisen in both the United Nations and the Council of Europe human rights machinery.

Much more so than in the 1920s, the present phase of the Northern Ireland conflict has come to the attention of the international community. It has not been a major issue of international concern, unlike countries such as Lebanon or Somalia. The international community has refrained from direct military involvement and generally from direct political involvement. Nevertheless it has not been insulated from international influence and we would argue that such influence has operated in the way that the external constitution commonly operates in the modern United Kingdom. That is, it involves a range of entitites which operate not through direction but through the provision of incentives, setting norms and monitoring performance. Below we examine the different manifestations of that international interest and how they have affected the governance of Northern Ireland.

---

[9] For a discussion of this see Guelke, *Northern Ireland: The International Dimension* (1988), chap. 1.

The European Dimension

The European dimension consists of two aspects in particular, the European Union and the Council of Europe. The impact of the first has been primarily political and economic, that of the second primarily legal via the mechanism of the European Convention on Human Rights.

THE EUROPEAN UNION

When Northern Ireland, as part of the United Kingdom, joined the European Economic Community at the same time as the Republic of Ireland in 1973 there were great hopes of the impact that this might have on sectarian conflict within Northern Ireland. Differences between unionist and nationalist might become less significant once we were all Europeans. The border itself might lose any real importance in a Europe of free movement of goods, workers and capital. Though such sentiments were to be repeated in 1988 as Europe moved towards the completion of a single market and possible political union, the intervening 15 years had not borne out such prophecies. Instead, the border actually assumed greater economic significance as Ireland entered the ERM in 1979 and ended partity with sterling. In addition, opportunities to collect Monetary Compensation Amounts (MCA) each time agricultural produce or livestock was exported led to a lively trade in smuggling and deception along the Irish border.[10] On the political front elections for MEP's from Northern Ireland served only as an opportunity to rerun the constitutional issue and contributed to the strengthening of the fiercely anti-European Ian Paisley's claim to be leader of Northern Ireland's unionists (he has regularly topped the poll). Unionists actually complained over the decision to allocate Northern Ireland three MEP's (a slight over representation of its population) as they feared this would ensure a seat for a nationalist. Northern Ireland has, in fact, sent two unionists and one nationalist to the European Parliament at every election since 1979. Indeed the measure to which involvement in Europe has not contributed to the reducing of differences is shown by the fact that efforts to begin or continue political

---

[10] For a discussion of the way in which Monetary Compensation Amounts could be claimed, illegally, in respect of the same produce on both sides of the border see Aughey, Hainsworth and Trimble, *Northern Ireland in the European Community: An Economic and Political Analysis* (1989), p. 42.

talks always assume greater urgency just before the beginning of a European Parliament election campaign. The assumption everyone holds is that once such a campaign is under way all parties will be anxious to reassure the more sectarian wings of their supporters and will be in no position to continue negotiations. By adding another election at which differences can be stressed again, Europe has arguably done more to prevent the reconciliation of such differences !

However, as we have argued throughout this book it is a mistake to see public power as being shaped only by the decisions of politicians as crystallised into law. Just because Northern Irish politicians have generally sought to "domesticate" the European dimension, to utilise "Europe" as just another site for playing out the same constitutional debates, this does not mean that Europe has been without influence. Such influence has been exercised through political, financial and legal channels. Though we are careful not to overestimate this influence, nevertheless it has been another element in setting the parameters of government policy in Northern Ireland. In turn Brussels is increasingly becoming a site for those who seek to influence government policy in relation to Northern Ireland, something which raises new questions about accountability and representation.

The political influence has been intermittent. The Council of Ministers and the European Commission have rarely devoted much direct attention to Northern Ireland, one exception being the Council's discussion of a specific housing aid programme for Northern Ireland in 1983.[11] The European Parliament has shown spasmodic interest, much of it due to prompting by John Hume (the SDLP leader and MEP) or a number of MEP's from the Irish Republic. The Parliament has passed a number of resolutions, for example one calling for a ban on the use of plastic bullets and another critical of government handling of the 1981 Maze hunger strike, which have embarrassed the United Kingdom government. It has also commissioned a number of reports on economic and political conditions in Northern Ireland. One of these, drafted by a Danish MEP, Niels Haagerup, anticipated many of the provisions of the Anglo-Irish Agreement in that it advocated agreement among political parties in Northern

---

[11] This was done via the mechanism of an Urban Renewal Regulation, for a discussion see McGurnaghan, "Integrated Operations and Urban Renewal: The Belfast Experience 1981–5" (1986) 34 *Administration* 505.

Ireland in the context of greater co-operation between the British and Irish governments including joint responsibilities in a number of fields.

The Parliament's adoption of the Haagerup report in 1984, followed by its endorsement of the Anglo-Irish Agreement by 152 votes to 27 (with 11 abstentions) in December 1985, demonstrated a solidifying of European views about the best way forward in relation to Northern Ireland. This was clearly away from unionist domination and towards a greater role for the Irish government, at least in discussions over what an acceptable settlement was. In turn this emergence of a consensus view in the European Parliament made it increasingly difficult for the United Kingdom government to contemplate any other approach to Northern Ireland. As Guelke observes, the support of the European Parliament was one of the things which

"locked the two Governments into the [Anglo-Irish] Agreement through the embarassment they would suffer internationally if either repudiated what international opinion had endorsed with their encouragement".[12]

As the former Irish Taoiseach Garret Fitzgerald has observed, the very fact that involvement in Europe led to more regular contact between British and Irish ministers and officials made it more likely that the two governments would work more closely in relation to the issue of Northern Ireland.[13] Both the Downing Street Declaration and the Framework Document of February 1995 envisage further development of this Anglo-Irish co-operation within the European Union in relation to the affairs of Northern Ireland.[14]

The economic influence has been more consistent but has also been of a light character. Northern Ireland has constantly remained a favoured region for the allocation of Community Structural Funds. Even when the 1988 revision of the criteria for entitlement to the Funds found Northern Ireland with a higher GDP than would qualify it for Objective One status (as one of the most seriously disadvantaged regions) it was still included "in

---

[12] See Guelke, *op. cit.* n.9 at p. 162.
[13] See *Irish Times*, December 4, 1993.
[14] Paragraph 26 of the "New Framework for Agreement" envisages that the proposed North/South body should be able to consider any EU matter relevant to the competence of either administration. In the section on "East/West Structures", paragraph 49 envisages that the Standing Intergovernmental Conference "will also be a framework for consultation and co ordination between both Governments and the new North/South institutions where the wider role of the two Governments is particularly relevant to the work of those institutions, for example in a co-ordinated approach on EU issues."

view of the special circumstances prevailing there".[15] Presumably this is a reference to deprivation related to the political conflict. The EU has also contributed 15 million ECU to the International Fund for Ireland and in December 1994 pledged a further £246 million for Northern Ireland and six border counties in the Republic to assist the peace process.[16] However, despite the views of some in Northern Ireland the European Union is not a crock of gold and its funding is not essential to the maintenance of the economy. Community spending has never exceeded 8 per cent of total governmental expenditure[17] in Northern Ireland and in view of the fact that Northern Ireland contributes revenue to Europe via taxes collected in Northern Ireland, doubts have even been expressed as to whether Community membership has proved financially beneficial.[18]

Commentators who have examined the use and impact of the Structural Funds in Northern Ireland have argued that European money has never encouraged the government to take action.[19] Instead, projects which have been the recipients of European funds (especially of the European Regional Development Fund—ERDF) have generally been infrastructure or industrial development projects which the government has already planned or even begun. Such lack of interest in European opportunites has also been seen as being manifested in delay in becoming involved in other European special project initiatives.[20] However, the nature of such influence is difficult to judge. Government may have been reluctant to begin such infrastructure projects without at least a strong belief that European finance would be available to complete them. Projects which EU economic requirements might have endangered have also been allowed to continue unhindered. The Commission raised no objections on state aid

---

[15] For a discussion of this see Trimble, "The Impact of the European Community" in *The Northern Ireland Economy*, (Harris, Jefferson and Spencer ed. 1990), p. 435.
[16] See *Irish Times*, December 12, 1994, which reported that 80 per cent of this aid would go to Northern Ireland.
[17] See Aughey, Hainsworth and Trimble, *op. cit.*, n.10 at p. 107.
[18] See, for example, Northern Ireland Economic Council *European Community Structural Funds in Northern Ireland Report* No. 94, Belfast, 1992. The report concludes that Northern Ireland has been a net beneficiary.
[19] See *op. cit.*, n.18 at p. 26.
[20] See *op. cit.* n.18 at p. 59.

grounds in relation to financial assistance to shipbuilding or the aircraft industry.[21]

Politicians within Northern Ireland have often criticised the government for not doing enough in relation to obtaining Sructural Fund assistance, especially in comparison to the Republic of Ireland.[22] Yet despite this there has been relatively little use of the Community "from below", from local government or non-governmental groups, to secure financial assistance or political influence. Farmers have had a consistent interest in the Common Agricultural Policy, but this has largely been channeled through the National Farmers Union in Britain. Local authorities in Northern Ireland, perhaps because of their limited powers and functions, have generally displayed less interest in Europe than their equivalents in Great Britain. A much lower level of ERDF funded projects originate with local government in Northern Ireland than in the rest of the United Kingdom.[23] Trade Unions and the voluntary sector in Northern Ireland have also been slow to engage with Europe. The former, in common with most of the British left, maintained a largely anti-European stance until at least the mid 1980s. This position also seems to be changing however. Following criticism of the rather exclusive process by which Structural Fund applications have been drawn up, a wider consultation exercise took place in respect of the application for the 1994–9 tranche.[24] Some local authorities have shown increased interest in European iniatives, especially as regards tourism, and the voluntary sector is also displaying an increasing interest in European mechanisms.[25]

---

[21] The relevant shipbuilding directive set state aid at a ceiling of 28 per cent. Government assistance to shipbuilding in Northern Ireland did not exceed 26 per cent. See Aughey, Hainsworth and Trimble, *op. cit.*, n.10 at p. 44. However this may be changing as the Commission has recently raised concerns about ERDF money being used to support public concerns which are subsequently privatised, such as Belfast International Airport, which was privatised in July 1994. See *The Guardian*, November 11, 1994.

[22] For a comparison of Northern Ireland and the Republic of Ireland as regards the structural funds see Trimble, *op. cit.*, n.15 at p.419.

[23] See Hainsworth, "The European Community as a Policy Area in Northern Ireland" in *Northern Ireland: Adoption or Adaption*, (Connolly and Loughlin ed. 1990), at p.93.

[24] See chapter four for further discussion of this.

[25] For an example see Oliver, *Fortnight*, June 1992, p.22, on the work of the Northern Ireland Anti Poverty Network within the European Anti Poverty Network.

THE COUNCIL OF EUROPE AND THE EUROPEAN CONVENTION ON HUMAN RIGHTS

The European Union has also had a legal impact on Northern Ireland. Perhaps its most significant impact is via provisions on sex discrimination and equal pay. The Equal Opportunities Commission for Northern Ireland has utilised European law, notably through a reference to the European Court of Justice in a sex discrimination case against the RUC, to bring about significant changes in at least the legal position of women in employment in Northern Ireland.[26] The use of European law in such fashion is a classic example of the external constitution reaching not only into the public obligations of the state but into the private lives of its citizens. Another area where this has occurred and which has raised issues of government policy more specific to Northern Ireland, has been in the jurisprudence of the European Commission and Court of Human Rights. Since the United Kingdom signed the Convention in 1953 and especially since accepting the right of individual petition in 1966, it has earned the reputation of having had more adverse findings by the European Court of Human Rights than any other Member State. Although the Convention is not incorporated into domestic law and hence the legal obligation to implement it exists only on the international plane, the United Kingdom government has generally respected Strasbourg decisions. At least in letter if not always in spirit.[27]

Over 30 cases from Northern Ireland have reached at least the stage of a finding on admissibility since 1968. Most, but not all, of these have concerned challenges to aspects of the security policies adopted to deal with political violence in Northern Ireland. One case which did not, that of *Dudgeon v. United Kingdom*,[28] actually indicated in a particularly clear fashion the potential of the Convention to bring about change even in the teeth of political opposition. Dudgeon challenged the failure of the United Kingdom government to extend de-criminalisation of homosexuality to Northern Ireland.[29] Despite strong government arguments that in the light of opposition amongst both protestants and catholics in Northern Ireland

---

[26] See *Johnson v. Chief Constable RUC* [1986] E.C.R. 1651.
[27] See *op. cit.* n.5.
[28] (A/59): (1983) 5 E.H.R.R. 573.
[29] Dudgeon's application actually went a little further than this as he argued that not only should the decriminalisation of homosexuality be extended to Northern Ireland but also that the age of consent should be the same for homosexuals as for heterosexuals.

to the legalisation of homosexuality the Court should find the government's decision to be within its "margin of appreciation", Dudgeon's right to privacy was found to have been infringed. The Court indicated that as a "most intimate aspect of private life" was implicated only the most compelling grounds would justify government intervention.[30] As a result of the decision the law in Northern Ireland was brought into line with that in the rest of the United Kingdom. Although some protests continued there has not been significant public support for calls to repeal it.

Most of the cases, though, have concerned aspects of security policy. This is not entirely surprising. Given the limited parliamentary scrutiny of emergency legislation and the inability of courts to review such legislation within the British constitution, those who wish to challenge such emergency powers have seen Strasbourg as a more inviting outlet. They have also been encouraged to do so by a number of successes.

The most spectacular occured in 1978 when the European Court of Human Rights concluded that the interrogation of some of those detained in 1971 amounted to inhuman and degrading treatment.[31] The case had been brought by the Irish government and centred around five sensory deprivation techniques employed to gain information from detainees. The techniques had been approved by two judicial inquiries, even though the majority on one of them concluded that the techniques probably did violate Article 3 of the European Convention.[32] Neither the Commission nor the Court accepted such claims. While the government's argument that, in light of extensive terrorism in Northern Ireland, it was necessary to derogate from the Convention was upheld,[33] the Strasbourg institutions indicated that the non-derogable provisions of Article 3 had to be given

---

[30] In *Dudegon* itself such a compelling interest was discerned in the protection of young people and the Court therefore refused to equalise the age of consent for homosexuals and heterosexuals.

[31] See *Ireland v. United Kingdom*, (A/23): (1978) 2 E.H.R.R. 25. The Commission had concluded that the use of the five sensory deprivation techniques amounted to torture.

[32] See *Report of the inquiry into allegations against the security forces of physical brutality in Northern Ireland arising out of events on August 1971* Cmnd 4823, (1971) (the Compton report) and *Report of the Committee of Privy Counsellors appointed to consider authorised procedures for the interrogation of persons suspected of terrorism*, Cmnd 4901, (1971) (the Parker report). Lord Gardiner dissented from the findings of the latter report.

[33] Article 15 permits derogation "in time of war or public emergency ... to the extent strictly required by the exigencies of the situation, providing that such measures are not inconsistent with its other obligations under international law". The derogation was entered in respect of Article 5 (the right to liberty) as detention without trial had been reintroduced in 1971.

effect. Even claims that use of the five techniques had produced valuable information which helped to save lives was not enough to sway the Court from giving effect to this fundamental right.

Though the decision in the five techniques case was rendered in the very politically charged atmosphere of an inter-state application, challenges to security policy by individual applicants have also proved successful. In *Brogan v. United Kingdom*[34] four people arrested and held for a variety of periods under the Prevention of Terrorism Act prevailed in their claim that the Act violated the requirement in Article 5(3) of the Convention that anyone arrested be brought "promptly" before a judicial officer.[35] In response the government, which had revoked all its derogations in 1984, had once again to enter a derogation in 1989 in respect of the PTA's detention provisions. The 1990 decision of *Fox, Campbell and Hartley v. United Kingdom*[36] found the United Kingdom again to be in breach of Article 5, this time in respect of a provision in the Emergency Provisions Act which permitted arrest of someone on "suspicion of being a terrorist".[37] The European Court ruled that this violated the guarantee contained in Article 5(1)(c) that arrests could only take place if a person was "reasonably" suspected of having committed a criminal offence. This decision overruled a House of Lords judgement which upheld the lawfulness of the same provision.[38] The Lords however, could only consider the interpretation of the statute, not its compatability with a higher law. A third arrest case in which the applicant prevailed before the Commission but lost at the Court stage is *Margaret Murray v. United Kingdom*.[39] Therein the Commission held challenges based on Articles 5(1)(c) and 5(2) admissible in respect of an arrest by a soldier under section 14 of the Emergency Provisions Act 1978 following a house search. By a majority the Court concluded however, that the authorities did arrest the applicant on reasonable suspicion of having committed an offence, even though the domestic court did not make a finding on this issue. Another Murray was more succesful in the Commission decision of *John Murray v. United*

---

[34] (A/152B): (1989) 13 E.H.R.R. 439.
[35] The periods of detention varied between four days six hours and six days sixteen hours.
[36] (A/182): (1990) 13 E.H.R.R. 157.
[37] The arrest was based on section 11 of the Emergency Provisions (Northern Ireland) Act 1978.
[38] See *McKee v. Chief Constable for Northern Ireland* [1985] 1 All E.R. 1.
[39] Case No. 143210/88, Decision of the Commission February 17, 1993, Decision of the Court October 28, 1994.

Kingdom.[40] Therein a majority of the Commission found that drawing inferences from a defendant's silence in a police station, coupled with the denial of access to a solicitor for 48 hours under emergency powers, amounted to a breach of the right to fair trial. This again was a case where a challenge to the law in question had failed before the House of Lords.[41]

The majority of applications from Northern Ireland have, however, proved unsuccesful. A large number of prisoners' applications in respect of failure to transfer them back from England to Northern Ireland have been ruled inadmissible.[42] A number of challenges to the use of lethal force by the military have failed to get beyond the admissibilty stage,[43] though recently the Commission has ruled admissible an Article 2 application in respect of the shooting of three unarmed IRA members by soldiers in Gibraltar in 1989.[44] The 1980 prison protest (a forerunner to the 1981 hunger strike) also produced a case that the Commission was eventually to rule "manifestly ill founded". This was *McFeeley v. United Kingdom*[45] which raised a number of claims relating to strip searching, regular disciplinary punishments, the prisoners' living conditions and their claim for political status. While rejecting the prisoners case the Commission did issue a warning to the government that

"the Commission expresses its concern at the inflexible approach of the state authorities which has been concerned more to punish offenders against prison discipline than to explore ways of resolving such a serious deadlock."[46]

These words were to acquire greater poignancy a year later when 10 prisoners starved themselves to death. The most recent setback for European challenges to security policy occured in *Brannigan and McBride v. United Kingdom*.[47] In *Brannigan* the applicants challenged the justifiability of the derogation entered after the *Brogan* case. While the Commission ruled

---

[40] Application No. 18731/91, Decision of the Commission June 27, 1994.

[41] See *Murray v. Director of Public Prosecutions* (1993) 97 Cr. App. R. 151.

[42] See, for example, *Kavanagh v. United Kingdom*, Application No. 19085/91, Decision of the Commission December 9, 1992.

[43] See *Stewart v. United Kingdom* (1985) 7 E.H.R.R. 453, *Kelly v. United Kingdom* Case Number 15579/90, Decision of the Commission January 13, 1993.

[44] See *McCann, Farrell and Savage v. United Kingdom*, Application No. 18984/91, Decision of the Commission March 4, 1994.

[45] (1981) 3 E.H.R.R. 161.

[46] *ibid* at p. 201.

[47] (A/258-B): (1994) 17 E.H.R.R. 539.

the application admissible, both it and the Court were to conclude that the government prevailed on each of the limbs of the Article 15 test. These were that a state of emergency existed (a point not challenged by the applicants) and that the decision not to bring someone arrested on reasonable suspicion of terrorism before a judge for up to seven days was a measure "strictly required by the exigencies of the situation".

In general therefore Strasbourg has upheld the legitimacy of the security policies pursued by the United Kingdom government in Northern Ireland. Given that the United Kingdom is a democratic state faced by a more prolonged and intense terrorist campaign than that faced by states such as France, Italy or Germany (or even probably Spain) this may not be totally surprising. As that campaign is also totally opposed by the Republic of Ireland, which generally endorses the security measures adopted by the United Kingdom, for the Commission or Court to go against such a European consensus would be unlikely. The Commission's conclusion in *McFeeley*, that a right to recognition as political prisoners could not be founded on Article 9 and that intolerable conditions were primarily the fault of the prisoners indicated that the Strasbourg institutions would not interpret the conflict from the perspective of many Irish Republicans. However, the concern expressed at government inflexibility in dealing with prison protests also showed that the European Convention organs would not give carte blanche to policy adopted in Westminster and Whitehall.[48] Decisions such as *Ireland v. United Kingdom*, *Brogan* and *Fox, Campbell and Hartley* demonstrate that the Commission and Court will place limits on the security policies that the government decides to adopt. In its way even the *Brannigan* case, although the government prevailed in it, upholds this trend. In *Brogan* the Court refused to let the government succeed with its claim that prevailing conditions in Northern Ireland justified a limitation of rights if not their formal derogation. In *Brannigan* the government, having now derogated, still had to establish the validity of that derogation. It did so, but acknowledging that a state of emergency exists creates an obligation to bring it to an end, to recognise that such a situation is temporary. This is in marked contrast to the way emergency powers in relation to Northern Ireland have been treated over the past 20 years within the Westminster system.

---

[48] The Commission also became involved in the second hunger strike after an application had been filed by Bobby Sands' sister. When Sands refused to proceed with the application the Commission's involvement came to an end.

It is also noteworthy that decisions such as *Fox, Campbell and Hartley* and *John Murray* overturned decisions of the House of Lords while *Brogan* raised an issue that was hardly justiciable in United Kingdom courts. They thus forced the government to explain policies in relation to fundamental norms of human rights in a way that is largely unavailable in the Westminster system. In contrast to the autonomy which we have observed security policy makers and the security forces themselves normally enjoy in Northern Ireland, the Convention has provided a vehicle whereby citizens can seek to make them accountable, if not to the populus, then at least to certain well accepted principles.

Many people in Northern Ireland may not see it that way. They may argue that the government has won most of the cases taken to Strasbourg. Even where it has lost they may suggest that this was only after the policy had already been changed—the five techniques had been renounced by early 1972 and the EPA had already been altered before the *Fox, Campbell and Hartley* or *Margaret Murray* cases were heard. They might suggest that even the most clear rebukes for the government have not brought real change. Allegations of police mistreatment in Castlereagh Holding Centre were already on the increase when the *Ireland v. United Kingdom* court reported[49] and after *Brogan* the government simply derogated and kept the same powers in place. This however, is to miss the way in which we claim public power is being reshaped. The Convention has contributed to this by setting the parameters within which government acts in Northern Ireland. No senior figure is now likely to express the indifference to Article 3's absolute prohibition on torture that Lord Parker demonstrated in 1972.[50] The government has largely sought to keep its policy within the confines of the Convention and more draconian security policies, notably internment, may well have been ruled out because of potential European problems. This is despite the fact that they might have proved very popular on political and even security grounds. The influence of the Convention on the framing of policy again indicates that it is no longer true that parliament can do what it wants, even when it may want to do it. The ability of individual applicants to use the Convention to challenge government policy also demonstrates that the number of ways avenues available for citizens to influence that policy is widening beyond political parties.

---

[49] These were to lead to an inquiry by Judge Bennett, *Report of the Committee of Inquiry into Police Interrogation Procedures in Northern Ireland*, Cmnd 7947 (1979) which called for the strengthening of safeguards against ill treatment.
[50] See *op. cit.* n.32.

Defects in the Convention system, notably its limitations in dealing with primarily factual disputes and the delay involved in getting a decision from Strasbourg, means it may not have proved all that some people have hoped. Its influence, though, has been substantial. If a Bill of Rights is to form part of a political settlement in Northern Ireland then many believe that the Convention could be a starting point, though its anti-discrimination provision would need strengthening to deal with Northern Ireland's divisions.[51]

The United Nations

In contrast to some other significant conflicts around the world the United Nations has had a very minimal role in relation to Northern Ireland. Calls for the withdrawal of British troops and their replacement by a UN peacekeeping force, while popular with some on the British left, have received little discussion within the UN itself. Given the number of serious conflicts on its agenda, the UN has seemed happy to regard Northern Ireland as a European problem and has left Europeans to deal with it. Again the approach of the Irish government has been vital. After making some attempts in 1969 to have the Northern Ireland issue discussed in the Security Council and the General Assembly (efforts effectively rebuffed by the United Kingdom) the Irish government has seemed content not to raise issues relating to Northern Ireland in this forum. With the British government treating the issue as an internal question and the Irish government not seriously challenging this notion, it is unlikely that any other government would make Northern Ireland an issue within the United Nations.

Whereas the Security Council and General Assembly are highly politicised bodies, where the intervention of a Member State is essential to produce any sort of development, the United Nations human rights machinery does allow for greater input by interest groups. In recent years this machinery has come to devote more attention to Northern Ireland, prodded by both domestic and international human rights agencies such as

---

[51] Article 14 of the Convention only prohibits discrimination in the exercise of the rights guaranteed by the Convention. A more general prohibition on discriminatory action by government is probably needed in Northern Ireland and is already prefigured by developments discussed in chapters four and five.

Amnesty International, Human Rights Watch and the Lawyers Committee for Human Rights.[52] Northern Ireland has come to play an increasingly prominent role in the scrutiny by expert committees of a variety of reports submitted by the United Kingdom government under treaties such as the International Covenant on Civil and Political Rights, the Convention on Torture and the Convention on the Elimination of Racial Discrimination. Such committees have often been sharply critical of the United Kingdom in relation to matters such as the treatment of suspects in police stations in Northern Ireland and threats to defence lawyers.[53] Since the non-exhaustion of domestic remedies rule does not apply to such reporting mechanisms (unlike litigation before the European Court of Human Rights) these committee hearings may be better able to elicit facts and patterns of official behaviour or policy implementation than the European human rights mechanisms.

Domestic NGOs at least would argue that criticism by the UN has had an impact on what happens in Northern Ireland, for example, that complaints of ill treatment by suspects in Castlereagh police station decreased sharply after the Committee Against Torture hearings in November 1991.[54] As with the European experience using the UN human rights mechanism has appeared to offer interest groups within Northern Ireland a more effective way of influencing government policy than is available within the domestic structure. It is a process therefore which is only likely to continue.

The American Dimension

With a large population of Irish descent, many of who left Ireland to escape famine or persecution, the United States of America has always had an interest in developments in Ireland. Irish Fenians in the mid nineteenth century attempted to extend their campaign against the British to North America by invading Canada. Eamon de Valera raised money and support

---

[52] See, for example, Amnesty International *Killings by the Security Forces and Supergrass Trials* (1988); Helsinki Watch, *Human Rights in Northern Ireland* (1991); Lawyers Committee for Human Rights, *Human Rights and Legal Defense in Northern Ireland* (1993).
[53] In relation to treatment of suspects see the views of Rapporteur Burns during the hearing of the United Kingdom Report to the Committee Against Torture, CAT/C/SR.91 at p. 5, Geneva 1991 and in relation to threats to defence lawyers those of Sub Commissioner Palley, Geneva 1992.
[54] See Committee on the Administration of Justice *Annual Report* (1992) at p. 2.

in the United States for the Irish Republican cause in the 1918–20 period. In the most recent phase of violent conflict the Provisional IRA has also raised money and obtained arms from supporters in the United States, though on a less extensive scale than is popularly believed.[55] Yet Britain is also perhaps America's closest friend, a relationship strengthened by the two world wars. As a result American government policy in respect of British action in Ireland (until 1922) and Northern Ireland thereafter has been fairly restrained. However, the importance of the United States is clear. Both British and Irish politicians spend considerable amounts of time in trying to influence United States policy in relation to Northern Ireland, probably more than they spend trying to influence the policy of any European state, or indeed the European Union. Also, lobbying by non-governmental groups from both within and without the United States in relation to Northern Ireland has produced the adoption of policies at various levels of American government that have had significant impact on the exercise of public power in Northern Ireland.

The Federal government and the United States State Department in particular have pursued a cautious course in relation to Northern Ireland. Although several Presidential candidates, have indicated an interest in pursuing a more activist line this has rarely translated into deeds once the Irish-American vote has been secured. President Clinton has perhaps gone furthest in this regard, eventually honouring in 1994 a campaign pledge in 1992 to appoint a special envoy for Northern Ireland and agreeing to sponsor a conference on investment in Northern Ireland in the spring of 1995. Presidential support has been warmest for actions that have the backing of both British and Irish governments. Thus President Reagan strongly endorsed the Anglo-Irish Agreement and encouraged the appropriation of money for the creation of the Ireland Fund. The development of a peace iniative by the Irish and British governments in late 1993 was also strongly encouraged by the United States State Department. The decision by the Clinton White House to grant Sinn Fein leader Gerry Adams a visa to visit the United States in early 1994 has been seen as an important breakthrough on the way to the peace process. Since then different levels of the United States government have met many of the players in Northern Ireland's political discussions. One other area in which American governments have shown some willingness to intervene in

[55] See J. Holland, *The American Connection: US Guns, Money and Influence in Northern Ireland* (1987).

Northern Ireland has been in connection with allegations of human rights abuses. In 1979 the State Department suspended arms sales to the RUC in response to lobbying within the United States arising from allegations of police mistreatment of suspects in Castlereagh. President Clinton also expressed concern about allegations of human rights violations in his first meeting with John Major.

For the Federal Government (especially under Republican administrations) however, Northern Ireland remains a very minor issue and one which is clearly at the mercy of broader geopolitical questions. Despite concerns about possible human rights violations in Northern Ireland the Reagan administration pushed through a supplementary extradition treaty between the United States and the United Kingdom in 1986 which made it easier to extradite those charged or convicted of IRA related activities. The administration's strong stand on the treaty stemmed as much from its desire to convey a clear anti-terrorist message and to reward the British government for the use of airfields for an attack on Libya, as from views on what was most appropriate for Northern Ireland. In Congress such geopolitical concerns have a little less sway and some of those Congressmen with an Irish-American background or a strong Irish-American constituency have shown a consistent interest in the issue of Northern Ireland. Guelke credits the "Four Horsemen" (leading Democrat Senators Edward Kennedy and Patrick Moynihan, Speaker of the House Tip O'Neill and Governor Hugh Carey of New York) with prodding Secretary of State Humphrey Atkins into a political initiative in 1979, via support from President Carter.[56] The Four Horsemen and the group with which they are associated, the Friends of Ireland, have in turn been regularly prodded by SDLP leader John Hume—a further example of a politician in Northern Ireland bypassing the Westminster system to exert more effective pressure on the government for change within Northern Ireland. Congress has also held hearings on allegations of human rights violations. An ad hoc committee hearing on allegations of a "shoot to kill" policy by the security forces which took place in Washington in the autumn of 1991 being a good example.

Yet perhaps the most significant impact on the shaping of public decision-making within Northern Ireland has come at the level of state and local government. This has been the McBride Principles campaign, which began in late 1984. The Principles called upon employers in

---

[56] See Guelke, *op. cit.* n. 9 at pp. 140–2.

Northern Ireland to take a number of positive steps to end discrimination and ensure greater representation of catholics in the workforce. The Principles were signed by a number of people prominent in Northern Ireland and the Republic, including Sean MacBride (a former Minister for External Affairs in Dublin) and Inez McCormack (a leading trade unionist in Belfast). Within the United States the Irish National Caucus (a strongly pro-nationalist interest group) in particular lobbied individual American companies which did business in Northern Ireland to adopt the principles. It also sought to have city councils and state legislatures adopt the Principles and refuse to invest public money in companies which refused to sign or operate the Principles. The campaign proved very succesful with legislatures in significant states such as Massachusetts, New York and New Jersey adopting legislation requiring compliance with the Principles.[57] This was in the face of stiff opposition from the British government which flew many politicans and other public figures from Northern Ireland to the United States to lobby against the adoption of the Principles. The government argued that the Principles were illegal under the prevailing fair employment law in Northern Ireland (a matter of some doubt and one on which a New York judge found otherwise) and that adopting them would only hurt investment and increase deprivation in Northern Ireland. The latter was a powerful argument with which even nationalist politicians in Northern Ireland and the Irish government had some sympathy. Nevertheless the campaign continued to gather momentum, fuelled by a number of studies in the mid to late 1980s showing that there had been little movement in rectifying religious imbalance in the workplace. Though the point is still denied by ministers and officials in the United Kingdom, it is clear that seeking to dilute the impact of the MacBride campaign was one of the main factors responsible for new legislation on fair employment in 1989.

Unlike the European Union, the Council of Europe or the United Nations, the United States has no formal, legal right to produce legislation or decisions which have an impact on the exercise of public power in Northern Ireland. Nevertheless it is clear that pressure from the United States, from a variety of different levels of its polity, can have an important impact on government decision-making in relation to Northern Ireland.

---

[57] By the end of 1994 20 state legislatures had passed legislation endorsing MacBride and more than 30 cities had passed resolutions or ordinances on the topic. See Bierne, "Negative Action", *Fortnight*, June 1994, p. 24.

This is despite the fact that Northern Ireland is not high on the list of American foreign policy concerns. In a world in which communications are ever more rapid, politicians and interest groups in Northern Ireland have noticed this development and have sought to court political and media decision-makers in the United States. In turn the United Kingdom government has also engaged in a persuasion exercise in Washington. The sight of British, Irish and Northern Irish politicans of all political affiliations travelling to the United States in the immediate wake of the ceasefires of 1994 showed widespread acceptance of the idea that American influence was an important factor in Northern Irish politics. Even where it does not take a legal form the external dimension of domestic policy-making is clearly a factor that is here to stay.

The Irish Dimension

The external influence which has the most regular and intense interest in developments in Northern Ireland is, of course, the Republic of Ireland. With the Anglo-Irish Agreement of 1985 this interest was formalised in a way, which unionist politicians constantly point out, is quite unique to the constitution of the United Kingdom. No agreement exists whereby a foreign government is given a formal right to make proposals regarding legislation or policy in respect of England, Scotland or Wales. The Agreement thus recognises the internationally disputed character of Northern Ireland, the way in which it is special within the United Kingdom, while asserting in Article 1 of the Agreement that the constitutional status quo of Northern Ireland will remain unchanged unless a contrary view is expressed by a majority of people within Northern Ireland. The Agreement establishes an Intergovernmental Conference within which the two governments can discuss issues of political concern, security and related matters, legal matters and the promotion of cross-border co-operation,[58] with respect primarily to Northern Ireland though developments in Ireland or Great Britain may also be considered. Under the Agreement the Irish government may make representations and put forward proposals for legislation and policy developments in Northern Ireland, at least where no devolved government exists in Northern Ireland with responsibility for such matters. The Irish government can also put

---

[58] See Article 2(a) of the Agreement.

forward views as to the composition of public bodies within Northern Ireland whose members are appointed by the Secretary of State.

As Article 4 of the Agreement states the Intergovernmental Conference is to be a framework within which each government will work together for " the accomodation of the rights and identities of the two traditions which exist in Northern Ireland". The Agreement is thus in itself a recognition of the shift in government policy we have discussed elsewhere in this text, towards the recognition and reinforcing of two identities in Northern Ireland. It is less clear however, that the operation of the Agreement itself has operated to produce this. Although the goverment did repeal legislation which privileged displays of the Union Jack, as opposed to the Irish Tricolour, in relation to public order law further entrenchments of equal respect, such as allowing street names in Irish or funding Irish language schools, have been slow in comming. Considera-tion of mixed courts, the harmonisation of the criminal law of the North and South and special measures to attract catholics into the RUC, all of which are referred to in the Agreement, have also failed to materialise. At the level of producing institutional or policy changes within Northern Ireland then it seems that the Agreement may have had a limited sig-nificance.[59] Both governments have instead tended to use the Intergovernmental Conference either to raise individual cases or to pursue ways forward as regards the "big" question of the constitutional status and structure of Northern Ireland. The Downing Street Declaration of December 1993 and the Framework Document of 1995 have carried forward the latter process and given additional recognition to the claim of the Irish government to have a say in the affairs of Northern Ireland. The Framework Document commits both governments to work together with political parties in Northern Ireland "to achieve a comprehensive accom-modation" (paragraph 13). It also indicates an intent to maintain a standing Intergovernmental Conference which will "provide a continuing institu-tional expression for the Irish Government's recognised concern and role in relation to Northern Ireland . . . [and] . . . will be the principal instru-ment for the intensification of the co-operation and partnership between both Governments". Thus it envisages that until any new political institu-tions in Northern Ireland are in place the Irish government will continue to have a consultative role with respect to developments in Northern

---

[59] See also K. Boyle and T. Hadden, *The Anglo Irish Agreement* (1989), pp. 72–5.

Ireland. Even after such institutions are established the Irish government will retain a role with respect to matters remaining within the competence of the Secretary of State. This is likely to include issues of law and order for some time to come. The character of Irish involvement raises interesting questions for public lawyers. Previously citizen challenges to aspects of Anglo-Irish policy have been confined to the respective jurisdictions (although, since Ireland treats all those born in the island of Ireland as Irish citizens, people from Northern Ireland have been able to raise constitutional questions in the Irish courts).[60] Whether joint bodies should have special or overlapping jurisdiction is something that remains to be worked out. Certainly at the moment there is no formal way for anyone other than representatives of both governments to have any formal input into the workings of the Agreement, though informal contact with ministers and officials may lead to issues being raised.

Conclusion

External influences have always played some role in shaping domestic law and policy. Since the dawn of the democratic age governments have faced a need to deal with external pressures posed by military threats and trade rivalries. However, since the Second World War the nature of that external influence has changed in two ways. First there has been a growth in formal intergovernmental organisations and mechanisms. The United Nations, the Council of Europe, the European Union and GATT are only the most prominent examples of formal co-operation at the international level. Each of these organisations have been created by treaties which have often had direct implications for national law and policy. The organisations themselves have been able to expand that influence through directives and judgements arising from the original treaty obligations. In the case of the European Union the capacity to grant financial assistance provides a further instrument to influence developments within Member States.

---

[60] See *McGimpsey v. Ireland* [1990] 1 I.R. 110.

The second change is that these external influences have become more accessible to individuals and interest groups within Member States. No longer does a state automatically represent all its citizens on the international plane. Rather, one can now find people seeking to invoke and extend the influence of international institutions against their own governments. This use of an external influence by sections of the polity within a state seems normally to take one of three forms. The first is seeking to influence how the state deals with the international mechanism in question, and thereby alter domestic priorities, such as consultation regarding E.C. Structural Fund applications. The second is seeking to invoke the international mechanism directly against the domestic government to reshape its actions—as with the use of international human rights committees or courts. Finally, the third seeks to utilise the international mechanism to bypass the domestic government and produce a redistribution of public power and reources—as with seeking grants from the Ireland Fund or direct financial assistance to local authorities from the EU.

The external dimension is thus changing in character and is assuming increasing importance. Practice however, has run ahead of theory. Discussion has been polarised over whether the influence of the European Community or United Nations human rights mechanisms is "good" or "bad". Clearly such influences are here to stay and the debate should now be about what role such intervention should play and how far it should extend. The predominant vision, notably in E.C. market regulation or UN human rights provisions, is of producing universal rights and obligations for people in all Member States. This is stressed either because it is seen as realising a universal ideal (as with human rights norms) or because it is the best means to achieving an end which all may be agreed upon (as with the single market of the EU). In Northern Ireland this has certainly been one way in which the internal dimension has been utilised, especially as regards the use of international human rights law to seek to fill a vacuum left by the lack of adequate protection of rights in domestic law. However the experience of Northern Ireland suggests a second role for the external dimension. This is to offer a different avenue for those who seem to be shut out of influence in the domestic polity. Those who feel they have little chance of altering domestic political decision-making may appeal to international standards and institutions in the hope that their case will receive a sympathetic hearing. Nationalists in Northern Ireland are an obvious example of this, and the SDLP proposal in the 1992 constitutional talks for a European Community appointed commissioner to be one of an executive committee of six to run Northern Ireland[61], clearly demonstrates a view that an external influence might be more likely to protect minority interests. However, even Northern Ireland as a whole plays this sort of game within the European Community, where all Northern Irish politicians and interest groups seek extra finance to compensate for their minority position within the United Kingdom.

As with other ways in which we have observed public power being reshaped there are dangers as well as opportunities with these developments. The greatest danger is that those who seek to use external influences to alter national law or policy may find themselves sucked into an even less accountable and ultimately less accessible structure. Clearly there is a need to review the way in which bodies such as the European Commission and the United Nations are accountable to those in whose name they exercise power and to explore to what extent such institutions can be democratised. The concept of European Citizenship, which some have begun to explore,[62] may provide one part of the way forward in this area. However it is important that such democratisation does not simply amount to an increased role for political parties as opposed to national governments. One of the encouraging ways in which the European Union, in particular, has developed recently is in a greater openness to the emerging politics of interest groups, civic associations and local identities. It is around such forms of association, where the possibilities of co-operation across national boundaries are greater, that structures to encourage greater participation might be built. However, the failure to make much progress with the idea of Europe of the Regions, announced in the Maastricht Treaty, suggests that resistance remains to any formal recognition of representation in policy-making that is not at a nation state level. Northern Ireland is one region that might benefit from a change of approach.

---

[61] The others were to be: three directly elected from Northern Ireland and one each appointed by the British and Irish governments.
[62] See, for example, Meehan, *Citizenship and the European Community* (1993).

Chapter Seven

Northern Ireland and the English Problem

Introduction

In the earlier section of this book we were unenthusiastic about joining in the debate on constitutional reform that is presently undergoing one of its perennial revivals. This is not, of course, because we are satisfied with arrangements as they are or even because we are hostile to many of the ideas put forward. Indeed, we believe strongly in the idea of constitutionalism. Institutions and processes should be structured with safeguards that protect against arbitrary government or simple majoritarianism. People should be involved as closely as is convenient with decisions and actions that affect them and retain the ability to call to account politically and financially those who exercise power on their behalf or spend their money. However, we argue that in many important ways the suggestions for reform do not completely address this agenda. It is certainly true that parliament and the mechanisms of representation and accountability there are in need of review. Government does exercise significant prerogative powers without adequate checks and civil liberties might be more secure from potentially authoritarian government if they were written down and policed by a special court. However, this agenda does not account for all the areas in need of change. It does not even cover what are now the major problems.

We have argued that power has moved away from the traditional sites of central government. Any process that is based ultimately on simply reinforcing the institutional controls on big government and, in particular, on reviving the role of parliament, is no longer addressing the major issues of constitutionalism. Power has moved away from central government and the remit of parliament to external and european sites. Many international and transnational bodies appear uncertain of their future role but, at the same time, the European Union, the ECHR and other bodies are increasingly defining the lives of people in the United Kingdom. It seems that now there are a whole range of centres of authority or sovereignty as in medieval times when church, king and baron exerted competing and overlapping influence. Simultaneously, power has leached downwards towards a new and more vital civil society which not only often acts as a counter to the organising power of central government but can not any longer really be contained within the traditional frameworks. As we have seen, in some areas government has sought to delegate what was the exercise of public functions to semi-state or wholly privatised bodies. In others, the effective withdrawal of the state from the delivery of public services has led to an expansion of the role of voluntary associations or private corporations. In these circumstances the boundary between public and private power becomes blurred, facing traditional notions of public law with particularly difficult problems. The actions of many "private" bodies may have "public" consequences. They may engage identities, organised along gender or ethnic lines for example, which are poorly expressed in established representative politics and its institutions. As Amitai Etizoni points out, "men, women, and children are members of many communities—families; neighbourhoods; innumerable social, religious, ethnic, workplace, and professional associations; and the body politic itself."[1] The investment plans of a multinational corporation, the decision of a pharmaceutical company not to engage in AIDS research or of a charity not to provide housing for the young homeless may engage some of those identities more than the decisions of government or political parties. Yet the state is often implicated in such decisions through its powers to purchase, subsidise, grant aid or regulate. The tasks of public power are changing. Government is increasingly about steering rather than rowing; it is about guiding social forces rather than powering them. Public law too must change. It is now less about organising and holding back the supposedly mighty power of the state on the behalf of the individual. Public law needs less to consider how to restrain government from intervention than to consider what values and normative standards might influence how and when intervention occurs.

---

[1] *The Spirit of Community: Rights, Responsibilities, and the Communitarian Agenda* (1993) at p. 253.

Even that power that does remain more closely within government is subject to change and development. Government now operates at a distance and responsibility is relinquished or avoided. Government is increasingly a regulator rather than a provider or even organiser. There are now a whole range of quangos, regulators and agencies, rather than government in the traditional sense, standing between people and the rather skewed version of market that exists to deliver many of the basic utilities and services. Even within government itself the influence of market is brought to bear through the new public management structures and relationships. Ideas of citizen's charters and a variety of performance indicators are increasingly the tools that must be used to create and control a new relationship between state and individuals. Any concept of constitutionalism that still sees itself focused exclusively on the institutions of central and local government will increasingly miss the opportunity to exert control on public power as it is actually exercised.

Of course these changes are not complete. What we are describing is a tendency within the mainstream rather than an accomplished fact. However, these changes are significant and they are accelerating. Existing constitutionalism, even in a reforming guise, is already in difficulty trying to accommodate the most obvious developments within its parameters. The struggle to acclimate European law and the effort to stretch the concept of ministerial responsibility to the new government structures provide only two examples of the difficulties that will soon overwhelm the whole project of orthodox constitutionalism. A re-think of the scope and nature of the British version of constitutionalism is required: a degree of even radical reform to the main institutions is not enough.

We argue that the experience of the British version of constitutionalism in Northern Ireland is instructive. There one can observe the endgame of Westminsterism in a crisis that is similar although more spectacular and advanced than in the rest of the United Kingdom. It is there too, primarily in looking at how the business of government is actually carried on, that it is possible to discern signs of a nascent form of constitutionalism that may enrich and invigorate the mainstream. In this chapter we will draw together the threads of the new constitutionalism in Northern Ireland and begin to set out how it might be translated into a wider context. We look first at how Northern Ireland prefigures developments in Great Britain. Then we sketch out, primarily by outlining the new range of levels at which law must now operate, what might make up the seeds of an alternative and more effective way of reshaping public power within the United Kingdom.

Northern Ireland Prefiguring Great Britain

Northern Ireland is the same as other parts of the United Kingdom and yet different. It is part of the United Kingdom but not unequivocally like the rest. Those visiting Northern Ireland often see this clearly. Belfast shares much in common with other northern Victorian cities and, while there is much that is familiar, it can seem somehow oddly different, like seeing a London bus in Nairobi or a British bobby in Bermuda. Some aspects, such as armed police or street names in Irish, obviously set the place apart. At the same time a whole range of British institutions from the BBC to Marks and Spencer's are to be found in Northern Ireland and often, particularly with government offshoots, they are more marked than in mainland Britain because regional policies establish headquarters notwithstanding a relatively smaller population. This sense of being different and yet the same extends to the institutions of government in Northern Ireland. The courts and legal system are broadly similar but yet there are important discrepancies. The substantive law is often the same but may vary slightly in detail or in format. The civil service mimic much of what happens in Great Britain but yet operate within a special context with a particular local structure. The monarchy is taken very seriously but is often the focus for stronger feelings on wider issues. The issues facing government and people are the same but yet there is always a sense that they may be overtaken by the conflict that is endemic in such a strongly divided society.

Most significantly the constitutionalism in Northern Ireland shares this same-but-different quality. The Northern Ireland constitutional debate is generally framed in terms of all the traditional stuff of Westminsterism: borders and sovereignty, the effectiveness of big government and the checks upon it, and, most of all, how to fit political parties into structures of rule. Of course the actual circumstances of Northern Ireland fit very uneasily into this paradigm. It clearly is not working in practice. However, as we noted above,[2] most of those constitutional writers who give any attention at all to the Northern Ireland problem generally persist in seeing it as simply an aberration from the mainstream. For them, direct rule is a temporary stop-gap and a version of Westminsterism remains the solution. The only issue is how far it needs to be mutated—for example, by protections for minorities or structures for cross community

---

[2] See above pp. 111–115.

involvement—in order to accommodate the veneer of special circumstances that cover a polity that is essentially similar to that in Great Britain.
We argue instead that Northern Ireland is very far removed from Westminsterism. But so too is Great Britain. In fact the two jurisdictions share
many features in common and often these can be seen in more advanced
form in Northern Ireland.

So how exactly does Northern Ireland prefigure Great Britain? Some
people see Northern Ireland simply as a caricature of a dependent state:
relying on external funding, external ideas and external initiatives.[3] There
is something in this view but it does miss out on much of interest. There
are many ways, some obvious and some more subtle, in which what is
happening in Northern Ireland mirrors more general trends in the rest of
the United Kingdom and foreshadows possibilities there. There is the
sense in which Northern Ireland has been used as a testbed for a number of
innovations ranging from anti-terrorist law and modifications to the
criminal justice system to punitive debt legislation and changes to local
government. Beyond this, however, there are a range of more interesting
features which foreshadow more significant trends. These relate essentially
to the sort of society in Northern Ireland, the extent and nature of
government and the relationship between the two that has been worked
out in the difficult circumstances of having to get the business of government done when the survival and legitimacy of the state was under very
severe threat. Many of the sort of changes in state and society in Great
Britain that we outlined in chapter two are, often for different reasons,
more advanced in the context of Northern Ireland.

First and most obviously there is a crisis of legitimacy within the
Westminster approach, which is present in both Great Britain and Northern Ireland, but has manifested itself most spectacularly in Northern
Ireland with 25 years of armed conflict and an uncertain future as a highly
politicised and polarised society struggles over the details of rule. The
result of this conflict is presently a system of direct rule from the parliament
at Westminster and an executive headed by minsters drawn from there but
with no direct democratic nexus with the people of Northern Ireland.
While the formal democratic deficit is most striking in Northern Ireland it
is not different in kind to that in Great Britain, where all the reformers,
charterists and auditors of democracy complain of a remote parliament

---

[3] See for example, Collins and McCann, *Irish Politics Today* (1989) at p. 97.

going through the empty rituals of representation and accountability for a disempowered people. Future prospects for each part of the United Kingdom are not dissimilar either. Discussion of the constitutional future of Northern Ireland is corralled into a peace process that needs to reconcile the irreconcilable and then turn this into a grand level structure.[4] Meanwhile in Great Britain, nineteenth century style constitutional reforms to parliament and the electoral process are expected to bring control and accountability to a post-modern constitutional condition. In both Northern Ireland and Great Britain real politics and governance— that relating to how power and resources are actually distributed and used—carries on at levels that are largely untouched by both mainstream constitutionalism and any reforming tendency. In Northern Ireland, as we have argued, the necessity of having to get the business of government done has meant that new structures, techniques and strategies have been more apparent and developed than in Great Britain. There the façade of parliament as representing a homogeneous people, and all the rest of the crumbling edifice of Westminsterism, can hide for longer both the reality of power moving out and away, and the need to do something about this.

Since the necessary abandonment of the straightforward Westminster solution of devolution in line with the 1920 scheme, the process of developing new techniques and structures to get the business of government done in Northern Ireland has been uneven and often contradictory. As we noted in chapter four, a variety of strategies, ranging from the straightforward application of "British Standards" to a more subtle "security, economic support and community relations" approach have been tried, abandoned and developed as particular exigencies and pressures seemed to require. What cannot be denied is that there is often "more" government in Northern Ireland and always government of a qualitatively *different* kind to that of traditional Westminsterism. If we use public spending as an index of government activity it can be clearly seen that the welfare budget (not to mention the security expenditure) indicates a highly interventionist government. That does not simply mean however that Northern Ireland has remained an oasis of the Keynesian welfare state while market forces raged elsewhere. The nature of government activity has been more subtle and complex.

---

[4] See above pp. 103–111.

As we have discussed in earlier chapters, there has been a movement to depoliticise a whole range of basic issues such a housing, education, industrial investment and the provision of basic social goods. Within the context of Northern Ireland such matters have invariably appeared as constitutional issues going right to the very heart of the state and its legitimacy. By ceding these to quangos and voluntary agencies, government can to some extent bypass the constitutional and legitimacy issues and at least get the business of government done. (There is a cost in terms of a democratic deficit in relation to the formal processes but the machinery is always described as "temporary".) The task of government can thus be depoliticised and rendered possible in particular moments of crisis. It is this objective (even more than the economic and political goals that are occasioning similar structures in Great Britain) that has led to Northern Ireland having a highly developed and sophisticated quango and voluntary sector. This is a structure of government at a distance. The exigencies of the situation have produced a de-politicised form of governance that is similar to, yet more advanced than, that in Great Britain—although there it arises in different circumstances.

And yet there is more. In the Northern Ireland context the possibility has remained open to re-politicise government— although now on safer and officially sanctioned lines. Here the "two traditions" approach which we critically reviewed earlier comes into play. Generally this seeks to endorse as legitimate a catholic, nationalist identity as well as a protestant, unionist identity and thus leave as illegitimate (and ideally marginalised) a less easily managed republican or loyalist identity. As we noted, this approach exists not only at the high constitutional level of the Anglo-Irish Agreement and the Downing Street Declaration but also at the basic community level where funding is provided for educational programmes and voluntary groups who advance this agenda (and sometimes withheld from those that do not). The uniquely important position afforded to the quangos and voluntaries as emanations of the state, but not subject to the same legitimacy problems, has produced the possibility that government could use them by staffing, feeding and funding them in line with policies advancing the two communities analysis and solution. This removal of politics from government, and its reintroduction along officially sanctioned lines through quango representation and state sponsored community groups, is reinforced by a series of other strategies that also reinforce the idea of there being two legitimate identities deserving protection in public space and a broadly equal or at least fairer access to social goods. Thus there is legislation proscribing certain organisations, controlling the expression of opinion in public places and creating an offence of incitement to religious hatred.[5] There is the law and machinery designed to monitor and police employment practices to ensure an equal access to work opportunities.[6] Above all this there is the constitutional legislation which places limits on the exercise of power by any devolved administration that might eventually be created.[7] The examples of a deployment of a two-traditions approach within a wider context combine with their use at the grassroots to produce a potentially interesting direction in the use of public power.

All of this is part of a developing rather than developed tendency. We are not yet arguing that there is in Northern Ireland a wholly coherent, new form of constitutional regulation which operates with a range of partners beyond the moribund structures of the central state by deploying values and categories in a complex process which augments the use of traditional legal mechanisms with techniques of structuring and funding or by setting standards and sustaining identities. Such a picture of social partnership does not accord with the most obvious reality of a democratic deficit and a largely authoritarian state. It would also underestimate the extent to which such changes have been influenced by pressure from elements within civil society. What we are suggesting though, is that the seeds of such a new constitutionalism are present. Northern Ireland has been forced to recognise, in order to survive, that the old assumptions of Westminsterism do not hold. In place of the myths of Westminsterism that we discussed in chapter one and chapter three there is a breakdown of formal institutional level politics, including a significant reduction in the role of local authorities, a growth of government at a distance through quangos and community groups and a forcible recognition that society is not homogeneous but racked by conflict between a number of groupings. There has also been an appreciation of the international and transnational quality of many aspects of political and social life within any modern polity. While central government may still be involved to a considerable extent in propping up the whole state, it has developed a steering role in addition to its traditional rowing one. Now it is involved in facilitating,

---

[5] See Northern Ireland (Emergency Provisions) Act 1991 s. 28 and The Public Order (Northern Ireland) Order 1987.

[6] See above p. 140-3.

[7] The anti-discrimination provisions are presently contained in Part Three of the Northern Ireland Constitution Act 1973.

empowering, funding, regulating as well as simply delivering big government and law. Values and principles have become much more of a focus in the absence of the structures of government which normally preoccupy constitutional lawyers.[8] Now an important part of government's role is to create, or at least reinforce, a range of identities and provide for these identities protected space and opportunities to share equally in social goods. Beyond guaranteeing fair employment standards and a sphere of protection, the state offers these groups some limited access to the institutions of government at a distance. This produces a sort of corporatism where, instead of guilds or employers and employee organisations being given a privileged status in government, it is representatives from the "two traditions" who are brought into government in a limited (and, at present, largely legitimising) way. In the absence of a genuine pluralism, where groups exist meaningfully and separately, and can organise their own representation in government without intervention from the state, this seems an important development, although presently its democratic potential is largely undeveloped. Standing above this new level of government activity there is also an appreciation of the transnational context of political life and increasing involvement with brokering international interests and concerns.

All of this is new and potentially instructive in the context of Great Britain. Certain aspects of the experience in Northern Ireland are suggestive of a new form of exercising public power that could translate to the rest of the United Kingdom. In Great Britain there has not yet been any recognition of a somewhat different process bringing similar results. However the accelerating breakdown of any coherence within traditional constitutionalism may soon require a new understanding and the Northern Ireland experience stands as a model. As we noticed throughout the first two chapters of this book, the constitutional landscape in Great Britain is changing as dramatically as the thinking about the constitution is standing still. While the state has always been a problematic issue in Northern Ireland it is increasingly appearing so in Great Britain too. The British state now appears as simultaneously too small and too big as international codes and supranational structures appear alongside global

---

[8] It is perhaps significant that the debate over a Bill of Rights in Northern Ireland is largely over with almost every shade of political opinion modestly in favour of such a development—with the exception of the present Conservative British government. The short shrift given in the Framework document to the idea of a comprehensive bill of rights disappointed many.

problems and, concurrently, issues become too specific and local for the
national institutions. Indeed, as we have argued, it is increasingly difficult
to think of the people in the United Kingdom as a homogeneous
population of British citizens (or subjects) who are effectively represented
in domestic institutions. The international tendency to vote along ethnic
rather than class lines is highly developed in Northern Ireland but it is
occurring in Great Britain too, with whole sections of the polity, particularly in the celtic fringes, preparing to peel away altogether. Beyond even
such expressions of nationalism there is now a wide diversity of people
mobilised around a range of local, national and international issues who are
largely escaping the categories of major political parties with their agendas
for running the national state. In Northern Ireland, as noted in chapter six,
there has been a realisation that social, financial and, indeed, constitutional
issues cannot be dealt with in sovereign isolation. While the Westminster
approach that still dominates most constitutional thinking about Northern
Ireland remains hostile to aspects of this, it is increasingly accepted
elsewhere, in the actual practice of government, that an international
dimension provides a necessary site for development.[9] If such a conjecture
can be approached in Northern Ireland it would seem to be something that
constitutionalists in the rest of the United Kingdom could reasonably
aspire to fairly soon.

The mechanisms of governance in Britain too are increasingly to be
found beyond the traditional sites. We have already noted how central
government has, of course, relinquished much of its welfare state role and
throughout Great Britain there is less of a role for local government.
Quangos and committees, charities and voluntary organisations and a
variety of partnerships between private and public take over roles that
were once in the public sphere. Central government influence is achieved
not by running and funding everything but by setting standards, goals and
performance indicators. For example, in education Local Education
Authorities remain, but increasingly they are required to test and teach in
line with national standards, and developments, such as league tables
introduced in the name of consumer choice and control, distort and

---

[9] It is perhaps revealing that the Ulster Unionist Party, which must use the word "sovereignty" even more frequently and routinely in its political rhetoric than even the
Euro-sceptics in the Conservative Party, has recommended incorporation of the ECHR and
the adoption of both the Council of Europe convention on national minorities and the
Organisation for Security and Co-operation in Europe's standards on communities and
minorities. See *A Blueprint for Change* (1994).

diminish the autonomy of local bodies and individual schools. This sort of exercise of power is occurring all over the constitution in all the interstices of public and, increasingly, private life. In Great Britain much of this change was, at least initially, economically driven. In contrast the process in Northern Ireland was necessitated originally and mainly by a more fundamental need to simply maintain the functions of the state. Despite the different origins of the processes much of their effect has been similar. Of course, in Northern Ireland the facade of Westminsterism has not been available to hide the significant shifts of power that have occurred (although there is always the reassurance that any aberration is temporary only). Without such cover to offer a degree of legitimacy a little more attention has been paid to shoring up the mechanisms by quasi-democratic measures and steering their operation in line with more general principles. Thus it is that the ground rules for government are already set in terms of principles of non-discrimination in policy-making as well as employment that can be enforced by law. Law making involves the circulation of draft orders to all interested parties (although without guarantee that any representations received will be considered). Beyond this there have been efforts to ensure that the boards of quangos are staffed by a range of worthies reflecting what is perceived to be the two official traditions. Of course much more could and should be done in terms of openness, responsiveness, redress and the dispersal of power. However, the circumstances in Northern Ireland where such bodies are the only significant institutions of power has perhaps forced a great recognition of these issues than in Great Britain. Of course these developments have not necessarily led to a feeling in Northern Ireland that a more (post) modernist democracy is already in place. But they have produced a greater openness to new possibilities of constitutional change, change which could galvanise the structures that presently are occupied on a more informal and ad hoc basis.

Reviving Constitutionalism

We argue that a similar, although more coherent and sustained, process could and should happen in Great Britain—only at an earlier stage. The impact of the globalising state and new forms of civil society should be accommodated within new structures, mechanisms and controls. The various mechanisms of government at a distance need to be addressed. However, a new constitutionalism in Great Britain would be about not just recognising that the sites of power have moved but engaging with the questions about how to control power as it is now exercised there. Northern Ireland provides some indications, not only of what might be done but of what might be avoided.[10] For example, while the idea of protecting and sustaining identity and guaranteeing equal access to social goods through enforceable rights is a powerful one in the context of the new civil society in Great Britain, it requires a richer and more complex idea of identity and citizenship than that provided within the rather narrow compass of the two official identities in Northern Ireland. Simple discrimination law and related ideas of balance (between religious or even gender groups) that can be offset by simplistic ideas of quotas provides an impoverished interpretation of the range of communities that people belong to. Similarly, the idea of bypassing the moribund electoral institutions and ensuring representation by appointment to quangos in the areas where power is actually being deployed has attractions for Great Britain too but, like the utilisation of the voluntary sector to do the work of government, it has obvious dangers in that the traditional mechanisms for checking power, feeble though they might be, are bypassed.

Of course, the reality is that the sites of power have already moved and what any new constitutionalism must be about is not simply challenging this but also producing principles and mechanisms that follow public power to its new sites. There is a need to face the new agenda on its own terms. The mechanisms must be detailed and appropriate to all the different levels where power is now exercised, from the international and transnational to the nitty-gritty of contract management and performance indicators in public service contracts. It is only in the detail of the whole range of arenas in which power is now exercised that basic ideals of constitutionalism can be rediscovered in the forms most effective and

---

[10] Beyond the useful, if flawed, example of Northern Ireland there are developments elsewhere in the world which should be drawn upon. There is the experience of a revolution in public management in New Zealand. See Wistrich, "Restructuring Government New Zealand Style" (1992) 70 *Public Administration* 119 and Greer, *Transforming Central Government* (1994) Chap. 8. See also above p. 77–83. There is the Swedish example of securing a version of traditional accountability for new forms of executive agencies. See, for example, Burkitt and Whyman, "Public Sector Reform in Sweden: Competition or Participation", (1994) 65 *The Political Quarterly* 275. There is also the new thinking on public management in the United States which, although somewhat over-hyped, does at least have the advantage of potentially following the issues right down into the detail of how power is used. See Osborne and Gaebler, *Reinventing Government* (1992). See also the discussion of this in a British context offered in "Reinventing Government: A Symposium" in (1994) 72 *Public Administration* 263–289 and in (1994) 65 *Political Quarterly* 242–274.

appropriate for their new application. Thus ideas about measuring social value and guaranteeing it in the delivery of services through legal and other measures of redress are important. So too are notions about transparency and about distributing power rather than concentrating it and equality of outcome and equal treatment.[11] These values now apply to private as well as public areas and while traditional ideas of participation and accountability to elected forums remain of importance they are certainly no longer to be seen as the sole key to enlarging the space, freedom and autonomy of individuals within society.

Despite the fact that the agenda has so clearly changed, much of the academic writing is still centred around the idea of returning all power to local government or a reformed Westminster. However, this no longer accords with the views of most people outside the academy or think-tank. They are aware that something has changed in the exercise of public power, particularly since the beginning of the 1980s. Privatisation, the work of agencies such as the Child Support Agency, contracting out, changes in the organisation of health and education services, the rise of the quango and the growing influence of the European Union have all been extensively covered in the media and have directly affected the lives of many people. Yet while the architects of many of these changes have claimed that their aim is to make the exercise of public power more responsive to the needs and desires of citizens this is not how many perceive it. Instead there appears to be widespread concern that the changes of the last few years have transferred power away from central and local governments of limited accountability to even more remote and secretive bodies. Moreover the speed and apparent ease with which central government has achieved this has exposed the weakness of existing constitutional checks on government action which lacks widespread consensus or support.

While we share much of the popular unease about the perceived failure of public accountability we cannot join with those who argue that the appropriate response is to return all power to Westminster and to local government, even to a Westminster reformed along the lines advocated by some of the reformers we have discussed in chapter two. However, this does not mean either that we endorse the polar opposite of such a

---

[11] Some of these ideas as they apply to newly privatised industries have been briefly sketched out in Morison, "Privatisation and the New Politics of Control", *Revue Europeenne De Droit Public/ European Review of Public Law* Special Number 1994, pp. 117–127.

response— the privatisation of all aspects of the state—as the appropriate response to this changed context. As we observed in chapter two this appears to be the preferred approach to institutional reconstruction of Conservative governments in Britain since the mid-1980s and it is an approach whose merits and modes of operation has not perhaps received the attention from constitutional lawyers that it should have.[12] In addition to the privatisation of previously state owned bodies and the contracting out of certain services formerly in the public sector this approach includes the establishment of NHS Trusts, opted out schools and the hiving off of civil service departments to become agencies (who are charged with the duty of considering whether the service they offer could be moved to the private sector). Ultimately this sort of strategy appears to envisage government withdrawing from most areas of direct service provision, including perhaps even the most traditional public services such as' policing, and instead simply raising taxes and using them to pay for services delivered to the public from a selected contractor. While this vision of a "contract state" has a certain coherence to it, and has stimulated fresh thinking on the delivery of public services, we feel that strong arguments can be raised against the idea that contracting is the solution to all the problems of governance as we move into the twenty-first century.

THE LIMITS OF CONTRACT GOVERNMENT

There are a number of reasons why we would wish to limit the role of contract in government. First there is the legal ambiguity of such arrangements. Some are claimed to be legally enforceable contracts while others are not, either because one of the "parties" to the arrangement is not a separate legal entity or the terms of the arrangement are particularly vague.[13] Even if the terms are legally enforceable the controlling mechanisms for enforcement, beyond terminating the contract and giving it to someone else, are underdeveloped. If constitutionalism in the United Kingdom has suffered from an absence rather than a surfeit of legal regulation, contracting is unlikely to offer a remedy.

---

[12] See the criticisms of Harlow, "Changing the Mindset: The Place of Theory in English Administrative Law" (1994) 14 *Oxford Journal of Legal Studies* 419.
[13] These problems, and those government by contract generally, have been drawn attention to by a number of writers. Notably Harden, *The Contracting State*, (1992) and Freedland, "Government by Contract and Public Law", [1994] *Public Law* 86.

A second problem relates to the fact that while government by contract has the capacity to make visible the actual costs and benefits of public decision-making, it may also tend to "flatten" complex decision-making and exclude important participants from it. Take the problems which have arisen in relation to the management of the recently agentised prison service in the United Kingdom in late 1994 and early 1995. With each crisis that has arisen, whether in relation to prison security or disturbances, the question of whether it is the Home Secretary or the Director General of the Prison Service who is responsible has been posed. Yet as key decisions appear to slip between being defined as matters of "policy" and hence within the Home Secretary's remit or matters of "operations", where they become the Director General's responsibility, no clear answer emerges and ultimately no one seems responsible. Even if most matters do end up as being for the Director General to decide, the issue of whether he or she has any responsibility to the public, as opposed to a "contractual" responsibility under the framework document to the Home Office, is shrouded in even greater mystery than the application of the doctrine of ministerial responsibility. If this is so for the Prison Service, which remains formally an aspect of the state, it is even more so for private companies to whom formerly public functions are contracted. Can it be said that Corrections Corporation of America owes any responsibility to the public or even to prisoners for the way it runs its prisons in the United Kingdom? In theory the Home Office, in awarding and monitoring the performance of these contracts, can represent the public interest but as the details of such contracts are not made public, for reasons of "commercial confidentiality", the public may end up having even less knowledge of what happens in prisons than in the days when the notorious section 2 of the Official Secrets Act 1911 blocked all inquiries into state prisons. The invocation of "commercial confidentiality" symbolises the shift to notions of a private arrangement to which only the parties to the contract may be privy. Other groups such as prisoners, prison staff and the general public, who may be affected by the decisions reached by the contracting parties are largely excluded from them. A similar problem is discernable in the development of the health care system and the arrival of the "purchaser/provider" split associated with the introduction of NHS Trusts. As a result of this individual consumers may gain clearer rights to available health care, depending on the legal status of patients charters, but they also seem set to lose any influence over the initial allocation decisions which determine what sort of health care will be available. Such an outcome may be acceptable to those who can obtain sufficient health care from the market, what Will Hutton has recently described as the "secure 40%" of the population, but it may leave the remaining 60 per cent vulnerable to the social risk of ill health without adequate social insurance.[14]

A third, related problem arises with the nature of contract as a means of social organisation. As Teubner[15] observes, following McNeil and institutional economists like Williamson, contract works best for specific transactions which are time limited in character and involve limited investment on both sides. Where the task involved resists clear specification, is open ended in time and likely to change over time and requires a high level of investment by one side or the other, contract is less likely to operate adequately unless the parties renounce sharp edged exchange relationships in favour of a more co-operative style of contract management. Instead of one side directing the other to do certain things in return for a specific payment there must be a willingness to modify constantly the arrangements in the light of changing circumstances and to share risks and rewards. The implication of this for the contracting of public services is that unless the tasks to be done can be described with a relatively high level of precision, and can be detailed in such a way that does not require a high level of investment (or makes use of investment already made by service providers), then contract may not prove a successful mechanism. If the state wishes to preserve some freedom to choose among service providers it is likely to find itself receiving a poor level of service as providers concentrate on some definable aspects of the task and economise on investment. Alternatively it will find itself locked into a more co-operative relationship with a limited number of service providers who have made the investment necessary to provide a higher quality and more flexible service. Over time the split between purchaser and provider in such a relationship is likely to erode and rather than specifying what it wants from a service provider the state is likely to find itself increasingly defining its requirements in line with what the provider is prepared to offer. Health care and training are two areas which immediately spring to mind as potential candidates for such a scenario. Indeed, it already seems that lack

---

[14] See Hutton *The State We're In* (1995) p. 105 for the idea that only 40 per cent of society has sufficiently secure income and employment prospects to provide for their own health, housing and education. Hutton sees a further 30 per cent as marginalised and insecure while a bottom 30 per cent is permanently disadvantaged.

[15] Teubner, "The Many Headed Hydra: Networks as Higher Order Collective Actors", in *Corporate Control and Accountability: Changing Structures and the Dynamics of Regulation* McCahery, Picciotto and Scott ed. 1993), pp. 41–60.

of investment and autonomy has crippled the operation of Training and Enterprise Councils.[16] If all this contracting is done under the cloak of commercial confidentiality important public decisions regarding the type and range of some public services may essentially be made by private corporations. While this is clearly a new way of exercising public power, it is not clear that any gain in accountability flows from it.

Nevertheless, where discrete tasks can be identified and adequate public review mechanisms built in, contracting can play an important role in the reconstruction of the constitution. Moreover, seeking to identify services or tasks that could be hived off or contracted out will often prove to be a valuable technique for learning more about how government actually operates. However as much governance in the twenty-first century state is likely to involve complex co-ordination activity it would seem unwise to rely upon it as the only advisable institutional principle. Moreover it is a principle which, if carried to its limits, seems more likely rather than less likely to substantiate fears of public power becoming increasingly remote and inaccessible.

A CONSTITUTION OF VALUES

While we would give government by contract only a qualified welcome we would not argue for any one, alternative institutional form. Indeed, it has been one of the arguments of this book that constitutional law in the United Kingdom has been bedevilled by a focus on institutions at the expense of values. This is why it has been unable to cope with the new forms of public power developing above and below the levels of Westminster and Whitehall. Attempts to plug the activities of quangos or the European Union back into the mechanisms of accountability to ministers or parliament have largely failed and have deepened the sense that the new sites of power are beyond our capacity to control them. It is time to recognise that many of the institutions of the constitution were designed for a different time and a different place. Only a shift to a focus on the values which the constitution is designed to espouse can help us to guide the development of the new forms of public power and ensure that they remain the servants rather than the masters of the public. To the extent that the present institutions fail currently to advance these values we must look for new ones.

---

[16] See Hutton, *op. cit.* pp. 189–190 for a discussion of the rise and fall of TECs.

The issue of what values the constitution should, or does already espouse, is a large one and a full discussion of it is beyond the compass of this book. When they have moved away from an exclusive focus on "restraining state power" it is the type of debate that the various chartists and auditors we describe in chapter two have usefully engaged in. We agree that devising a list of values that a society aims to protect, and reproducing these in a charter of rights, is an important and valuable endeavour. However at this point, drawing especially upon the experience of Northern Ireland, we want to focus only on one aspect of this endeavour.

This is the issue of what values should be respected in the *making* of decisions affecting the use of public power. The values which we see as most important, though often most absent in the new sites of public power, are subsiduarity, participation and transparency. All speak of what Anthony Giddens has called the development of reflexivity and detraditionalisation in society.[17] Giddens argues that as societies become more complex and knowledgeable people become less willing to accept that others, notably governments and politicians, know what is best for them. They acquire more information about their own situation and are likely to seek greater involvement in decisions which directly impact on their lives. Such a development may lead to a breakdown in belief that powerful institutions can discern and act upon a monolithic public interest that is in the interest of all. Such a belief was at the heart of the traditional image of the British civil service, for example, and its societal weakening may explain why there has been so little public resistance to the changes wrought on the civil service in recent years. Yet the decline of belief in the capacity of institutions to discern and implement a public interest does not mean that we are all reduced to the status of atomised consumers seeking only to achieve individual projects, as exponents of the contract state may suggest. Instead, as we have suggested throughout this book, it has led to a proliferation of identities and interest groups. People still see the need for common action and for institutions to represent common interests. Yet they are more likely to combine and act specifically over issues that affect them and their sense of identity directly than see themselves as represented by governments or political parties which may be pursuing a broader and different agenda. Feminist and environmental politics are two classic examples of this, politics which tend to engage tactically and specifically

---

[17] See Giddens, *Beyond Left and Right: The Future of Radical Politics* (1994) pp. 80–87.

with existing political structures but which seek to avoid being subsumed by them. It is the extent to which the new forms of public power accommodate themselves to these new ways of acting politically that we can say they represent a qualitative advance over our old forms of constitutionalism.

Hence the importance of the value of subsiduarity, the idea that decisions be taken as close as possible to people affected by them. This also requires that decisions be taken at the level at which the people affected can have an effective voice. Hence decisions about environmental pollution might be best taken at a European level, those about schools at a city level. Such a value encourages the fragmentation of the state which we have discussed earlier in this book and can facilitate greater popular involvement in the way that it reaches its decisions. It accords with Unger's call that "To every crucial feature of the social order there should correspond some form and arena of potentially destabilizing and broadly based conflict over the uses of state power".[18]

To subsiduarity must be added values of participation and transparency as regards all the new sites of public power. Rather than assume the capacity of the new regulators, contract managers or agency directors to discern and act in the name of the public interest, it is important to require that decision takers consider all the relevant interests and reach a decision in line with their stated objectives. Thus far the development of the new sites of power has been associated with a level of secrecy as great, if not greater, than that which attended Westminster and Whitehall. Only if this is changed will an increasingly well-informed public avoid becoming an increasingly cynical one.

The exposition of these values is likely to lead to a greater role for law. However it is law which will be involved less in curtailing government activity than prompting it, or facilitating others to become involved in it. This should come as no surprise. As we move towards what we have called the "communicative constitution", where the state seeks to influence others to do things rather than do them itself, law is likely to be one of its main forms of communication. In the communicative constitution the state is likely to become more enmeshed with civil society through its actions of funding, licensing, regulating or providing information (consider the recent dispute as to whether government statistics should be

---

[18] See Unger, "The Critical Legal Studies Movement" (1983) 96 *Harvard Law Review* 561, 592.

available on a market basis), further blurring the line between public and private and setting new challenges for public lawyers. The extent to which public values of participation and transparency should also apply to those "private" organisations which interact with the state or assume its functions is likely to figure as chief among these challenges.

To return to Northern Ireland, we can see that several of the conditions we have identified above are in an advanced state. The notion of a clear public interest has been shattered by arguments over the legitimacy of the state and claims that it has been biased to serve one set of private interests. Political parties have ceased to be many peoples' primary form of public involvement, instead voluntary organisations and community groups have assumed a greater role. Already many people are used to interacting with more than one level of government. Moreover we can see that potential exists for some of the new institutions of public power to play the sort of role we advocate.

In Northern Ireland turning over the delivery of important public services such as health, education, housing or industrial development to appointed bodies may have seemed a retrograde step from the point of view of promoting orthodox ideas about democracy but it has arguably resulted in policies which are more inclusive than might have been obtained if such decisions lay in the hands of elected majorities. Still many in Northern Ireland continue to see such bodies as remote and inaccessible. This criticism has force mainly because such bodies have not clearly established their autonomy. Their most important relationship tends to remain with their sponsoring government department and they remain generally reluctant to act in a way which might disturb that relationship. If the logic of fragmentation were to be pushed further however, such bodies could become the sites of more focused and extensive conflict over key functions of the state. Such a development could be a way of energising the emergent "new politics" around issues such as health, sexuality and ethnicity which increasingly appear relevant to many people, particularly to women often excluded from traditional politics, but which sit uneasily with current forms of party politics in both Britain and Northern Ireland. For such a development to occur fragmentation of power needs to be pushed further in two directions.

First such government units need to be distanced more fully from existing government departments. This might require a clearer legal and budgetary framework within which the body could operate. It would follow the logic of agentisation of government but make such agencies autonomous bodies with a public responsibility to deliver a service rather than the clients of a government department. Central government would retain a co-ordination function in respect of the claims of different interests in society and therefore would have the power to set budgets, give general directions and operate as one check on an agency exceeding its remit. However, rather than the agency simply taking its lead from central government, it would now expect to lobby for resources and negotiate with government as to its functions. To make such a prospect realistic such bodies would need to be staffed by people of expertise in the area who would work on a full time basis. This would obviously involve a departure from the part time membership of most current quangos where ability and expertise in one field, normally business, is taken to be a sign of expertise in any other. If such bodies were to have increased powers then it is likely that the representative character of their membership would come under even greater scrutiny and that many would seek to ensure that the membership was directly elected. We believe that this runs the risk of these bodies falling hostage to traditional party politics and should be resisted. While electing some members might be wise to maintain contact with the world of mainstream politics, there should also be scope to nominate people whose main claim for selection is expertise in the relevant field of activity. Lest this is felt to be unsatisfactory in democratic terms, their nomination could be made subject to the approval of the legislature, much in the same way as judges and many executive appointments in the United States are made subject to Congressional approval and the European Parliament has recently taken to doing with appointments to the European Commission. Furthermore, vetoes and minimum conditions of consensus, perhaps emphasising the importance of those who actually consume services or are in some way vulnerable or otherwise disenfranchised, could be built in to ensure that experts feel the need to carry with them those actually affected by their work.[19]

The second direction in which such institutions need to develop is in becoming increasingly transparent to the public as regards their decision-

---

[19] We can draw here on the work of those who regard democracy as a mechanism privileging certain groups over others and seek to develop instead strategies to deliver effective power in a "strong" democracy where public life is repoliticised in such a way as not to require the creation of a unified public realm or universal citizenship but rather an alternative emancipatory politics where difference is acknowledged in new hierarchies of power and privilege. See further, for example, Iris Marion Young, "Polity and Group Difference: A Critique of the Idea of Universal Citizenship", (1989) *Ethics* 99; *Justice and the Politics of Difference* (1990); A. Phillips, *Engendering Democracy* (1991); *Democracy and Difference* (1993) and Barber, *Strong Democracy: Participatory Politics for a New Age* (1984).

making. As our discussion of the Northern Ireland experience shows, many people are unaware of how key quangos operate or who sits on them. The law is not of much help to them in finding out. Frequently it imposes only minimal reporting obligations and fails to afford meaningful rights to participate in quango decision-making. As a result quangos tend to operate in a relatively cosy world to which only the government and large professional associations or voluntary organisations have access. If public engagement with the exercise of public power in these areas is to take place such reformed bodies need to be more porous and afford a wider range of groups the opportunity to influence decision-making.

Law can play a role in facilitating the access of more voices to such decision-making and ensuring the transparency of the decisions that are taken. To do so under present legal doctrine, however, would require a greater liberalisation of standing rules and rights to consultation than has hitherto been permitted.[20] It might acquire greater force to do so with the passing of a charter of rights, an idea which also has found greater acceptance in Northern Ireland than in Great Britain so far. As we have seen in chapters three to five government in Northern Ireland already acts under greater normative constraints than is true in the rest of the United Kingdom, especially as to the need to ensure that its policies ensure equal treatment of the two main communities (even if this derives more from administrative directives such as PAFT or TSN than legal imperatives).[21] There is widespread political support for a charter of rights as part of any political settlement, a charter which would mark a significant break with established traditions of constitutional law in the United Kingdom by putting certain matters beyond the reach of political compromises.

Charters of rights have often been seen as encouraging greater individualism and a turning away from the more participative style of politics we have been advocating. However there is no reason why this should

---

[20] Stewart, "The Reformation of American Administrative Law" (1975) 88 *Harvard Law Review* 1667, identifies the relaxation of standing rules as the most important factor in ensuring greater public access to agency decision-making. Perhaps the best opportunity for this to occur in the United Kingdom comes from the domestication of European concepts of administrative law into English law or from the emergence of a pan-European administrative law. (See further Schwartze, *European Administrative Law* (1992). See also Cappelletti, *The Judicial Process in Comparative Perspective* (1989) and Richardson, "The Legal Regulation of Process" in *Administrative Law and Government Action* (Richardson and Genn ed. 1994) for more general arguments that judges can bring popular input into government decision-making.

[21] See above p. 142 and pp. 157–8.

necessarily be so. Canadian commentators have spoken of the phenomenon of "Charter Canadians" to denote the way in which the exercise of
rights under the Canadian Charter, notably its equality clause, has provided a focus around which a number of groups, such as women, the
disabled, native Canadians and ethnic minorities have been able to organise politically and seek change. Such groups often found themselves shut
out of established politics. Moreover the type of rights protected need not
be limited to the type of civil and political rights displayed in nineteenth
century constitutions. Unger, whose work we have referred to above,
envisages a number of different types of rights as being part of the
constitution of what he refers to as "empowered democracy". These
would include "immunity" rights, "solidarity" rights, "market" rights and
"destabilisation" rights.[22] The last are especially interesting and potentially
important. Their inspiration lies in competition laws and in the complex
structural injunctions that American courts have been prepared to order
after findings of constitutional violations by large institutions such as
prisons, mental hospitals or school boards. Such injunctions have often
required significant reorganisation of the institution in question. Unger
asserts that destabilisation rights

> "protect the citizen's interest in breaking open the large scale organizations or
> the extended areas of social practice that remain closed to the destabilizing
> effects of ordinary conflict and thereby sustain insulated hierarchies of power
> and advantage".[23]

Such rights are clearly intended to impact both on "private" areas of
entrenched power as well as "public" ones. If elements of formerly public
activity are privatised or turned over to market activity such rights could
play an important role in ensuring that areas where it is essentially public
power that is being exercised do not gain autonomy from democratic
accountability.

Finally the experience of Northern Ireland suggests the need for a more
focused engagement with the external dimension of the constitution. As
we have observed, some individuals and groups have sought to make use
of the external dimension, notably in Europe, the United States and the
Republic of Ireland, as a way of influencing or bypassing the exercise of

---

[22] For a detailed discussion of the content of these different types of rights see Unger *False
Necessity: Anti Necessitarian Social Theory in the Service of Radical Democracy* (1987), pp.
513–38.
[23] *Supra* at p. 530.

domestic political power. Europe, in particular, for them has not been the remote intrusive bureaucracy often portrayed in the British media but a means of bringing a fresh perspective to a domestic conflict. Moreover it is arguable that there are some public issues, such as environmental regulation or refugee policy, that might best be decided at a European rather than a national level. Nevertheless many people still see decision-making in a European context as a rather remote activity. Some of the most important decisions in relation to the new Europe, such as the establishment of European Monetary Union or the Schengen Agreement on internal borders, have been produced outside even the European Union's fairly limited review and scrutiny mechanisms. There is clearly a need for Europe to democratise its decision-making procedures. Such obvious affronts to the transparency of government, as the fact that Council of Ministers meetings still take place entirely in secret and without many of the relevant documents being made available to the public, can not be defended. The Maastricht Treaty has given the European Parliament more powers but due to the fact that voters have yet to identify with European elections as being concerned with European rather than domestic affairs (Northern Ireland being an especially good example) it is likely to remain a long way from being an adequate forum for the representation of European citizens' views. Instead it might be better to structure more opportunities for representation and participation in decision-making around functional activities and interest group lobbying. There, in the women's movement, the poverty lobby, environmental politics and even in some trade unions, examples already exist of co-operation and cross-European thinking.[24] Just as in the domestic sphere, the challenge in the European domain is to define institutions which accommodate the development of such new politics.

The potential constitutional landscape we have sketched here is complex and somewhat messy. We do not believe it could be otherwise. The forces we have identified as leading to a reshaping of public power are themselves diverse and uncertain in their effects. Any institutional programme which responds to them likewise needs to be flexible and hence cannot be specified in detail in the abstract but only in detail in practice. One of its most significant features is likely to be a continuing competition over power with different "levels" of the constitutional structure,

---

[24] See Meehan, *Citizenship and the European Community* (1993), p. 152–3 for examples of cross border co-operation and organisation in Europe.

national, regional, functional and external competing for influence and allegiance. There is unlikely to be in the future any neat separation of powers where different branches of government have clearly defined areas of competence and constitutional lawyers need only patrol agreed boundaries. Rather it is clear that the constitution will be an untidy and unruly affair and constitutional lawyers, if they are to have anything of relevance to say, must continue the move that some have made away from an exclusive focus on the workings of parliament, the cabinet and the courts. Instead of pursuing the vanishing agenda of Westminsterism through a vision of constitutional law that no longer accords with the way the world really is, they must continue to erode the divisions between constitutional and administrative law and between domestic and international law. Legal scholars must be prepared to examine the workings of all the institutions in which public power is exercised. As the boundaries between public and private become increasingly blurred it will be necessary to re-think the extent to which the focus on constitutional law should remain exclusively on the activities of the state. In order to explore the normative basis of the newly emergent constitution and the relationships between institutions and structures within the new framework a more daring approach is required. Although daunting, this is an exciting agenda, certainly more challenging than the exposition of supposed traditions and the hankerings after the constitutions of other states which has so far constituted the bulk of both conservative and critical scholarship in public law this century.

Appendix One

A Brief Political—Constitutional Chronology

Clare Palley has argued, in what has become a seminal work for lawyers on "The Evolution, Disintegration and Possible Reconstruction of the Northern Ireland Constitution",[1] that both the "Irish Question" and the "Ulster Question" together reflect a complex of divisive socio-political forces. These can be analysed by reference to imperialism and colonialism over a three hundred year period. For strategic and economic reasons England as an imperial power introduces a large garrison of settlers into Ireland for its own defensive purposes. Then, as these imperial interests change, it begins to withdraw but it gives the settlers a measure of support via a system of devolved government whereby a local administration assumes control over many matters under the supervision of the British parliament. Finally it feels the need to abandon its former possessions as support is found to be costly and politically difficult. Such an analysis simplifies much but does perhaps suggest the deep-seated nature of the conflict, the idea of two communities who still retain different (and opposing) traditions and the current position of the British government who are reluctant to stay but afraid to go.

The summary that follows is necessarily simplistic. It might, however, afford a very brief overview.

---

[1] *Anglo-American Law Review*, 1972 at pp. 368–9.

Late Sixteenth Century

The earliest settlements by the land hungry Norman barons and their retainers with their relatively loose attachment to the English Crown were on the east and south coastal areas. This left much of the country to the native Irish. The Protestant Reformation during the reign of Elizabeth I involved the church, with its bishoprics, buildings and land, passing into protestant hands. Protestantism, however, made little progress among the native Irish who remained faithful to the Roman Catholic church. With the ever growing importance of sea power and the growing strength of Catholic Spain there was continuous concern that the native Irish, allied to a foreign power, first Spain and later France, might threaten English dominance of the seas around the British coast and in the North Atlantic. (Indeed, this English concern persisted through the following centuries and Irish bases in both the South and then the North were to prove vital in both the 1914–18 War and in the Second World War.) During the reign of Queen Elizabeth intermittent and indecisive conflicts between the settlers supported by the English and the indigenous Irish occurred. In the northern province of Ulster a rebellion by the Earl of Tyrone in 1595, aided by the Spanish, was only successfully suppressed in 1601.

Seventeenth Century

Four years after the succession of the Scottish King James I in 1603 the leaders of dissident native faction went into exile in France and, on the lands forfeited by these fugitive Earls, colonies were planted. The official colonies, made up of English and Scottish settlers based in the West of Ulster (where the main city in the region was renamed Londonderry to mark its association with the City of London and its companies) were augmented by an unofficial influx of largely Presbyterian Scots who were dissenters from the Established Protestant church. The present day demography still reveals traces of this pattern. However, during the reign of James I Ulster, which had been the last bastion of Catholic Gaelic resistance to the Elizabethan reformation, became the stronghold of a powerful Protestant colony.

This position was strongly and bloodily contested on both sides and, after the Royalists had been defeated in England, the Parliamentary general Cromwell brutally suppressed Irish rebellion. The restoration of the

monarchy in England, and the more favourable climate there towards
Catholicism from Charles II and James II, was interrupted by the "Glori-
ous Revolution" of 1688 which saw the throne pass to William of
Orange.

1688–1690

In Ireland, however, William was not acknowledged as King until 1690.
With Protestants in Londonderry, influenced by rumours that Catholics
were planning a massacre, loyalties were divided. In 1688 King James sent
a new regiment to garrison the city: a catholic regiment. The Protestant
city authorities felt obliged to admit the army but were thwarted on
December 7, 1688 by 13 apprentice boys who locked the gates of the city
in the face of King James' troops. The town was besieged, and while the
commander of the Protestant garrison was prepared to surrender the city,
the citizens rejected his authority. William of Orange sent a fleet which
eventually relieved the city in July 1689. King William followed and
routed the armies of King James at the Battle of the Boyne in July 1690.

The events of this period have left an indelible mark on the history and
culture of Northern Ireland. They established the political dominion of
the Protestants over the Catholic majority in Ireland and continue to
supply a focus for protestant politics and catholic antipathies in the present
day.

Eighteenth Century

Ireland was ruled by a parliament and a Lord Lieutenant responsible and
subordinate to the Parliament at Westminster. Penal Laws were introduced depriving Catholics of power and property. However, in 1782
"Grattan's Parliament" offered a forum for government in Ireland that was
freer of London, although still largely restricted to the Protestant ascend-
ancy. Demands for Irish independence, along less sectarian lines, were
advanced through Wolfe Tone's United Irishmen movement founded in
1791 but military action supported by France to achieve a break with
English domination for a more widely emancipated Irish nation was finally
defeated at the Battle of Vinegar Hill in 1789. The Acts of Union of 1800
extinguished the Irish Parliament and instead provided seats in the Westminster Parliament where Irish members would be in a permanent
minority.

Nineteenth Century

Independence movements continued in various forms. Robert Emmett's attempt to seize Dublin Castle and proclaim a Republic in 1803 led to his execution and that of his fellow conspirators. Daniel O'Connell's broadly-based and peaceful Catholic Association led to the Act of Emancipation 1829 removing the ban preventing catholics from taking seats in Parliament. However, the wider aim of removing the Act of Union was overshadowed by the Great Famine of 1845–1849. The small-scale and ineffective rebellion in 1848 by the Young Ireland Movement was one of the few political gestures in a country numbed by disaster. The Fenian rising of 1867, which took up the mantle of this earlier movement through the creation of the Irish Republican Brotherhood was no more successful than its predecessors.

The series of revolutionary failures paved the way for more successful movements for reform by constitutional means. Home Rule, self-government under the British Crown, became focused under the leadership of Charles Stewart Parnell. The Liberal government of W. E. Gladstone was persuaded to introduce a Home Rule Bill in 1886 but this was defeated and Parnell's leadership was fatally compromised when he was cited a co-respondent in a divorce case. An election in 1882 gave Gladstone's Liberals a sufficiently large majority to carry a second Home Rule Bill in 1893 but this was defeated in the House of Lords leaving Irish nationalism a seemingly lost cause and the Ulster Unionists and their supporters in the English Conservative party victorious.

Irish nationalism then began a significant turn against the goal of simply achieving Home Rule under the British Crown and towards the setting up of an Irish Republic. The Irish Republican Brotherhood was re-established and invigorated by the Gaelic League aimed at creating a distinctively Irish Culture.

Twentieth Century

Nevertheless, at the turn of the century most politically active Irish people were not yet Republicans. Arthur Griffith formed an organisation called *Sinn Fein* (We Ourselves) in 1905 but it urged merely that Irish M.P.s should withdraw from Westminster and set up their own parliament under the Crown. Asquith's Liberal government abolished the House of Lord's veto powers in 1911 and the third Home Rule Bill was passed through parliament in 1912. Ulster Protestants under the leadership of Edward Carson strongly opposed this and almost half-a-million protestants signed the Ulster Covenant and Declaration promising determined resistance. Conservative British leaders pledged support. The Ulster Volunteer Force was formed and armed. British Army officers garrisoned in Ireland announced that they would resign rather than obey orders to coerce Ulster. While the Government of Ireland Act (arranging Home Rule) was given the Royal Assent on September 18, 1914, a Suspensory Act was simultaneously given Royal Assent delaying its operation in light of the war.

The First World War

During the war soldiers from both parts of Ireland enlisted. However, a radical anti-war minority of Irish Volunteers under Padraic Pearse joined with James Connolly's Irish Citizen Army to stage an uprising in Dublin in Easter 1916. This small-scale effort, with limited public support, was followed up by executions of 15 of its leaders and this action converted many moderate citizens into convinced nationalists. One of the those involved in the Easter Rising, Michael Collins was released from prison at Christmas 1916 and reorganised the Volunteers around an Irish Republican Brotherhood which joined with Arthur Griffith's Sinn Fein movement under the command of Eamon de Valera. It was committed to much more than simply the unimplemented Home Rule Act of 1914 and, following victory for Sinn Fein candidates in elections after the Armistice, the majority of those elected met in Dublin, proclaimed themselves *Dail Eireann*, the Irish Parliament, and declared Ireland an independent Republic with De Valera as its first President.

Before the *Dail's* proclamations could turn into reality, a period of brutal conflict between the Republican movement and the Crown, which supported the police with irregular forces and martial law, took place alongside attempts to extend the effective rule of the self-proclaimed government. At last in 1920 a legislative measure for Home Rule was passed in the Government of Ireland Act which provided for separate parliaments for the 26 counties of the South and the six of the North. In the South it was an irrelevance but it came into force in the North where a bicameral legislature was elected with an executive performing the role of a devolved government.

The 1920 Settlement

This settlement in the north of Ireland was to persist for 50 years. However, on the southern side of the partition it required the Anglo-Irish Treaty of 1921 to end the guerilla war between the Irish Republican Army and Crown forces. Following negotiations with Lloyd George and the British cabinet the Irish Free State (Agreement) Act was passed in 1922 giving dominion status to the new Irish Free State. Nationalist factions violently contested the extent and value of this settlement and a brief but bloody civil war ensued. Meanwhile unionist fears over a Boundary Commission's review of the border's final form led to widespread violence in Belfast. When the Free State government eventually suppressed the anti-treaty elements of the IRA, De Valera founded *Fianna Fail* as a political party which in 1932 secured a majority in the *Dail*. There it began to alter the Treaty provisions and move towards complete independence. In 1937 a new constitution was drawn up, which in Articles 2 and 3 made a not entirely unambiguous claim over the north of Ireland. In 1948 the Irish state was renamed the Republic of Ireland and withdrew from the British Commonwealth.

Southern and Northern Ireland thus existed as two distinct political identities: as a "catholic" state and a "protestant" state. Within the northern state a unionist regime effectively controlled the domestic agenda and modest conciliatory gestures towards the catholic minority begun by the government of Terence O'Neill were insufficient to halt the development of a civil rights organisation and a People's Democracy movement in 1968. The actions of these groups were violently contested by a protestant opposition and violently suppressed by the police force. The British Army was brought in to be initially welcomed by catholics as protecting them from protestants and the largely sectarian local police. Widespread civil unrest began and the IRA and a variety of other paramilitary organisations, both catholic and protestant, re-emerged. Internment without trial was introduced in 1971 later to be replaced by the "Diplock Court" system of a judge sitting without a jury. Following terrorist bombings of civilians in Northern Ireland and British Army targets in England and an operation by British paratroopers in the Bogside area of Derry which left 13 people shot dead, the British Prime Minister Edward Heath recalled law and order powers to Westminster. The Stormont government resigned and the Northern Ireland Parliament was prorogued. Direct Rule from London was imposed through The Northern Ireland (Temporary Provisions) Act 1972.

Continuing Direct Rule

Later in 1972 a government discussion paper on *The Future of Northern Ireland* was published. This suggested the restoration of devolved government, but with executive power shared between representatives of both the majority and minority communities. It also referred to an "Irish Dimension" linking the interests of Northern Ireland and the Republic of Ireland. The status of Northern Ireland within the United Kingdom was reaffirmed.

The ideas in this paper have remained the basis of the British Government's policy in Northern Ireland. All subsequent initiatives have operated within this fundamental framework, although sometimes in particular political conditions, different aspects have been emphasised relative to others in order to attempt to secure the political agreement necessary to proceed.

In March 1973 a plebiscite on the issue of the border was conducted which produced a majority among those that voted for remaining within the United Kingdom. This was enshrined in the so-called "constitutional guarantee" in section 1 of The Northern Ireland Constitution Act 1973. The main function of this Act, along with a Northern Ireland Assembly Act 1973, was however to provide for a single chamber Assembly of 78 members elected by the single transferable vote system of proportional representation. The Assembly was to have legislative powers over a limited range of local matters and an executive representing both sides of the community was to be drawn from it. Simultaneously discussions between the British and Irish governments and the leaders of the Northern Ireland parties over the Irish dimension provided the Sunningdale Agreement with a structure for a Council of Ireland. In January 1974 the Northern Ireland Assembly and Executive began operating under their transferred powers. Despite widespread popular opposition, the Assembly approved the Sunningdale Agreement. In February 1974 the Heath government called a general election. Unionists opposed to Sunningdale and power-sharing won 11 out of the 12 Westminster seats (with only 51 per cent of the Northern Irish vote). A unionist coalition was formed against power-sharing and the Council of Ireland and the Ulster Workers' Council called a general strike supported and enforced by loyalist paramilitaries. When essential services were threatened Unionist members of the Executive resigned and the power-sharing experiment ended after only five months. Direct rule was resumed, initially under the 1973 Act and then through The Northern Ireland Act 1974, and has continued until the present day.

The Range of Initiatives

Since then there have been initiatives to bring in structures to realise the basic objective of eventually achieving devolved government containing an Irish dimension with direct rule being only a temporary arrangement. In 1975 and 1976 a Constitutional Convention was convened. In 1979 Northern Ireland representation at Westminster was increased from 12 to 17 members to improve direct rule while a White Paper for a conference was published. In 1980 the "Atkins Conference" led to a further White Paper entitled *Proposals for Further Discussion* and summit meetings occurred between the British and Irish Prime Ministers. In 1981 the Anglo-Irish Intergovernmental Council was established. In 1982 the Northern Ireland Act was passed and an Assembly was elected, initially with a scrutinising role only but able to take on such functions of government as were widely agreed upon. Following the deliberations of the New Ireland Forum in 1983 and the publication of its report in 1984 the Anglo-Irish dimension was developed. In 1985 the Anglo-Irish Agreement was signed and the Anglo-Irish Intergovernmental Conference established. Unionist opposition became focused upon this aspect and the potential for restoring devolved government through the Assembly receded with the Assembly finally being dissolved in 1986. A variety of talks and "talks about talks" initiatives failed to bring significant political progress. Although direct rule remains a temporary expedient, with devolution being the preferred option, it is strongly in place. In July 1993 Unionist members at Westminster provided support for a Conservative government beleaguered over European issues and achieved better scrutiny of direct rule through a Northern Ireland Select Committee. In December 1993 the Downing Street Agreeement between the governments of the United Kingdom and the Republic of Ireland was signed. This further establishes the legitimacy of two traditions and seems to commit the governments to the idea of unification of Ireland only with the consent of the people of Northern

Ireland. Following on this, and in recognition of the role of the government of the Republic of Ireland as persuaders in the process towards eventual reunification, the republican paramilitaries and then the loyalist paramilitaries agreed what was interpreted as a permanent cessation of violence. In Dublin the Irish government organised a Forum for Peace and Reconciliation attended by non-unionist representatives. Further talks about the future of Northern Ireland were held in Belfast, Dublin and London and in December 1994 representatives of Sinn Fein met with British Government representatives. In the spring of 1995 the *Frameworks for the Future* documents were published. These contained suggestions for restoring devolved government to Northern Ireland and expressed the joint position of the British and Irish governments on the Anglo-Irish dimension. The *Framework for Accountable Government in Northern Ireland* document proposes a 90 member assembly with legislative and administrative powers. It will be elected by proportional representation and an elaborate system of checks and balances across its proposed system of departmental committees is suggested. The document also contains the idea of a panel of three who will exercise some sort of unspecified monitoring and refereeing role. The *New Framework for Agreement* documents sets out the shared position between the British and Irish governments and is intended to assist discussion and negotiation involving the Northern Ireland parties. It endorses ideas of two traditions. It again puts the idea of the consent of the people of Northern Ireland at the centre of any change to the constitutional status of Northern Ireland. The government of the Republic of Ireland has undertaken the potentially difficult task of ensuring that its constitutional legislation is consistent with this position. A new North–South body, drawn from both the Assembly and from representatives in the Republic of Ireland is suggested. This will have a harmonising and consultative role but also an executive role in a limited range of matters. A standing Intergovernmental Conference is to be created and maintained to reflect "the totality of relationships between the two islands" (para. 39). While both governments pledge to encourage the development of a Charter or Covenant of rights there is no commitment to a bill of rights for Northern Ireland.

It is these frameworks that provide the agenda for on-going talks which now promise to include a whole range of views including those from former paramilitary organisations who have renounced violence.

Index